BHARATHIPURA

First published in 1973, *Bharathipura* is about the practice of untouchability in a traditional society that is evolving into modernity through new economic forces brought in by a certain class of people. The story revolves around the life of an 'enlightened' modern Indian, Jagannatha. Violent and unexpected events follow Jagannatha's attempts to revolutionize everyone and everything by linking his own transformation to the changes he wishes to orchestrate. Emotional, fast-moving, and deeply philosophical, this novel by one of India's most famous living authors, himself the grandson of a priest, confronts every kind of reader with India's greatest tragedy: caste.

U.R. Ananthamurthy, a teacher of English literature and one of India's leading contemporary writers, does all his creative writing in Kannada. Author of five novels, including the widely acclaimed *Samskara* (English translation, OUP 1976), he has six collections of short stories, five collections of poems, a play, and sixteen volumes of critical writings. He was Vice-Chancellor, Mahatma Gandhi University (Kerala) and President, Central Sahitya Akademi.

'one of the important novels that shaped Kannada modernity in content and form, it had employed a fresh idiom to explore the experience of the new individual ... hailed as a masterpiece for its multi-layered structure and extensively nuanced treatment of the caste question'

—*The Hindu*

'[*Bharathipura*'s] power resides in the way its universal ideas are worked out through the frame of the local.'

—*The Wall Street Journal*

BHARATHIPURA

U.R. ANANTHAMURTHY

TRANSLATED FROM KANNADA BY
SUSHEELA PUNITHA

WITH AN INTRODUCTION BY
N. MANU CHAKRAVARTHY

EDITED BY
MINI KRISHNAN

Oxford University Press is a department of the University of Oxford. It furthers the University's objective of excellence in research, scholarship, and education by publishing worldwide. Oxford is a registered trademark of Oxford University Press in the UK and in certain other countries

Published in India by
Oxford University Press
YMCA Library Building, 1 Jai Singh Road, New Delhi 110 001, India

First Edition published in 2010
Oxford India Paperbacks 2012
Second impression 2013

ISBN-13: 978-0-19-808202-6
ISBN-10: 0-19-808202-9

Typeset in 11.5/13.5 Perpetua Std
by Excellent Laser Typesetters, New Delhi 110 034
Printed in India by Rakmo Press, New Delhi 110 020

MR. Omayal Achi MR. Arunachalam Trust was set up in 1976 to further education and health care particularly in rural areas. The MR. AR Educational Society was later established by the Trust. One of the Society's activities is to sponsor Indian literature. This translation is entirely funded by the MR. AR Educational Society as part of it aims.

Dedicated to the hope that
we may see ourselves in others . . .

Contents

Author's Note

I am deeply intertwined with the memories of childhood. I seem to have an inexplicable metaphorical connection with that world. Whenever I talk of caste and untouchability—both of which have bothered me a lot—I remember my grandfather who had a complex notion of purity and pollution. He would go around carrying me on his back and, on one such occasion, he told me this, as if it were a story: 'We Brahmins had the *shapanugraha shakti*. That is, we were capable of slapping a curse (*shapa*) and showering grace (*anugraha*). Sadly, we have lost both.' And he blamed this on his desire for coffee, which was considered polluting. Caste, like coffee, is woven with many such ideas and notions. People truly believed it and I have been a witness to it in my growing years. As someone who was constantly exposed to the good and the bad side of these practices, I could neither become entirely anti-Brahminical as I am made out to be, nor could I save myself from becoming a sceptic.

I abhorred untouchability right from my childhood days. This feeling was so intense in me that it recurred in many of my stories as the theme of touch, as if it were an obsession. While I was in Mysore, I wrote the story 'Ghatashraddha' in which this little boy, Naani, goes to the forest in search of the widow, Yamunakka. It is night and the Dalit who accompanies him holds a torch. In the darkness illuminated by that meek patch of light, he assumes supernatural proportions for the little Naani. He is scared, wants to hold him tight, but the Dalit prevails upon him not to. Much later in the story, there is a point when Naani holds on to Yamunakka who is pregnant, much against the norms. The theme of touch is related to the caste system; it is also sociological. Even in *Samskara* touch is very significant; it sets people on journeys hitherto unknown.

Bharathipura also comes from my concern about untouchability. In order to love the past, one must also hate the past. There is a lot of love of the past in India, which is not based on any discrimination or suffering. If we intensely hate something from the past, then we know what we love in the past. Gandhi was a great example of intense love of the past. When we began to fight untouchability, he knew exactly how it could have worked in the past in a traditional society. That was something that influenced me greatly. If you ask me what is the worst of the Indian civilization, I would say it is untouchability. I can understand slavery—a slave can fight back—but untouchability gets internalized. The victim gradually begins to feel he is untouchable. I have seen this happening in my childhood. I grew up in an agrahaara, in a very orthodox set-up which practised untouchability. It grew in me as a strong repulsion and, in a very metaphysical sense, I began to obsess over everything that seemed the opposite of all this: to touch, to love, to come close.

Did I want to write a Gandhian novel? The answer is a no and a yes. It is not a Gandhian novel because the hero wants Dalits to enter the temple and destroy the belief of the people that God is all powerful and will make them vomit and die. So it is an attempt at deconstruction—the deconstruction of a myth. The original God is not Manjunatha, but a folk god which the lower castes worship. It is a Gandhian novel in the sense that it is a response to Gandhi as well as all the existentialists.

Just before writing *Bharathipura* I got the Homi Bhabha Fellowship. I had decided to write a long essay on the 'Search for Identity in Indian Fiction'. When I told R.K. Narayan this, he said, 'Don't write an essay, write a novel.' I took his advice. But after *Bharathipura* was published, there was a joke going around: 'Ananthamurthy was asked to write a novel, but he still wrote an essay!'

Having said all this, I must say that 'touch' is for me the most important thing. Whenever I think of it, there is one persistent image that keeps coming back to my mind and that is of Gandhi. He always put his frail arms around the shoulders of two girls as he walked. To me, it has always said many things.

I must thank N. Manu Chakravarthy, my student from Mysore, who has written the 'Introduction' to this translation. Manu knows more than I consciously know about my texts. Susheela Punitha, the translator of this novel, not just translated the work, but enjoyed the text and asked me searching questions as she worked on it. I am immensely grateful to Mini Krishnan for the interest she has evinced in getting this novel translated into English. She has enriched the entire process with her keen insight. My thanks to her.

October 2010 U.R. ANANTHAMURTHY

Translator's Note

It is one thing to translate such an intense novel as *Bharathipura* and quite another to theorize from it. On the whole, the process of translation was a retreat, an indwelling with my Kannada reading of the novel to rewrite it in English. Much of the transfer was intuitive; as I read the novel, I heard the author tell me the story in Kannada and I narrated it to readers by writing it down in English. I have tried to maintain the oral style of story-telling that is the mainstay of the novel.

But it was not always easy to fit a left-brain experience into a right-brain activity. Reading to write is not a passive skill. There had to be multiple levels of reading the novel that led to multiple levels of writing and rewriting. The spontaneity of retelling the story was stalled by the meta-reader in the translator seeing gaps in meaning, significance, and flavour during the transfer, and choosing from both languages to make the third language of the translation specific and distinct, to carry the burden of the story with as much ease as was possible.

The places in which the novel is set are an indication of the felicity with which English carries the story forward. The parts of the story based in England and Bangalore flow as fluently in English as they do in Kannada. In fact, Raghava Puranik, a character who lives in the virtual England he has built for himself in Bharathipura, speaks only in English much to the translator's delight. And the expressions in English that Jagannatha and his friends use act as signposts to the translation.

It is while translating the major part of the story set in small-town Bharathipura, a Brahmin stronghold, that English bends under the strain of the cultural signified for which there are no equivalent signifiers in English. And, so, familiar expressions like mantra and linga have been retained with footnotes to help along the way. But the computer-compliant spelling of 'dhoti' for the length of cloth worn by men to cover the lower part of the body had to be changed to *dhothi* as there is a phonetic difference between the two words in Kannada; the former pronunciation refers to a crook, the long stick with a hook at one end.

The choice was more deliberate in retaining Holeyaru for its connotative value. Though 'Dalit' has a modern pan-Indian political content in referring to the depressed castes, the socio-cultural Kannada term 'Holeyaru' has been retained as it refers to the community that cleaned toilets, for the story is about them. With it come its variants used in the text, Holeya (singular) and Holathi (feminine). In this context, human waste had to be translated as 'shit' in places where 'faeces' was too sanitized to carry the necessary revulsion.

And there was a problem with *gudi*, a touching instance of polysemy in the context of the theme. Gudi means 'temple' and it also means 'the dwelling of the Holeya', and yet the word could not be retained. To avoid confusion, it had to be translated as 'temple' or 'hut', whichever was relevant in the context.

And so it was with *garbhagudi*, literally, the 'womb of the temple'. Though my Christian background suggested 'sanctum sanctorum' or 'holy of holies', the Christian connotation of the expression is so strong that I preferred to use synonyms of the 'inner chamber of the temple'. Only once is garbhagudi rendered as 'womb'; the image is graphic and evocative where Jagannatha makes an attempt to take the Holeyaru there to be born anew.

As is natural to them, the Brahmin characters frequently quote Sanskrit slokas or refer to stories from Sanskrit texts, making the text trilingual. To maintain the flow of the narrative, all but one have been loosely translated. However, they are amply supported by footnotes.

But English breaks down completely while translating the world of the Holeya in the context of the Brahmins. Just as the footnotes and glossary help where the text is dense with intertextual references, the translator's note has to step in where translation has failed.

The idiom of Chouda's mother as she defends her dead son has no equivalent language variety in English. And, so, her pronunciation and style of speaking could not be transferred. Her lines are in 'chaste' English.

And there was no way of conveying the innate contempt Jagannatha, as a Brahmin, has for the Holeyaru. English grammar, unlike Kannada grammar, does not distinguish between human and non-human in the third person plural, 'they'. For example, in Kannada, 'they came' is rendered as '*avaru bandharu*' while referring to human beings and as '*avu bandhavu*' while referring to non-human living beings. The one context where expressions like 'avu bandhavu' are used for human beings is with reference to children—to express endearment, to be indulgent. In any other context, it would imply contempt, equating human beings with animals. And that is what Jagannatha thinks every time he sees the Holeyaru approaching him—'avu bandhavu'—as if they were a herd, not people. He who is all set to initiate a social change and hopes to become a wholesome person through it, fails to transform his own attitude towards them; he could be anyone of us. Jagannatha's inability to realize that he does not see the Holeyaru as human beings is central to the angst in the novel. And, yet, it could not be transferred to the English text because the language is not equipped to describe that kind of othering. And, so, 'they came', as it occurs in the translation, is neutral in attitude; it is not coloured with contempt.

This epiphanic revelation struck me when Mini Krishnan stalled my reading to seek a clarification. I was reading the novel and she was following it in translation. Now Mini does not know Kannada and the Kannada reader in me was too much of an insider to see the incongruity of the non-human third person plural with reference to the Holeyaru.

'What is *avu*?' asked Mini. And that was when I saw. As I was explaining to her the sophistication of a structure in Kannada grammar, I became aware of its implications in terms of meaning and attitude. I could become enough of an outsider to read the cultural significance of its use in the context. For this insight, and for so much more, I have to thank Mini. She invited me to translate the novel and as my editor helped me to refine the text. It grew in collaboration. It was she who suggested that I should create chapter headings to improve the overall presentation of the work, and her infectious energy in striving for excellence has honed the translator in me. What greater grace can a teacher ask for than that her student should be her mentor?

I would like to thank my dear friends N. Manu Chakravarthy and Deepa Ganesh for being there for me. Manu helped me understand the Sanskrit slokas and the finer nuances between brahminical belief and practice. Despite her busy schedule, Deepa has helped me fit the footnotes to the text as I am not computer-savvy.

My special thanks to the author, U.R. Ananthamurthy, for his invaluable support right from the day he read my translation of the first chapter as a sample of what I could do. But he could be disarmingly exasperating too, as when I asked him the meaning of the expression '*Jobadhra*' in '*Jobadhra Mundedhe!*'

'What do I know?' he said, 'That's what people say to scold children or to pet them.'

Did he have to use words that are so familiar that the meaning does not matter any more?

October 2010 SUSHEELA PUNITHA

Introduction

My works are a journey from the profane to the sacred ... from the quotidian to the abstract.

—U.R. Ananthamurthy

U.R. Ananthamurthy is one of the most significant writers of post-Independence India, characterized in political and cultural discourses as 'post-colonial' India. The intellectual world has been flooded with endless theories on the 'post-colonial' situation which is, in fact, a flourishing academic industry. One of the flaws of 'post-colonial' theory is the tendency to homogenize a 'post-colonial' society by overlooking its multiple complexities, dualities, contradictions, and paradoxes that defy reductionist and simplistic categorizations and challenge singular ideological constructs. Secondly, most 'post-colonial' theorists are highly selective in their choice of the texts for study, and, more crucially, for all their theoretical virtuosity, literally and metaphorically bend and bind texts only to foreground their narrow ideological positions. The living realities of communities become mere anthropological or archival material for theorists who, sustained by an apolitical academia that sustains such endeavours, have over the last few decades managed to privilege theory, systematically marginalizing texts and the complex socio-cultural and political realities they deal with. However, this hegemonizing nature of 'post-colonial' theory has always been resisted by many discerning intellectuals and, more significantly, by the creative works that have come out of all 'post-colonial' societies.

Ananthamurthy's novel *Bharathipura* (1973) is one such act of resistance and confrontation.

This translation of *Bharathipura*, his second novel, comes long after the fairly well-known translation of his first novel *Samskara* (1965). This introduction attempts to locate the work in its specific socio-cultural context on the conviction that creative writing unfolds experiential dimensions that are in no way inferior to the epistemological elements that the social sciences claim to contain while 'objectively' studying societies and cultures.

Thinker, Writer, Critic, and Teacher

Ananthamurthy has published five novels, six anthologies of short stories, five volumes of poetry, sixteen collections of critical writings, and a play. In addition, there are three volumes of his translation into Kannada of the poetry of Yeats, Brecht, and Rilke. Also, he edited a highly-acclaimed Kannada literary journal, *Rujuvathu*. More importantly, for nearly six decades Ananthamurthy has shaped the consciousness of generations of readers in Karnataka by his incisive writings on various aspects of culture, including politics. No cultural and intellectual history of Karnataka, especially of the last six decades, can be written without a full negotiation with the insightful, provocative, and controversial ideas that Ananthamurthy has brought the Karnataka public face-to-face with.

The fiction of Ananthamurthy has altered the sensibilities of several writers in a major way. Many of his contemporaries and several young writers of the present, who have already gained considerable reputation as writers of distinction, have always openly acknowledged the impact his fiction has had on them, especially during their formative years.

With a strong socialist background, Ananthamurthy has also involved himself with environmental activism and civil liberties movements. But it is the nature of his involvement in politics that has really made him a major figure in the cultural life of Karnataka.

As a professor of English, Ananthamurthy was arguably the most brilliant teacher among other very distinguished teachers, spending the most creative part of his teaching life in the department of English at the University of Mysore. It was as a teacher and a research guide that Ananthamurthy produced a number of scholars, many of whom are now accomplished critics.

It was mainly because of Ananthamurthy who drew great inspiration from several teachers at Birmingham, that the department of English at the University of Mysore always integrated literary studies with a genuinely liberal political consciousness. Much before one had heard of modern theorists, or had become familiar with Edward Said, one had learnt to correlate the text, the critic, and the world.

The other outstanding contribution of Ananthamurthy as a teacher and a critic, and certainly as a cultural icon in Karnataka, was to make the students and the other teachers of the department realize that English literary studies as a discipline in India would become derivative, unimaginative, and pedantic if it did not open itself to literatures from Latin America, America, Africa, Australia, and, of course, from the various Indian bhashas. During the 1970s, for Commonwealth Literature to become an integral part of the English literary studies programme in India, the courageous pioneering efforts of C.D. Narasimhaiah at the University of Mysore—also Ananthamurthy's guru—have to be acknowledged. The student further radicalized his great teacher's early efforts by his forceful arguments concerning the value of studying literatures from all over the world, and, in particular, literatures produced by the so-called Third World countries.

The Influence of English

It is not a matter of coincidence or accident that a significant part of all the modern literary movements in Karnataka has been greatly influenced by teachers of English. Bilingualism has always been one of the central features of modern Karnataka literature, and, in our own times, Ananthamurthy has been the most vehement spokesperson for those advocating the cause of bilingualism in India. Ananthamurthy has constantly resisted the overwhelming hegemony of the West, and, in our own context, the rather exaggerated status accorded to Indian writing in English. His interrogation of Eurocentric models and many confrontations with English can by no stretch of imagination be interpreted to mean an attitude of parochialism or linguistic chauvinism. On the contrary, it suggests the recognition and validation of the autonomy of diverse traditions, cultures, and experiential and epistemological centres. To state it differently, it is the great belief in the idea of decentralization and the actual experience of being with living traditions that generate such an adversarial position in Ananthamurthy, who has always fought hierarchies and binary opposites of all kinds. The apparent irreconcilability between national and regional, centre and periphery, tradition and modernity, religion and secularism, global/universal and local, and several other oppositional categories sustained for long as valid and justifiable propositions by many epistemological centres, especially in the social sciences, emerge as unsustainable, untenable, and artificial constructs in Ananthamurthy's creative works. In fact, binary opposites metamorphose into complex, inseparable paradoxes of communities and societies transforming one another in a manner that defies conventional intellectual reasoning and understanding of the lives of individuals and the dynamic nature of the cultures and societies they are a part of.

For those who are deeply conversant with the range and depth of literatures produced in the bhashas in India—and, of course, with the literatures of other parts of the Third World—the richness and diversity of local cultures and the dynamism with which these cultures manage the new forces brought by alien cultures are well-known issues. It requires an insider to fully comprehend and experience them with a sense of immediacy. This is one of the reasons why many scholars commenting on the Indian colonial experience recognize it as a cultural encounter wherein local cultures freely negotiate with the dominant alien culture without any kind of neurotic anxiety or inferiority complex crippling their responses to the hegemonizing forces unleashed by the colonial masters. The manner in which local cultures organically evolved while negotiating with the dominant culture of the colonizer is a truly fascinating story, told in a subtle and perceptive manner by the bhasha writers, of whom Ananthamurthy is, arguably, the most significant. The fictional works of Ananthamurthy are profound narratives that depict the cultural encounters of our times, and what is of great interest is that these encounters are located in specific socio-cultural contexts and mark various points of time. In other words, the encounters carry sharp particularities of space and time, the spirit of which is continuously evolving. It is indeed the story of alterities.

Kannada: Language and Literature

One must, even if briefly, make an attempt to understand the genius of Kannada, as a language and a culture, to come to terms with its rich and complex identity. Kannada identity, linguistically and culturally, has been shaped by several kinds of confrontations and negotiations.

Kannada has had an interesting relationship with other languages and cultures. There are linguists who are of the opinion that the Kannada language is part of the Dravidian family of languages. It has also been argued that the Dravidian family of languages spread from Finland to mid-Mongolia. The journey one of the branches of this family made, and the many other systems of languages it entered, is an incredible one. One cannot go into all these here. But it has been suggested that around the second or third century BC this particular language started branching further. Consequently, Tamil came into existence first, and Kannada, later, as an independent language. For a long time Kannada had to deal with Sanskrit, recognized as the *Marga* (the classical), and other native languages, called Desi (the folk). What is remarkable is that Kannada borrowed from the other languages freely and certainly did not grow in isolation and in a hostile and antagonistic relationship with them. Kannada had an open relationship with Sanskrit and, it must be stated clearly, created its own directions and movements without being intimidated by the classical language. In the ninth century Kannada produced *Kavirajamarga*, a text that talked of the uniqueness of the Kannada language even as it recognized that this language was an essential part of the whole world. Kannada identity, over the centuries, has been shaped by the consciousness that uniqueness and inclusiveness are complementaries and not categories in strict opposition to each other. Even to this day it is this understanding of the growth of a language and a culture that continues to nourish Kannada identity, and all the great cultural figures of Kannada have sustained this wisdom in their creative and intellectual endeavours.

The literary tradition, too, has evolved along these lines. The Kannada literary tradition is quite an extraordinary amalgam of several other traditions and cultures. Modern Kannada literature, in particular, has, in the areas of poetry, drama, fiction, and criticism, drawn extensively from Greek drama, French fiction, English drama, fiction, poetry and criticism, and Russian fiction—to name just a few. Homer, Aeschylus, and Sophocles; Alexander Dumas, and Victor Hugo; Shakespeare, the British Romantics, Victorians, and modernists; Tolstoy and Dostoevsky—among several other writers, and a whole body of criticism and philosophy from the ancient to the modern periods—have shaped the spirit of Kannada literature and culture. These have not figured as mere influences from outside. What is of absolute importance is that the cultural and literary traditions of Kannada received ideas from the West, as freely as they did from other Indian languages, in consonance with their imagination, concerns, and attitudes. Moreover, the Kannada genius always ensured that its strong idiom built over centuries did not become insignificant in the process. Whatever came from outside was internalized with a fine understanding of the native sensibility and a proper and full sense of one's own tradition. The great feature of modern Kannada literature is that it found its relevance in the contemporary world by evolving in an organic manner conflating the past and the present.

From *Navodaya* to *Navya*

Kannada literature witnessed a great shift from what has been recognized as the phase of romanticism of the pre-Independence era, called *Navodaya*, to the post-Independence phase, described as *Navya*. It was the Navodaya Movement that opened up Kannada literature to the West in a prominent way. Between these two phases there was the emergence of the Progressive Movement, known as *Pragatisheela*, which was influenced, in a broad sense, by Leftist ideology. What one needs to understand today is that these literary movements brought into Kannada literature diverse thematic preoccupations, stylistic concerns, and ideological positions. It is necessary to add here that these phases do not indicate rigid, static, and definable positions. One must be fully aware that there is a problem with the use of this kind of terminology.

The Navodaya writers, with all their familiarity with and understanding of Western philosophy, were rooted in their culture. All the major works, especially in fiction, of the Navodaya period show how the writers were negotiating with their own local realities and little cultures. The Navya phase was different from the earlier one in many ways, though it cannot be argued that it differed from the Navodaya in an absolute manner. However, sharper and more rigorous distinctions were introduced by the Navya writers when it concerned questions of form, style, structure, and the narration of the existential predicament of individuals and communities. Also, the major preoccupations of modern literature such as despair, alienation, loss of identity, and angst constituted the core of Navya writing. Though the Navya writers drew from the European existentialists and quite heavily from Western schools of criticism, it is very wrong to equate them with European existentialism, realism, and symbolism. For all the influences at work on them, the Navya writers were profoundly situated in the socio-cultural and political realities of post-Independence India. The dualities and contradictions in the lives of individuals and communities became their concern in thematic and aesthetic terms and, in a very major way, shaped their literary sensibility throughout. The Navya writers moved away from great pan-Indian narratives, vague and amorphous ideals, and turned to the paradoxes of social life and the dichotomies built into the lives of individuals. The best of Navya attempted to catch the transitoriness of life as it manifested in a society that was experiencing various kinds of upheavals.

Ananthamurthy and *Bharathipura*

Ananthamurthy is one of the most important symbols of the Navya phase. It was in the early 1950s that Ananthamurthy began his writing career and, over the last nearly six decades, has undergone such a metamorphosis that he defies all categorizations as a Navya writer, and, more significantly, has made the term Navya itself a very problematic one. The outstanding range of his fiction has altered many perceptions, once believed to be fundamental and definitive, about the nature of Navya literature. This has been possible for the simple reason that Ananthamurthy is one of the few writers who have constantly evolved with the changing nature of India as a society and a culture as a thorough insider. He has always juxtaposed antithetical positions without resorting to simplifications and reductionist ideological positions. His creative works deal with all the illogical, irreconcilable aspects of an entire society in the most ambivalent manner. In fact, the novel *Bharathipura* brings us face-to-face with a number of issues of the Nehruvian and post-Nehruvian era.

Bharathipura is about modernization, a growing economy, socialism, and the struggle of individuals to move beyond their caste and class interests. The novel centres around an enlightened modern Indian who wants to break free, get rid of his personal burdens, and, in order to do so, has to do scandalous things, which also means desecrating many sacred things that have come down from the past. What is of importance in all these is that such an urge to break the burden of the past leads to a tragic, ironical situation. When Jagannatha, the protagonist, driven by the intense impulse to break the oppressive caste hierarchy of his small town, decides to act by forcing the untouchables, the polluted ones in the upper-caste dominated society, to gain their liberation by touching a sacred object and polluting it, what follows are strange reversals, irrational developments, and unexpected twists of circumstances, by which the object becomes more sacred and powerful than it was earlier, leaving the untouchables more vulnerable than before. Jagannatha's moral act is incorporated into the deeper illogical and arbitrary patterns of belief and irrational systems of a cultural order that generates power, whenever necessary, to subvert whatever challenges its authority. Ananthamurthy's work is a fascinating revelation of how the contemporary world recreates and reconstructs the past to protect its hierarchical structure. The complex dialectics created by social systems, whether of the past or the present, is what every fictional work of Ananthamurthy foregrounds. This is one of the reasons why Ananthamurthy journeys from the present to dwell in the past in most of his works. For him the return to the past is one of the most crucial aspects of understanding the present, which, as one ought to know, is a legacy of the past. As Camus brilliantly put it, nostalgia is a rebellion against an oppressive reality and an ontological search for the essence of one's being.

The first two novels of Ananthamurthy—*Samskara* and *Bharathipura*—deal with the existential predicament of two individuals located at different points of time and the moral choices they have to make to gain some authenticity of the self. The two have to transgress their social order if they are to arrive at any acceptable notion of their being. The two works, in different ways, are open negotiations with an Indian reality that has, apparently, moved from the past into the present in a linear manner. But Ananthamurthy's works draw our attention to the essential anachronistic nature of the present, also described as 'the modern', which, for a sensitive mind, carries many traces of the traditions of the past, making it impossible to separate the two. Such a complex philosophical understanding of the element of anachronism embedded in cultures and societies is precisely what lends a metaphorical/allegorical dimension to his works. Beyond a certain point, social realism makes way for the symbolic in his fiction. The symbolic dimension in Ananthamurthy operates at thematic and aesthetic levels, and his late works—the last novel *Divya* (2001) and the short stories 'Suryana Kudure' (The Stallion of the Sun), 'Jaratkaru', 'Akkayya', and 'Bete Bale Mattu Otiketa' (The Hunt, the Bangle, and the Chameleon)—push the metaphorical dimension to a point where 'reality' is registered mainly through its abstract dimensions. What it means is that social realism finds a perfect transmutation through images and symbols in Ananthamurthy's fiction, compelling the reader to comprehend the metaphysical dimensions of physical manifestations.

Bharathipura is about the practice of untouchability in a traditional society that is evolving into modernity through new economic forces brought in only by a certain class of people. Hence, cultural and economic practices are controlled by the ruling class, which has appropriated gods and temples too. To break one of them inevitably means breaking the others, simultaneously. Jagannatha cannot confront the caste system without shattering the economic order of the feudal town and desecrating its sacred symbols. While depicting all these, Ananthamurthy does not offer modernity as a great alternative, for it carries in its framework greater dehumanizing forces—a theme worked out in his third and fourth novels, *Awasthe* (1978) and *Bhava* (1994). The modern urban world is as bad as—if not worse than—the feudal order, and the politics of modern democracy is as manipulative as the tyranny of feudal societies. It is for this reason that the works of Ananthamurthy remain ambivalent and open-ended when they juxtapose tradition and modernity, the rural and the urban, the feudal caste order and the depersonalized cosmopolis, for contemporary Indian reality is an odd mixture of all these irreconcilable elements that merge, fuse into one another, yet, at the same time, diverge and contradict one another. The ambivalence in Ananthamurthy operates as the only legitimate metaphor that can mirror all the contradictions, dualities, and paradoxes of Indian life as perfect antinomies. And it is through Ananthamurthy's ambivalent symbols that the complexities of Indian social and political realities reveal themselves fully. *Bharathipura* is a major work that decades after its publication carries all the vital and subtle resonances of a society and a culture that seem to engender greater contradictions and more complex dichotomies with the passage of time.

I must thank M.R. Rakshith for his outstanding support throughout. It was Rakshith who recorded and transcribed my long interview with U.R. Ananthamurthy. His contribution has been invaluable. I am deeply touched by Mini Krishnan's concern, warmth, and editorial support. I thank Mini for all that, and being with me in many other way.

October 2010 N. MANU CHAKRAVARTHY

ONE

Homecoming

When he was on his own, Jagannatha never walked around puddles . . . he jumped right across. And in the tender sunlight of chilly December, he loved to walk briskly.

The moment breakfast was over, he had said to his mother's younger sister, 'Chikki, I'm going over to see Sripathirayaru,' and had set off towards the town. He was racing downhill, pinching leaves from wayside shrubs, sniffing the heady scent, and wondering how to put across to Sripathi Rao something he had been mulling over for about a month now. That was when he ran into Narahari Rao of Belthangadi—turbaned head, studs in ears, wrinkled face, and anxious eyes.

'Are you going to the temple for a *darshana*?'[1] asked Narahari Rao as his palms met in a greeting even as he held both bag and umbrella. The umbrella, patched in a hundred places, had turned a weather-beaten grey, one stud had a pearl missing, and his dusty feet had no chappals.

[1] A 'viewing' of the deity.

'No, no, just here … to the town,' Jagannatha replied, waiting for him to say something more. Instead, Narahari Rao put his hand in his pocket, anxiously trying to ferret out something while Jagannatha wondered, is it proper for him to walk away from here without asking Narahari Rao home for a cup of coffee?

'Why don't you go over to my house and have something to drink? I'll be back by the afternoon,' he said, and picking up the hem of his *dhothi*[2] and tying it firmly around his waist, he looked at Narahari Rao, in a hurry to move on. But the man was preoccupied with searching his pockets, one after the other, and Jagannatha could not guess what he could be looking for. Finally, from over a hundred slips of paper, Narahari Rao pulled out a letter and held it out to him, and said apologetically, as if it was improper for him to speak at all, 'Perhaps you've written this way because you were upset I hadn't yet repaid the loan I took from your father. But what could I do, you tell me? I'm worn out with getting five children married. And the crops have failed this year.'

That was when Jagannatha understood the anxious expression. Perhaps he had not explained himself clearly while writing a hundred or a hundred and fifty such letters. 'Che, che, no Naraharirayare,' he said, 'I really meant that you shouldn't pay back the loan. You see, this business that my father carried on, and then his accountant after him, of giving loans and then collecting an interest on it and offering it to Manjunatha[3] at the temple … I don't like it at all. I've written similar letters to the others too. Why don't you go to my house now? We can talk about it later.'

It didn't look as if Narahari Rao had quite grasped what Jagannatha had said. His expression continued to be subservient; only his toothless mouth stretched to a smile because it wanted to. He brought his palms together in obeisance, bag and umbrella dangling from one of them, and then fumbled awkwardly to make small talk.

'Go home and rest awhile,' Jagannatha said to ease the embarrassment and walked on.

[2] A length of cloth worn by men round the waist to cover the lower part of the body.

[3] Or Manjunathaswami: the local deity, another name for Shiva. 'Swami' is a suffix meaning 'Lord'.

As he was tearing up all the promissory notes, Jagannatha had thought about this problem: writing off these loans was like breaking a vital link with these people. He would have to forge another way of keeping in touch with them; but then, first, he would have to look for a different kind of relationship ... Now, sipping Chikki's coffee, Narahari Rao will try to make sense of this perplexing situation: why did Jagannatha let go of loans running into thousands of rupees? What's to be our plight when we need to borrow again? ... Even Chikki was sure to be worried. She might secretly shove some sanctified amulets under his pillow. She might even make a few more vows on his behalf. She knew he had resigned from his position as a trustee of the temple. After all, it had been whispered all over the town. When the President of the country visited the temple to worship Manjunatha, Jagannatha had received an invitation to meet him. And Chikki had been all excited about it. But when he had sent word that he would not attend, she had been very upset. He had resigned from the trusteeship that very day.

Striding rapidly, Jagannatha walked down the hill and reached the road. The town was just another furlong away. Beyond the tollgate was another world of other smells. Small restaurants filled with the smoky aroma of *dosés*,[4] hair-dressers displaying comical concave and convex mirrors that made the faces of passers-by appear narrow and then, wide ...

Jagannatha walked on, looking neither this way nor that, for he felt some people might feel obliged to stand up respectfully, ask how he was doing, and say, 'How is it you've come walking all the way? You could've driven down.' Some might even think it proper to walk some distance with him. They might feel boorish, might feel a kind of awkwardness; *what will he think of us if we don't?* And surely, just to feel neighbourly, all of them would try the usual opener, 'On your way to the temple?'

Jagannatha went past the Vokkaliga[5] Students Hostel. To the right was the High School run by the Shri Manjunatha Trust where he had

[4] Pancakes made of rice, dhal, and beaten rice. It is a typical south Indian snack.

[5] An Indian caste or social group found mainly in the Old Mysore region of southern Karnataka. A dominant caste, they are basically a farming community. Some of them have the surname Gowda.

studied. There were some boys playing volleyball. The school had not grown at all, except perhaps for two new rooms. Just the previous week, Gurappa Gowda, the MLA, had said cajolingly, 'Why don't you add a wing in memory of your mother?'

'Let's see,' he had replied.

He had wanted to argue if it was right to waste public money doing up the road to the temple just because the President had made a visit to Manjunatha, but he had not.

Beyond the High School, on a hillock, was a Traveller's Bungalow. Once, when Gandhi had visited, arrangements had been made for his stay there. But Gandhi, on reaching the town, had headed straight to the Holeyaru[6] settlement on the outskirts. And so, even Jagannatha's father, as an elder of the town, had had to go there to be with him. Later he had gone through the *panchagavya*, a ritual cleansing. Jagannatha had heard this story from Sripathi Rao. Gandhi was the only person who had visited the town without making a visit to Manjunatha. These days, not a minister on an official visit left the town without receiving the prasada[7] from the temple.

From here the road split into a hundred stinking lanes leading to the central marketplace set in the valley. It had been born through Manjunathaswami's bounty and had grown haphazardly spreading tentacles at random, with the stench of urine in every street corner and the walls defaced with the age-old advertisement, 'Liver Cure!' and the more recent, 'Vote for Gurappa!' The streets around the marketplace had an air of excitement.

People from the nearby villages had come in cartloads for a day in the town. Hanging around the shops were farmers, and Deeva women, with the edge of the sari just a little below the knee, large ear studs, nose rings, and tightly plaited hair loaded with strands of flowers. Perhaps they had come for a wedding in the temple or perhaps to ask their god, Bhootharaya,[8] to foretell their future, or to buy saris and

[6] A community of low castes who cleaned dry toilets; Holeya (singular), Holeyaru (plural), and Holathi (feminine).

[7] A portion of the food, fruit, and flowers offered to the idol and returned to the worshipper as a blessing.

[8] Lord of the spirits; an awe-inspiring god of the lower castes. *Bhootha* is spirit.

ravikes. A boy was plaguing his mother to buy him a balloon; he had seen another boy blowing one. After doing whatever they had come to do, these people would stop at any one of the small eateries to eat some fried bhajis, down it with some coffee, and get something packed to take home. Jagannatha had lived in England for five years, and yet he had not forgotten any detail of the ambience of this place. Hasn't it changed at all? Or, is it that I can't see the change? Those who sat about in front of the shops felt a little awkward to see him pass by—what if he should see me? Shouldn't I stand up respectfully?

But Jagannatha walked past them briskly, as if he were on urgent business. He noticed a few youngsters in tight trousers, here and there. Perhaps those were children of the tourists who had come to the temple for Manjunatha's darshana. But the men who whiled away their time on the benches lining the shop-front were old familiar faces. They sat watching pilgrims, digesting their breakfast of seasoned beaten-rice or *dosés*, while their women sat in smoky wood-fire kitchens throughout the day. Here, on a bench in a bustling market-street, these men sat every day in companionable silence, watching the pageant of pilgrims on their way to the temple. Here they sat until it was time for lunch; then they would wend their way home, or, if there was some trouble at home, they would go to the temple for a free meal. This is how they lived, trusting in Manjunatha's bounty. They owned rice fields in some distant village; some landless labourer worked their soil and reaped their harvest for them. And fearing the wrath of Bhootharaya, the god of his people, he never failed to pay for his tenancy. He also gave them vegetables he had grown—pumpkin, cucumber, bunches of banana. Somehow the belly was filled; someone gave birth, someone died. In a year there were at least a few deaths, a few births, ten or more weddings. Somehow time moved on, hair greyed, teeth dropped out.

Jagannatha was disconcerted. In the letter to Margaret he was composing in his head, he said, 'Life has ceased to be creative here. Manjunathaswami is the cancer of our lifestyle; this very town is a cancer, growing for him.'

The first bus from Shimoga arrived, raking dust in its wake; it was run by the Shri Manjunatha Bus Service Company. It stopped at the end of the road. It stops in this manner at the end of every street. Brahmin boys, with a tuft of hair on their heads and a scrap of dhothi wrapped round their waists, crowd around it. 'Come and stay with us, please. Come to our house, please,' they plead with the pilgrims getting down from the bus. They pester in Hindi those who look as if they may not understand Kannada. There is a *choultry* for such visitors that Jagannatha's father had built. It was a free lodge but it was not large enough. After haggling over the rates, they strike a deal and lead the tourists to their homes, carrying their luggage for them. It is a package that includes a bath in the river for ritual cleansing, a visit to the temple, a ritual for the dead, a visit to the shrines, the fulfilling of a vow to Bhootharaya on the hilltop, and reservations on the bus for the return journey. The competition is so keen among these boys that, sometimes, two brothers pretend to be from different homes and dupe a customer into believing each fellow is offering him a better deal than the other. Little rascals! The tourists with their families follow these boys to their multi-storeyed homes, darkened with wood smoke. They may stay here for a day or two. This is an old marketplace that gets to see fresh faces every day.

'Jagannatharayare, namaskara! Looks as if you're on your way to the temple?'

Jagannatha turned and looked to his right. Are these people trying to make fun of me? Or is it just an attempt to be cordial, to make a connection? Nagaraja Jois stood at his door smiling at him. He was known in the town for casting the Hindu almanac. He was the one who, when the President had visited the town, had composed verses in Sanskrit praising him, had got them printed, and had presented them to him. His son was an advocate practicing in Shimoga. There was a story he always narrated with great relish: it was about the *matadhipathi*[9] who had excommunicated him for refusing to compute the movement of the planets according to the traditional Indian method and for using Western calculations instead; he had retaliated with verses in Sanskrit lampooning him. Jois was smart, he knew Jagannatha was modern in his outlook and the story would go down well with him. He even knew how to contend that God did not exist. Seetharamaiah, his cousin, was the chief priest at the Manjunatha temple, and so, naturally, he was jealous of him.

[9] Head of a religious centre, a preceptor.

Jagannatha climbed the few steps to the porch of Jois's house only because Jois was insisting on the visit. The younger son had just come home alone; he had not brought any pilgrims with him. 'A family from Bellary went to Udupa's house,' he said, sounding disappointed.

'That's all right, go and wait for the second bus,' said Jois to comfort his son—and to Jagannatha, 'I'll get you a chair.'

'Oh, don't bother!' said Jagannatha, 'A mat will do.' He did not want any coffee either.

'How is your elder son's practice doing in Shimoga?'

'Petitions are made only to Bhootharaya, aren't they? How do you expect any advocate's practice to flourish in these parts?' grumbled Nagaraja Jois. He edged close to Jagannatha bringing his face, with its ruby red ear studs and dirty red teeth, close to his. He was talking in a tone of great intimacy. Today must be an auspicious day; his face and head were freshly shaved. A necklace of *rudrakshi*[10] beads, strung in gold, hung round his neck. This was a sure way of enticing tourists—the ruby red studs, the gold chain, the disarming way of talking, and the feeling of fellowship he created by sitting so close to Jagannatha.

'You know, this claim that the idol of Manjunatha was installed here by Shri Parashurama?[11] That's a big lie, Jagannatharayare. If any researcher were to dig up the linga,[12] the truth will be out. Already it has developed a crack; it's been set only three inches deep. You know why? Because it was really Yedutheerthaswamy who installed it. You ask me and I'll tell you. Nobody accepts my argument because they think I'm jealous of my cousin, the chief priest ....'

Nagaraja Jois edged closer. He whispered even more secretively, his eyes wide-open, eloquent, 'Just look at it this way, Jagannatharayare. You're well read; you'll know what I'm driving at. Tell me. Is there any place for demon-worship in Advaita[13] philosophy? And now, who do you think is being worshipped here? Tell me the truth.'

[10] A berry, sacred to Shiva.

[11] Literally, Rama of the axe. He is considered to be the sixth incarnation of Vishnu and belongs to the period of the struggle between the Brahmins and the Kshatriyas.

[12] The symbol of Shiva's creative energy, in the form of a phallus; it represents Shiva in temples dedicated to him. It is worshipped by Shaivites.

[13] Nondualism, a doctrine that identifies the divine essence and the human soul as one.

Jois's voice became even softer, his eyes staring at Jagannatha as if accusingly, 'Tell me. Whom do the people fear? Whom did even the President of the country come here to worship? Who decides where the offerings to Manjunatha go?'

Jois stared at Jagannatha for a moment, in silence.

'All the worship offered to Manjunatha really goes to Bhootharaya, doesn't it? Tell me why the red rice offering is made to him. Why do the temple boys wear red clothes, you tell me?You know the *kumkuma*[14] that Bhootharaya wears on his forehead and chest as a blessing from Manjunatha? Tell me why it is red. What is the purpose in giving the blood-red kumkuma instead of the ash-grey *vibhuthi*[15] as prasada?'

Jois pointed to the red kumkuma on his forehead, a sign of blessing from Shri Manjunatha plus Bhootharaya. He sat quietly for a while and then said, 'What Bhootharaya used to receive in those days was blood sacrifice. If that be so, the question is: what's the relationship between Manjunatha and Bhootharaya now?'

Now Jois showed Jagannatha a photograph of Manjunatha hanging on the wall of the porch—a calm face covering a fist-sized linga, and on top of this face, a small gold crown.

Jois noticed Jagannatha staring at the picture and used the crown as an example to prove his argument.

'Let's take this very crown, for instance. When you were born, you were possessed by a bhootha. For three days you lay listless, as if in a coma. I put you on my lap and I myself said the Mruthyunjaya[16] prayer. Subbaraya Adiga was also with me at that time. If you don't believe me, you can check with him. We touched embers to different spots all over your body to exorcize the bhootha from you. Even that didn't help; you didn't come out of the stupor. Then it was I who had asked your mother to make a vow to offer a gold crown to Manjunathaswami. If I envied my cousin his position as chief priest and didn't want the temple to flourish, would I have suggested to your mother that she should make this vow? Why am I talking about all that now? Because

[14] A sanctified red powder that Hindus put as a dot between the eyebrows; a widow has to give up this auspicious practice.

[15] The ash of cow-dung given as a blessing to a devotee. Shaivites smear parts of the body with this sacred ash.

[16] Another name for Lord Shiva, meaning one who has triumphed over death.

I want you to know that though Manjunatha got the crown, it was Bhootharaya who was actually worshipped to save your life. What does that mean? That it is Bhootharaya who does all the work in the name of Manjunatha. Now you tell me, is it proper for a Brahmin to worship the god of the lower castes?'

It suddenly dawned on Nagaraja Jois that he had made a grave mistake. By using the crown as an example, he had found fault with Jagannatha's mother. He had not meant it that way but his own line of argument had stumped him. He felt ill at ease. He did not know how to continue. He tried to steer clear of further embarrassment, 'Anyway, I guess it's all a matter of belief. If such faith wasn't rampant all over, do you think the President of the country would've come here to visit the temple? He's worried about his cardiac problems. Did you notice how he was beaming before he left? He was very pleased with my poem in Sanskrit. I had it framed before presenting it to him. He took it with him in the plane.'

Jagannatha could not help feeling amused. Suppressing a smile he said, 'You were talking about some connection between Manjunatha and Bhootharaya, Shastrigale. Tell me more about it.'

'You know the original residents of this place? The ones who tie the dhothi right above the knee? Those who butcher chicken and goats and eat them? Their god is Bhootharaya. Our Brahmin priests installed Manjunatha over and above him and made them subservient to our interests.'

'Oho! So let's say that's the reason why every judgment of Bhootharaya is against the tenant farmer. Yes?'

Nagaraja Jois was a shrewd man; he could see Jagannatha was being sarcastic. However, he made one more attempt to get out of the muddle, 'Whatever that be, Manjunatha is an exacting god, very exacting, very exacting. He will not be taken lightly. Those who worship him must do it diligently. He should not become just an excuse to suit their ends. This is the gist of what I'm trying to say, nothing else.'

Jagannatha could see that Nagaraja Jois was trying to slip away. He stood up. 'You should write up all this as an article, Shastrigale,' he said.

'I need your support, Jagannatha,' replied Jois. 'It was your mother who published my book, *The Glory of Shri Manjunatha*. Would you like a copy? Shall I give it to you?'

'No, don't. I have one at home,' said Jagannatha, getting ready to leave.

'But you're leaving without a cup of coffee,' protested Jois.

'Oh, don't worry,' said Jagannatha, and getting down the steps to the street, raised his palms together to bid goodbye, and walked away.

The streets spread out in a circular network. They can't create anything, at any time. Even as the fame of Manjunatha spread, these streets have grown, without sewers, one leading to the other. If the Holeyaru struck work for even a week, and refused to fill the shit into baskets and carry them out on their heads, then these streets would be filled with such stench as would pervade even the innermost chamber of the temple where Manjunatha dwells. Jagannatha shuddered with disgust at the very thought. Not a single beautiful thing could be created in these towns where Brahmins and traders lived. Wonder why? Some ten miles from Bharathipura, there were masons who made pots and pans of stone, and woodcarvers who sculpted beautiful figurines from sandalwood. In a village just about two miles from here, lived puppeteers. But there was never ever anything beautiful in the town of Bharathipura except the main street paved with red mud when the President came to visit. And, anyway, even that had turned slushy after a few days. Jagannatha walked gingerly to avoid children's faeces and reached the somewhat broader Chariot Street.

The greatest creation of this town may be Nagaraja Jois's *The Glory of Shri Manjunatha,* written in the Sanskrit *anushtup*[17] metre. Remembering Jois, Jagannatha felt like laughing. How the fellow had tied himself up in knots! He must be so mortified now. In that book which Jagannatha's mother had published at two annas a copy, there was a description of the crown that had saved her son's life. There was also a prayer to the wearer of the crown, Shri Manjunatha, to grant her boy the grace of good health and long life. And then, there was a paean of praise for Bhootharaya for faithfully doing Manjunatha's work for him. There was also a whole chapter describing Bharathipura as an adornment to the world, like a jewel: with its attractive rangoli designs decorating the floor and tender leaves festooning the streets; with its good-looking

[17] A popular metre in Sanskrit poetry.

tribals, ascetics, ardent devotees of Bhootharaya; and with Sitadevi, the protector of orphans, the mother of Jagannatha.

No wonder nothing ever happens here, nothing new; God has made life sterile—Jagannatha added another paragraph to the letter he was composing in his head to Margaret. He must get down to writing that letter telling her everything; it had been a long time since he had written to her:

Some months ago, I was on my way to Delhi, dear Margaret. The plane was about to take off from Hyderabad when a person called Shirnali Baba got in. He's a godman, famous in the whole of India. Beside him sat a well-known scientist, a great devotee of the Baba. There were some wealthy businessmen in the plane and twenty vice-chancellors on their way to a conference. You have to see Shirnali Baba to believe his charisma. When the devotee-scientist raised his hand to turn on the light above him, Baba stopped him. What an embodiment of gentleness! Some four or five American hippie girls prostrated at his feet and, thanks to Baba's magical powers, their hands were filled with vibhuthi. They ate the sacred ash. Even the airhostesses prostrated before him. You know the kind of spiritual chivalry he has cultivated? He caresses the head of the devotee even before he touches his feet. He stretches out his hand with a smile sweeter than honey and leaves in the devotee's palm, vibhuthi or a gold thali, the symbol of marriage. This is the way the Baba has taken over the homes of all the governors. He has deputed devotees across the country to conduct bhajans. If there's any one person who all the people believe in, right from the President to the lowliest poor, it is this Baba. Dear Margaret, surely, unless we destroy God, we will never be creative. We are still embryos in the womb of God; we're not born at all. We're not yet caught in the churning of history. We should be.

'Hey, Vasu!' Jagannatha grasped someone's hand and shook it warmly. A friend he had not seen in ten years; the same teeth with gaps in between, the long face, the Hitler moustache, only the hair was scantier. He was walking into a restaurant. He had a spot of kumkuma on his forehead. Jagannatha couldn't believe his eyes. In Shimoga, when they were in the Intermediate college together, they used to sit up the whole night talking about revolution and change, eating spicy hot masala puri and washing it down with hot tea at Kaka's tea-stall. This fellow used to be bubbly, ready for any kind of sacrifice. For that matter, Jagannatha had been the timid one. For instance, during the Freedom Struggle of 1942, Vasu would not tell the police where he had hidden a postbox he had dug up and upended, even though they had beaten him up badly. Overcome by memories, Jagannatha gripped Vasu's shoulders, staring at his kumkuma.

'Hey, you rascal! Wearing this as a joke or what?'

'You're Jaganna, aren't you?' replied Vasu, slowly recovering from Jagannatha's overtures of friendship. He was in trousers and a bush-shirt.

'Come, let's go home,' said Jagannatha. He had quite forgotten he was on his way to visit Sripathi Rao. 'Why do you look so thin and worn out, Vasu? When did you settle here? Where do you stay? Nobody seemed to know where you were ...'

Vasu seemed preoccupied.

'I'm busy right now, Jaganna. See you later.'

Suddenly, Jagannatha felt disillusioned. It did not seem as if Vasu was as happy as he had been to meet again. Not just that; he looked weak and drained. Perhaps, his kumkuma from Manjunatha's shrine was not a joke at all. Instantly, Jagannatha felt an invisible wall rising between them. But, covering up his disappointment, he said, 'Come, let's have some coffee.'

'What! Will you enter such a tea shop?'

'What if I do? Don't be stupid!'

The manager stood up deferentially when he saw Jagannatha. Some of the farmers who were sipping coffee also rose to their feet. Jagannatha felt awkward. This was the first time he had entered a tea shop in the town. The manager himself did the honours, wiping clean the black stone top of the table, and drawing out the chairs for them. Some of the regular clients—labourers known to Jagannatha—moved to an inner room.

'Coffee!' said Vasu. The manager went in to see to the order personally.

'At least now do you know what an important person you are in this town?' teased Vasu. Jagannatha was pleased to hear the tone of banter in his voice.

'What're you doing? Tell me,' he said, sipping the warm, froth-capped coffee.

'You know I didn't complete my BA, don't you? My father had thrown me out of the house. That's when you went to England. I joined a theatre group. Then I started one of my own. I earned about thirty thousand rupees. And lost all of it. Those were the days of the Prohibition. I brewed and sold illicit liquor. Made money. Got married to a Shetty girl at the Registrar's. "Don't ever try to see me again," said my father. Now, I have three children. Tell me, what's the point in all that talk about revolution when I have to come home to a wife complaining, "There's no rice at home today"? Do you know how I feel? For sometime I sold brandy, pretending to be a chemist in a drugstore. Then I ran a "Bombay Show". Attracted by the girls in the show, many local businessmen and politicians became friendly with me. It was disgusting. I gave it up. Now I want to put down roots somewhere, so I've come to this town. Bhootharaya has asked me to set up a confectionary. And so that's what I'm doing now.'

'Your life sounds like a picaresque novel! Come on, do you really believe in Bhootharaya, Vasu?'

'Don't you also believe there's some mystery to it?'

It seemed as if Vasu was in a hurry to leave. 'Look, life is not easy, Jaganna. Tell me now, what're you doing? I heard you had returned; that you had gone back to farming your lands. There's even a rumour doing the rounds that you're married to an English girl. Is that true?' Vasu downed the last sip, lit a cigarette, and waited eagerly.

'I did live with an English girl. That bit is true. But I didn't marry her.'

'Good for you! You're smart, aren't you? You've had a gala time in England!'

An expression like 'gala time' from Vasu? Jagannatha felt depressed. How close they used to be! Who was that Vasu? And who is this? Wonder who I am! It is impossible to have a heart-to-heart with this man. It was true Margaret and I had lived as man and wife. It was also true that we weren't married. But it wasn't just to have a great time, just to be smart. It was something else. How could I explain it to Vasu? We can't be as close as we used to be. He doesn't need me now. He's depressed.

'Come home when you can make the time,' said Jagannatha and stood up. The manager said the coffee was on the house. Jagannatha shook hands with Vasu and left the place, walking towards Sripathi Rao's house. He would have to look for new links to find fulfilment here in this town. There was no other way. A stupor seemed to be spreading again. Was any kind of action possible in this place? The kind that belongs to history—that makes you belong to history? Action that makes you accountable to Time, that makes you bud, bloom, and bring forth fruit in the tender sunlight, sprouting fresh leaves again and again like a mango tree. In a gloom he could not fathom, there were dark-skinned faces with dishevelled hair, heads carrying baskets of human waste. Right ahead of him was the tip of Manjunatha's *gopura*[18], glinting in the sun. Beyond it, was the river with its clear water and the white sandy beaches that made you forget the filth of the town and the rocks—rocks that had taught his tender feet how to jump across.

On top of the hillock beyond the temple was Bhootharaya with hair wet and unkempt and body smeared with bright red kumkuma—holding a *singara*[19] and dancing in a fine frenzy—and in the inner chamber of the temple was Manjunatha, wearing the crown. And there was the bell, a gift from his forefathers to the temple, whose peals resounded through the town.

All these churned in Jagannatha's head forming a clear thought struggling to break free. He tried to see his idea from different angles.

Deciding to tell Sripathi Rao everything that was going on in his mind, Jagannatha walked in through the door of his house, stood in the dark entrance hall, and called out, 'Is Sripathirayaru at home?'

[18] Temple tower.

[19] A frond of areca flowers.

TWO

Sripathi Rao's Khadi Store

Sripathi Rao and Jagannatha's father, Anand Rao, had been childhood friends and grown up together. Even after Jagannatha's father died, Sripathi Rao continued to be a friend of the family, helping Jagan's mother, Sitadevi. And because Krishnaiah, the clerk who worked for the family, had also died by the time Jagannatha left home to attend college in Mysore, she never did anything without consulting Sripathi Rao. It was he who had advised Jagannatha to go to England to study further after his BA. At that time Jagannatha had been torn between two loyalties; he was his mother's only son, was it proper for him to leave the country? But then, should he not think of himself too, of widening his horizons? Sripathi Rao had discussed the issue with his mother and also with him, and had decided it was best for him to study abroad. 'You have wealth enough to corrupt you and ruin your peace of mind, Jagannatha. You don't have to waste your life adding to it,' he had said.

Sitadevi could see his point. She was worldly-wise and had managed the affairs of the family very well in Jagannatha's absence. Also, after Krishnaiah's death, Sripathi Rao had helped as much as he could to lighten her burden. And even when his mother had died suddenly. Jagannatha, who had been studying in England, had come home as soon as he had heard the news. And then he did not know what to do; whether to stay or to return. But it was Sripathi Rao who had sent him back to England. 'Go back and finish the course, Jaganna,' he had said, 'don't worry about anything here. Hasn't Chikki been living in your home since you were born? She's a child-widow. Isn't her elder sister's son like her own? She'll run the house, the *shanbogh*[20] as overseer and accountant will see to the affairs of the estate, and, anyway, I'm here. Why do you have to worry about anything?' Chikki had agreed with him.

And it was not just that. In so many other ways, Sripathi Rao was responsible for whatever Jagannatha was as an intellectual. During the Quit India Movement in 1942[21], Jagannatha had been in his final year in the High School run by the Shri Manjunatha Trust. (In fact, it was Sripathi Rao who had seen to it that the school was set up from the funds of the temple.) He was the regional leader of the Congress Party at the time. Jagannatha could even now remember him in a sit-down protest at the Taluk Office. Like his mentor, Jagannatha had worn a khadi *jubba*[22] and cap and joined the freedom struggle. He had gone about shouting '*Jai*' to court a two-day stay in prison. He had vandalized sandalwood trees and picketed liquor shops demanding their closure. Sripathi Rao had read writers like Ingersoll, Shaw, and Russell, and had sown seeds of scepticism in him. His mother had not objected to it. After all, he was influenced by Sripathi Rao, wasn't he? Anyway, his father too used to wear khadi. Now, even she began to wear white khadi saris. And she subscribed to the Harijan.[23] Every evening Sripathi Rao would visit their house to read the paper and explain the news to

[20] Village accountant.

[21] In August 1942, when the proposals of the Cripps Mission were rejected by Indians, the All India Congress Committee unanimously adopted this historic resolution.

[22] The word 'Khadi' is used specifically to designate the native homespun product as opposed to mill-made fabric from England. 'Jubba' is a collarless knee-length shirt, also known as the kurta.

[23] A newspaper run by Gandhi. Harijan, meaning people of God, was the name Gandhi gave to people of the lowest caste in the Hindu hierarchy. The British referred to them as Pariahs. They refer to themselves as Dalits.

them. His mother, his aunt, Krishnaiah, and he would sit around and listen to him.

But for Sripathi Rao, Jagannatha would never have known a world beyond that of Manjunatha in the mid-twentieth-century town of Bharathipura. Especially in his boyhood, there was no other way he could have known it. As one of the elders of the Congress Party in Mysore State, Sripathi Rao had sacrificed all his wealth for the country's freedom struggle, but after Independence he had been one of those cast aside. That was why Jagannatha was on his way to Rao's place to discuss with him the new plan struggling to take shape in his mind. He had thought about it on his own these many days and had, at last, decided to put it before his mentor. In those days, responding to Gandhi's[24] call to boycott British goods, Sripathi Rao had willingly emptied his textile store on the street and made a bonfire of it. So now, he would surely understand Jagannatha's inner turmoil to bring about a change. At least, Jagannatha hoped so.

It looked as if the husband and wife were having an argument in the kitchen. Jagannatha felt awkward. 'Rayare!' he called again, raising his voice.

As his eyes got used to the gloom, the room disclosed its mess to him: a bench against a wall to the right with rolls of mattresses piled high on it. They looked old, faded—too hard to be comfortable. There was a row of pictures on a wall; of Gandhi, Nehru,[25] and Subhash Chandra Bose,[26] each with a garland of dust-laden, homespun khadi yarn. On another wall was a picture of Shri Manjunatha with a garland of tiny cotton balls. Perhaps Sripathi Rao's wife, Bhagyamma, had made it for Him. The walls were stuck with nails. On them hung shirts of the four or five sons. On the reddened threshold were white rangoli lines delicately drawn with chalk-paste, and all along the edge of the four walls the black stone floor too was decorated with white rangoli designs. Sripathi Rao's eldest daughter, Savithri, might have drawn them: lacy run-on designs with delicate lines winding their way around tiny dots. And then there was the smoke—smoke that wrung tears from your eyes. You would have to walk gingerly with eyes in narrow

[24] The architect of Indian Independence; the Father of the Nation.

[25] Freedom fighter who later became the first Prime Minister of India.

[26] Freedom fighter from Bengal.

slits and face away from the direction of the smoke wafting from the kitchen. Most probably its acrid stink had settled permanently on the wet dhothi and the shirt Sripathi Rao wore, the shawl he wrapped around himself. His wife was muttering, he was shouting something in reply. Suddenly, there was silence. And then, the sound of Bhagyamma blowing into the blowpipe to start the fire afresh, the sound of the blowpipe being thumped on the floor in anger, the sound of a cough from a throat choked with smoke.

'Rayare?' Jagannatha called again. A fresh gust of smoke clouded his eyes. Someone came into the hall in a hurry, perhaps his daughter, Savithri. She rushed back closing the door behind her to keep the smoke from filling the hall.

'Who's that? Jaganna?' Rayaru came in rubbing his eyes with the strip of cloth wrapping his bare body. 'Damn the smoke! Come, let's go upstairs.'

The room upstairs was smoky too but, at least, it was brighter. Rayaru shut the door behind them and opened a few windows. He moved the clothes lying on the bed and said, 'Sit here.' Jagannatha saw the small cupboard by the bedside. It held some of Sripathi Rao's books he had known so well since childhood: Reynold's novels in very small print, two columns to a page; the novels of Scott; Goldsmith's *Vicar of Wakefield*; Edwin Arnold's *Light of Asia*; Shaw's plays. On a wall was Jagannatha's mother's photograph. It might have been taken soon after her wedding, perhaps during the annual town fair. In colour, developed in sunlight. It looked faded now, making the tender round face look even more sensitive. How tightly Amma used to pull back her luxuriant hair from a middle parting and knot it!

Rayaru did not talk. Generally, whenever they got together he did not talk. Neither did Jagannatha; they were quite happy to share a silence. At some point, Rayaru, while chewing on his betel leaves and nut, spiced with *sunna*,[27] would chuckle to himself and say something profound, distilling some ten or more lines of thought into one sentence, and Jagannatha would instantly grasp the essence of it. For instance, he might say something provoking like, 'Now, what did Gandhi say? But look at this Nehru ...' and that would be as if he had shared all his

[27] Quicklime.

views on the current political and economic situation with Jagannatha. And Jagannatha would respond with, 'Emotionally we're all Indians, no doubt; but our thinking is influenced by the West, isn't it?' stopping half way—and this comment would work on Rayaru's mind throughout the day and emerge the next day linked to a string of other ideas.

But today, Jagannatha guessed that Rayaru might have another reason for the silence; perhaps something was weighing him down. He pulled out some betel leaves and nuts from a khadi pouch; threw the nuts into his mouth and sat chewing on them as he smeared sunna on the leaves. Jagannatha lit a cigarette and looked around for some container in which to drop the ash. In a corner he found an old snuffbox. Everyone knew that Rayaru's wife used snuff in secret and never in her husband's presence. But, every month, it was he who would buy a box of snuff and put it in a place where she could find it. When Rayaru was in prison, it was Jagannatha's secret responsibility to replenish her supply. Perhaps Rayaru did not have to buy her the snuff any more now that her son had grown up and her daughter was a teacher in a Middle School.

White hair in a crew cut, bright eyes under bushy eyebrows twinkling with mischief even now, ears with hair sticking out from them, short, slim, and sprightly—that was Sripathi Rao.

He could be sitting on a chair but when he got all excited, he would draw up his legs and sit cross-legged, or get up and walk about. But there was no point in meeting him in his house; here, he was quiet and withdrawn. 'Come, Rayare, let's go out,' Jagannatha suggested.

'Wait a while.'

The door opened. Rayaru's wife, Bhagyamma, came in with two small brass tumblers of coffee. The stainless steel age had not yet stepped into Rayaru's house. These were well worn and dented, with the rim bent backward and gathering dirt in the groove. The jaggery coffee was barely warm, having lent its heat to the glass that held it.

'How are you, Amma?' Jagannatha asked her, sipping his coffee.

'As well as I can be,' said Bhagyamma, 'How is it we haven't seen you these ten or fifteen days?' She was wiping her nose-stud with the edge of her sari. She sounded bored or disgusted. She was a plump woman. Narrow forehead, small eyes—no one had ever seen her happy. Could she have lost what girlhood joys she might have had in years and years of sitting in front of a smoky wood fire and years and years of childbearing?

But then, how did Sripathi Rao remain supple yet wiry, like the fibre of the tamarind? This cold war between them to destroy each other must have been going on in this house for many years now. No wonder Rayaru perked up as soon as he set foot outside. 'Isn't it surprising that I can sense the sterility in their married life?' mused Jagannatha as he looked at Bhagyamma. She stood leaning against a pillar in the hall. She looked as if she was preparing to tell him something; Sripathi Rao seemed uncomfortable and fidgety. Jagannatha had guessed right.

'I'm sick of breaking my head, Jaganna. Why don't you try telling him? If I try talking to him, he springs on me like a tiger. They've transferred Savithri to Shimoga. He helps everyone with everything. Can't he speak to the DEO[28] and see that she continues to stay here? The education minister and he were in prison at the same time. Everyone has taken advantage of his part in the freedom struggle. Only we've lost out on everything. In those days I went along with his ideas; I threw into the fire even the four silk saris my father had given me. And now, whatever I may say, he sits quietly, as if in a stupor.'

Sripathi Rao was uneasy. 'That'll do. Go in now.'

'He stood for the municipal elections last time. Did you ask him what happened? When no one gives him even the least bit of respect, why should he be concerned with the welfare of this town, you tell me. When he doesn't have the clout even to keep his own daughter here ...'

'Let's see what we can do, Amma. I didn't know anything about this,'said Jaganna, to pacify her.

'It's not that, Jaganna. You can't get anything done by the DEO unless you bribe him. If he shows me the Government Order that says every person who has served in the same place for five or six years has to be transferred, then what can I do? Tell me.'

Bhagyamma raised her voice suddenly.

'Our daughter is old enough to be married but he hasn't done a thing about it. And there've been no proposals either. I'm not sure if it's because he spent time in prison or because we're not orthodox enough. Also, if she isn't earning, how can we run this house, tell me?

[28] District Education Officer.

If we have to bribe, we have to bribe. Aren't we ashamed to let our daughter earn this way to feed us?'

Jagannatha felt bad to see Rayaru seething with helpless anger. He felt it was best to get up and leave. To pacify her he said, 'Let's do something about this, Amma. I'm willing to go to Shimoga if you want me to …'

But she seemed not to have heard him at all. She started shouting. He was sad to see signs of hysteria in this aging woman.

'Who'll respect the pride of a man who can't even feed himself, Jaganna? Much like the saying, "a poor man's fury is a threat to his own jaw". The son has finished High School. Has he done anything to get him a job? It's true, the other day I had sent him to the bus to bring home some tourists to lodge with us, just as the other boys do. How can we live without any money? Ranganna brought home a family. He took them to the temple to worship. But as soon as they returned, you should've seen how this man was stomping about as if possessed by a demon. Is it wrong for me to have done what I did to feed my family? You should've seen how he thrashed me, Jaganna—me, who has served him without protest all these years. He's showing his power over me only because my parents are dead, isn't he? Those pilgrims had barely finished their worship at the temple; they had come all the way from Chitradurga, and yet he threw them out of the house. He even threw the food I had cooked for them into the compost pit. And the way he beat up Ranganna …'

Bhagyamma sank to the floor sobbing noisily. Savithri, who had been hovering by the door awkwardly, took her by the arm and pulled her into the kitchen.

'Come, let's go,' said Sripathi Rao, still in a daze. Jagannatha followed him, not knowing what to say. Both of them felt they could breathe more freely as soon as they stepped into the street. Right in front was the temple and they could hear the gurgle of the stream beyond it. 'Shall we go towards the river, Rayare?' said Jagannatha. He felt awkward even to look him in the face. And yet he felt it was not proper to leave Sripathi Rao alone at this point.

They walked on silently for a while. They stood on the bank of the river. Jagannatha shuddered at the stench of urine and faeces. Scorching sun beating down on the rocks and the white sand; flowing water, pure and clear, soothing the eyes, and its frenzy, as it dashed against the rocks, frothing and foaming, happy little boys bathing in it. Pilgrims gingerly letting themselves into the water. And the *purohits*,[29] reciting mantras, encouraging them to take a dip. Beyond the stream was the temple of Hanumantha. All along the bank, there were trees: mango, jackfruit, and teak. But wherever there was shade, there was the stench of human waste. Jagannatha could not take it any more.

'Let's go to your store, Rayare,' he said.

'Come, let's,' said Sripathi Rao.

'It's about two or three weeks since I met you last, isn't it?' said Jagannatha, trying to start a conversation.

'Oh, I've been through hell these two or three weeks. Sometimes I've even wondered why I shouldn't drown in the river and die, *Maharaya*.'

Jagannatha did not like to hear such things from Sripathi Rao. He felt sad to think that, perhaps, he would not have been so depressed if Bhagyamma had not created such a scene in his presence. He tried to change the topic.

'What do you think happened the other day? You know Rajanna—the one who looks after our affairs in the Kannada region? He came home very ill. Not to see the doctor, mind you, but to make a vow to Manjunatha. He squandered the five hundred rupees he had on the different rituals for the worship. Somehow I managed to take him to a doctor. He suspects cancer. But Rajanna doesn't have the money to go to Bangalore for treatment; I had to give him some. Yet somehow, I didn't have the guts to ask the dying man not to waste his money on Manjunatha.'

'See, Jaganna, when my son, Ranga, brought home the pilgrims from the bus, I felt as disgusted as if I had let my daughter become a whore, Maharaya. I've never raised my hand against anyone but that day I beat my wife. If Savithri hadn't stopped me, I think I might've killed her. I didn't even know I had such fury in me. Just see how this god tried to devour me in a weak moment.'

Sripathi Rao laughed as he spoke the last sentence. Jagannatha could see that both of them had touched on the same topic; he felt happy.

[29] Hindu priests.

And yet, he felt it was not proper to talk about his plans when Rayaru was so distressed. Perhaps it would be better to talk of things that did not touch either of them.

'Do you know anything about this Bhootharaya, Rayare?' he asked.

'There are different kinds of bhoothas, Maharaya. Pinjurli, Jumadhi, Baidhar, Kalkuda, Bobbarya, Jattigay: these are the bhoothas of the Shudras.[30] The Holeyaru too have their own bhootha called Kordubbusandhi or some such thing. Have you heard about the stories that are sung when a person possessed by a bhootha becomes a medium, speaking on its behalf? There's one such story song about this bhootha too, I believe. Anyway, the lord of all these bhoothas is Bhootharaya. And the lord of Bhootharaya is Manjunatha. If you want to know what Hinduism is all about, you should come to this temple.'

'Just look at this! We're making the Bhootharaya of the Shudras work for us just to keep them under our control. See how clever we are, Rayare!'

Sripathi Rao laughed. 'Did you meet Nagaraja Jois?' he asked pointedly. He had not yet heard of Jagannatha's plans. And when he did, he would not be afraid to try it out, for had he not burnt all he had to join the freedom struggle? He must somehow find a way to get Rayaru's daughter's transfer cancelled and also get his son a job in his own office. Or else Bhagyamma would surely send him off to get pilgrims to their home as paying guests. And Rayaru will never accept money from him. Jagannatha wanted to offer him some and say, 'You can pay me later, Rayare.' But he did not have the nerve.

They came to Sripathi Rao's Khadi Store in the town square. Ranga had opened it earlier and was seated there. In the store were bolts and bolts of khadi fabric, unsold, laden with dust; white caps hanging on pegs; a broken *charaka*;[31] a picture of Gandhi with his toothless smile; and khadi bags with Gandhi's face printed on them.

'Sit down,' said Sripathi Rao. Jagannatha sat down leaning against a bolster.

Seated in this very store, Sripathi Rao had once campaigned for freedom; he had shared his newfound ideas with young men like

[30] People belonging to the lowest caste.

[31] Spinning wheel; also a symbol of the non-violent, revolutionary struggle for Independence.

himself to fire them up. Now as he opened his pouch and smeared some sunna on a betel leaf, it seemed as if he had forgotten all about the embarrassing incident. His eyes, twinkling under those bushy eyebrows, showed signs of retrieving his usual verve. His quaint sense of humour resurfaced in the mischievous tone of his voice. No wonder Bhagyamma hated this creature who refused to be tamed.

The Shudras who had come shopping were hurriedly wending their way towards the temple in time for lunch. Watching them go by, Sripathi Rao said to Jagannatha, 'These are served in the courtyard of the temple—red unpolished rice and a curry with lentils. The Brahmins have their meal inside—rasam, curry, vegetables, and a sweet, usually some *payasa*. I think some eight to ten tons of rice are delivered to the temple from your house.'

Jagannatha nodded.

'I must do something to see that my wife and children don't have to go with their plates daily to the temple, Maharaya.'

There was pain in his sarcasm. *Dearest Margaret, we can restore dignity to man only by destroying this god. Or else ...*

'We haven't yet been involved enough in history to become creative, have we, Rayare?'

'With Manjunatha presiding over us, our lives are beyond history, with all the joys of eternity, Maharaya. Isn't that so, Ganesha? Isn't that what your father would say?' Rayaru addressed the questions to the young man at the door, teasing him. Ganesha, holding a bottle for some medicine and an old dog-eared novel, laughed inanely. Jagannatha stared at him: the head and face of a twenty-five-year-old in a boyish body. Hair barely enough for a tuft; a dhothi wrapped round his waist and another strip of cloth round his bare body; vibhuthi smeared on his forehead and large, pearly ear studs. Had he seen him somewhere before this? Jagannatha was not sure.

'Isn't your sister well, Ganesha? Did you go to Dr Anthony for some medicine?' And then, turning towards Jagannatha, 'Don't you know who he is, Jaganna? You know the chief priest of the temple, Seetharamaiah, don't you? This is his eldest son,' said Rayaru.

'Oho!' said Jagannatha.

'I should be going,' said Ganesha, bringing his palms together.

'Namaskara!' returned Jagannatha. And to Rayaru, he said, 'Come, let's have lunch at our place.'

'Look after the store, Ranga,' said Rayaru to his son, and picking up his pouch of betel leaves and nuts, he stood up. Vasu turned up right at that moment. 'Come, let's go home,' Jagannatha said to him too, and Vasu went along with them.

'What is this I hear, Jaganna?' asked Vasu, 'Did you really go to Nagaraja Jois's house? You should've seen his excitement at having the richest man in town visit him. He's been boasting about it to everyone he meets. But don't you ever trust him, Jaganna. Ask Rayaru about him, he'll tell you. He may have grown old but hasn't outgrown his craving for sex. He plagued his wife to death and now he's keeping his daughter-in-law, the beast that he is. Poor fellow, that son of his; he's slogging in Shimoga. Why can't he send his daughter-in-law to his son? He says he needs someone to run the house, for him to cater to his guests. That's an excuse. Look at me! I got married at the Registrar's in a right royal manner. And if I want a fling, I'll pay for it. I won't hide behind rituals of purity and be promiscuous on the sly like these sanctimonious old fellows. I heard he's planning to file a case to claim his right to be the chief priest of the temple. When Bhootharaya hasn't allowed even one case to go to court from anywhere here, why does this creature want to ruin this town, Jaganna? This place is full of such bastards, I tell you; they can't bear to see anyone else prosper. All they need is the Holeyara locality; they don't need places like this where the Brahmins live. All they do is take their *panch pathre*[32] and go to the temple for a free meal. That is all they know. Do they know anything at all about back-breaking toil?'

Jagannatha thought of the letter he was going to write to Margaret: Vasu is seething for no reason at all. Everywhere there seems to be an aggression waiting to break into the open. Surely, the Vasu who had refused to be cowed down by those lathi-charging policemen during the freedom struggle was someone else—not this man. Margaret, is

[32] A cylindrical glass made of five metals. It is gifted to Brahmin boys at the thread ceremony and to bridegrooms at marriage, to be used during evening rituals.

it ever possible not to be desecrated while coping with the very act of living? Think of the ruckus at Rayaru's house, the sense of persecution. How do we consider it vital for us to be a part of the action that keeps the wheels of history turning, despite being caught up in the ups and downs of daily life? Can I convince Sripathi Rao to prioritize pure, detached action, given his state of mind? Is my plan sound? If it is, how sound is it? I need to think about this deeply. And to do that, I need to be alone. But I need those nameless, faceless others too. Who are Pilla? Kariya? Mada? Inheritors of the Bhootharaya tradition. Will my decision be steady without the wisdom and the consent of an elder like Sripathi Rao? How can I persuade him? This town is an accretion of centuries of muck. We need to flush it all out, if necessary, with action; we need to push it forward, free it, and let it bloom again fearlessly.

Carts, loaded with sacks of paddy, were heading towards Shri Manjunatha Rice Mill.

'Namaskara!'

'Returning from a visit to the temple?'

'Looks as if we'll have good harvest of mangoes this season, doesn't it?'

'Can't really say. If it gets too cold by the new moon, the blooms might wither.'

A girl by the well, staring at nothing in particular, was wringing out some clothes; biting her lower lip, she was spreading them out to dry. Bhootharaya was dancing, smeared with kumkuma, dressed in red, hair all askew. See why he is dancing. Because we have to die one day or the other, we have to keep turning over the soil, over and over again. Plough, plant, turn over the soil. But only if the likes of Pilla, Kariya, Mada can hold their heads high; only if they can take the first step into the temple; only if they can scorn the practice of centuries with that one step and get the wheels of history turning again. How can I tell Rayaru how significant this step would be? Right now, someone squishes the soil and ploughs it; someone else eats the harvest here. The life force has become lethargic, fed on the fat of free-meals, thanks to Manjunatha's bounty. To protect this arrangement, Bhootharaya is made to dance, pointlessly. There goes the bell! The bell my forefathers gifted to the temple. Its sound reverberates through the octopus streets of the town. Bhootharaya is dancing, with the singara in his hand. One final benediction to Manjunatha, decked in the tender green leaves of the pathre. What a subtle change in these streets at the sound of the bell! A villager, checking out a bucket for holes before buying it, had put it down and was standing mesmerized. But the peal of the bell creates only an illusion of a renewal; it is really a gong reminding everyone that they are hungry for lunch. O God, who gets us out of our lethargy, who gets our tenants to pay their dues, who has promised a hundred years of life to the President of the country despite his cardiac problems, who is the crowned saviour of my life, O Lord of the gluttonous who falls on hundreds of banana leaves daily as red rice, as white rice; who feeds our bellies ... Jagannatha's face broke into a smile. Rayaru, who had been walking briskly, spat out the wad of tobacco he had been chewing. Somehow, I must get them to take that one step into the temple; let the change flow through me; turn everything over; get her back again; and together with her, Pilla, Madha, Kariya, liberating, gaining; together split open this rotting town; together shocking these apathetic people as if with a kick in the arse, as if Bhootharaya were dancing in every street .... But who's Mada? Who's Kariya? Who's Pilla? What links can I have with them with my vapid words? Through what kind of action can I forge a connection? Here, all I have to offer fearfully is this tentative plan. Bringing the words inside me to a boil, it waits to take shape.

Another bus came down the street and stopped at the toll gate. Brahmin boys crowded round it, hoping for prospective lodgers. 'If there's an easy job, this is it,' said Vasu. Gurappa Gowda, the local Member of the Legislative Assembly, got down. 'Namaskara, Sahukarare! Namaskara, Rayare!' he said, greeting Jagannatha and Sripathi Rao. With his white dhothi, jubba, cap, and a small paunch, Gowda had the bearing of a Congress leader. And on his forehead was the kumkuma, a blessing from Manjunatha.

'These guys used to be in the Justice Party in those days, on the side of the British. And now, they are Congress legislators,' said Rayaru bitterly, as Gowda disappeared round the bend. Jagannatha did not respond; he knew how such a comment would eventually descend to a pointless discussion on pro-Brahmin, anti-Shudra politics. He had noticed Rayaru's arguments imperceptibly acquiring overtones of caste prejudices; he was disgruntled with the corrupt current political situation. Feeling that his plan was just the right thing to renew people like Rayaru, Jagannatha walked on enthusiastically.

By the time they climbed the hill and reached the house, the leaves had been spread; they were pleasantly hungry too. As usual, it was an open house with around twenty people for lunch—those who had come into town to do some shopping and those who had come to visit the temple.

Chikki was happy to see that he had brought Rayaru home. Handing him a towel to wash before lunch, she said, 'It's about a month since you came this way, Rayare.'

THREE

Margaret

Jagannatha stretched himself on the bed and turned down the lantern. It felt so good just to stretch his legs, he was that tired. After lunch, he had tried talking to Sripathi Rao about his decision but could not; somehow the man seemed a bit too preoccupied.

As usual, the Holeyaru had come in the evening. But of the ten of them, did even one young man grasp the significance of what he had told them? There was no way he could know what was going on in their minds. Previously, they used to stand at the outer edge of the front yard, and it had taken him a week to get them to come closer. But perhaps they would never be willing to climb those few steps to the open porch and sit on a mat.

When Jagannatha was a boy, if ever he met this very Pilla's father, Bharma, on the street, the man would move aside immediately, hide behind a tree, remove his black shirt, and stand by the kerb with his head bowed as if it were a sin even to come into a Brahmin's view. And only when the lad was out of sight would he put on his sleeveless, collarless black shirt back on again. No, there was no point in these young men doing what I am asking them to do only to obey me, their master. They must be willing to do it; my action depends on it.

After dinner, he sat at his writing table, pen in hand.

First, let me write to the papers and tell them of my intention. Let Rayaru get to know my plans that way. Let me not foist anything on him directly. He may not have the courage to have the whole town against him. Moreover, it will keep him from feeling obliged to support me. I must do whatever I can on my own; others should join me only if they would like to. Jagannatha decided on this course of action and wrote a short letter to the newspapers. He wrote three drafts but tore them all up. When he tried to put down his ideas, they seemed too romantic, too idealistic. He felt naïve, as if he were living in a world of illusions. *People believe that Holeyaru will spit blood and die if ever they enter the temple of Manjunatha. They are convinced that Bhootharaya will hold such people by their feet and drag them around until they spew blood. Even the President of the country believes in the power of Manjunatha. Unless such faith in the power of this god is destroyed, Indians will never take responsibility for their lives; they will never learn to be accountable. Only in the anguish of losing faith in God can we become a creative people. This Majunatha, who has made Bhootharaya, the god of the lower castes, to work against his own devotees, must be ...*

No, it did not sound right. He tore up the letter and started another: *This temple is the primary enemy of a scientific temper. The god who exorcizes Jakani from women possessed by her is Bhootharaya; the god who gets the tenant to promptly pay the landlord for his tenancy is Bhootharaya. And the god who rules over Bhootharaya is Shri Manjunatha. He has kept our lives from becoming creative; He has kept us from participating in our history. Unless we demolish our faith in His miraculous powers, we can achieve nothing. True, trying to destroy the hold He has on us is much like putting a hand into a beehive. But it is this Manjunatha who has made it impossible for us to take any worthwhile social action in India. And because such meaningful action is impossible, social life seems totally pointless. By deriding the truth of our situation as a figment of a fevered imagination, we are living in self-deception. Therefore, if there is to be a revolution of any significance at all, the Holeyaru, the lowest of the lowest who live among us, must be able to stand, heads held high. The one step that they can take is the only change that matters. By taking this one step, these Holeyaru can change the course of a reality that is centuries old. For, however much the upper classes may prosper; we are still living in an illusion of progress ...*

Jagannatha tore up this letter too. *I must write only about what I want to do. Words like these sound pedantic, making me seem naïve. I should not build airy castles all over again, now that I have decided on this course only to rid me of all falsehood and to make me a truly strong person.* So Jagannatha wrote a short letter, describing only his plan of action:

Dear Sir,

I have decided to lead the Harijans into the temple of Shri Manjunatha, famous all over the country. I feel the festival on the third day after the New Moon would be the right time to do it because, on that day, devotees from all over the country gather here in Bharathipura. There is a belief that Holeyaru who enter the temple will spew blood and die. If we can prove to them how baseless this belief is, I am very sure a different mode of thinking will dawn in the minds of these people. For this purpose, I request the support of progressively-minded people.

Yours truly,
Jagannatha,
Bharathipura

He wrote two letters, one in English and the other in Kannada, put them in two envelopes, addressed them to two newspapers in Bangalore, and set out in the chill of night to mail them. He needed a flashlight to light his way down the hill to the post office, but the moment he dropped the letters into the postbox, Jagannatha felt exhilarated. He walked back home with a light heart, ran up the stairs to his room, and flopped on his bed. Even though the night was chilly, he was all afire, damp with perspiration.

But he could not sleep. His mind was whirling. The night was dark and deep. He turned up the lantern and continued the letter he had been writing to Margaret. *Then I thought, Margaret, that we all live in the womb of God and we will not begin to live unless we act and make our existence in society meaningful through such action.* No, that sounded a bit too pompous and so he scored it out. If he wanted to be honest with her, he should be able to write, *Dear Margaret, I've failed you because I'm not yet a man. Through the Holeyaru, in this act of getting them into the temple, I'll be a man again. ...* No, even that was not the truth. *I have not yet got over the sickness of being over-introspective. To put it symbolically, Margaret, I've been amusing myself with a mirror until now. I can't be true to myself if I don't have a mirror. When I was doing my BA in Mysore, Nehru was my mirror ideal. The way I spoke, the way I moved, even the way I stood; everything I did was a trick to attract attention to myself. Together with this mirror ideal, my obsessive introspection continually created images of me between these mirror images. My height, my long sleek hair, my wide wistful eyes, my winsome words, my ability to get engrossed in something— with all these I became more and more of a lie; more hollow, and more soft.*

Somehow, Jagannatha could not put all this down in the letter. He got up from the desk, walked out of the room on to the wide terrace, and paced restlessly. 'A spacious house atop a hill, boundless wealth, respect from others bordering on reverence, a tall impressive stature, I have grown up before these magnifying mirrors. I have never ever felt I have not been worthwhile in the sight of other people, but you don't know the canker in me, Margaret. I get so engrossed in an examination of conscience that I feel paralysed when I have to act. And the day I realized I'd do anything to solicit a moment's good impression of myself, I lost my peace of mind. What a whoring personality I must have! I haven't yet engaged in any action that will be a spiritual work out, Margaret, to burn away my smugness and to tone me up. What I feel right now is fear. My letter will be published in the papers. I'm scared that on reading it the people of Bharathipura may see me as a cur. Now that the zest I felt when I put that letter in the postbox has fizzled out, I feel I'm losing my bearings. But then, not to be doing anything at all was also distasteful to me, wasn't it?'

Jagannatha went back to his room, and sat once again in front of the letter he had been writing; he wanted to delve deep into his mind, to the very roots. Outside the window, beyond the hills, there was a sliver of a moon and the chirp of crickets. And a chill.

'What did I do during those six years in England? By being a subtle fraud, I got along well with both the whites and the blacks; by the time I had completed my MA, I was able to get my professor to talk of me as "the most charming and honest young man that I have met for years". I argued that a selfish, materialistic life was the only worthwhile way of living, and enjoyed the glamour of passing off as an existentialist. My black hair, black eyes, Italian complexion, the tone of my voice—I used them all to effect. I became a liberal, I read *The Guardian*. The reason? That way, I could easily justify my aimless, drifting lifestyle. I did not want to be attached to any one woman; I wanted to lose myself in many, but that was not possible. So I held forth on free love. I protested vehemently against the Puritanical mindset of the English—and praised the French for their love of life. I wanted to be self-willed, and so I said the way we live is absurd. I became a hero in the eyes of my friends who were still working their way through the various stages of seducing women. One of my Indian friends, who had been smarting at being spurned by an English woman, loved the way I criticized European culture. But all these were but a sham of attitudes to hide a host of secret desires. My life was one long masquerade, a debauchery.'

Jagannatha remembered the day he had first met Margaret at the London University Union Pub. Chandrashekar was with him. He had come to London, bored with middle-class life in Bangalore; to teach at slum schools, study at an evening college, and down draft beer till closing time at local pubs to while away his loneliness. A pro-Brahmin in Bangalore, in London he had become a strident socialist, condemning the racial bias of the British. Usually, when the two used to argue about why they should not bring out a monthly called *Protest*, Ruebens, a Jewish friend, used to be with them. But that day he was not there. That day at the pub, Jagannatha had been very depressed; he had not been able to tie up his dissertation on E.M. Forster. While walking down from the library, he had had a sinking feeling that he had nothing original to say about the novelist. Chandrashekar had been ranting; his British colleagues at the slum schools were an indifferent bunch, they could not appreciate the great Indian genius, the slum children were unteachable, neocolonialism was blighting Indian talent .... Jagannatha had been in no mood to listen to him that day. He had got up and got himself another half a pint of beer and some crisps, cheese and onion flavoured, and had lit his pipe. Chandrashekar was raving on and on. It had suddenly occurred to Jagannatha that he might never ever become an original; he was an out and out counterfeit. Everything he said was what someone else had spit out, every thought was borrowed. He did not have a single original thought about Forster.

Holding forth beguilingly on nothing worthwhile, being disarming with everyone he met, thinking like a foraging hog, living like a cat always on the look out for a cosy nook, soaring high on praise without any inner worth, getting smoother by the day. 'Bah!' he felt about himself in utter contempt. So like an eel. Every word, dressed up as thought, is a lie. My mind is full of desires half expressed, and that is the only truth about me. Being born to wealth, I have no direction, no goal. All this brash talk, these revolutionary ideas, these clever discussions on literature, all of them are merely mirrors to assure me that I am. But inside me, I don't have a single belief. I am forever looking for an audience to tell me my words ring true; that is my reality.

As Jagannatha sat belittling himself, Margaret had walked over to him. Holding a mug of beer in her hand, she had said, 'May I join you?' and drawing up a chair, had sat down beside him. Black hair falling over a cheek, black eyes, a plump body that, perhaps, spoke of her love of life, sweet lips—she stood up, took off her coat, and threw it on another chair. Around her neck was a chunky necklace of rudrakshi beads. She was wearing a light blue dress. She pushed her hair back from her cheek and, putting out her hand, gushed, 'I'm Margaret.' Even as he began to introduce himself, she said, 'I've seen you,' and added, 'Your speech at the Union on what it means to be an Indian in Britain was very sincere and moving.'

That day Jagannatha had talked about the subtle deceit an Indian uses to survive among the whites and the blacks, and about the psychology of the Indian abroad who would have conformed to caste restrictions in his own country, but would choose to be a rebel in England. He had explained why, though Nehru was emotionally an Indian, he thought like a westerner. As usual even on that day his pose, with his sweeping gestures and his eloquence, seemed to say it was heady to be a thinking being at all. In a way he had spoken about his own sense of being a devious person.

How strange! At the end of it all, even his honest appraisal of his inner turmoil had added to his stature as a speaker; he could see it in Margaret's comment. And she did not seem the kind who was free with her compliments. Her mod way of dressing and the way her hair fell all over her shoulders told him she was an independent spirit. He had also sensed a bite of sarcasm in her talk and that had made her approval doubly precious. Perhaps her critical eye might find him more appealing if he deprecated himself further; he could tell her his ancestors were really Nehru and Byron.[33]

[33] A British poet.

He had introduced Chandrashekar to her. She told them she was a teacher and in her spare time she was working for a Master's degree in history at London University.

'Oh, how thirsty I am!' she had said and downed half a pint of beer at one go and wiped her mouth with her hand.

Jagannatha's body and mind grew alert, she were saying, *Hey, I'm clamouring for your attention; I'm unattached, you know.*

He had stood up, picking up the three empty beer mugs. Margaret had also stood up.

'Let me pay, I'm earning, anyway,' she had offered.

'Don't,' he had said, moving towards the counter.

'At least let me help,' she had said and come towards him when he returned, delicately balancing brimming refills on a tray. She had also bought the cigarettes. Jagannatha had eagerly bent forward to light her cigarette and get talking. He had immediately noted the hunter in him taking over; he had just met a new girl and he was already doing his best to impress her.

How depressed I was just a few moments ago! But look at me now; the way I'm craning my neck, looking deep into her eyes, talking earnestly. I'm desperately trying to be absorbed into her. My compliance, or disagreement, or even my self-doubt, all are but strategies of stalking my prey.

Tossing back the hair falling over her cheek and stretching lazily to relax, Margaret had joined in the game. Without embarrassment, she had made her moves to entice him. Sometimes agreeing with each other, sometimes begging to differ, they had played out their new-found relationship with ease. They were hunting each other.

Chandrashekar could not handle his envy; he began to attack European liberalism: It was impotent, it was a sham; they needed a Che Guevara to expose the deceit. All this talk of the pointlessness of human life and this preoccupation with human inadequacies were games that decadent people played.

'Look at the way the two of you are carrying on,' he had continued, 'sitting here so cosily and discussing the human situation so animatedly. Could you have done this in Lumumba's Africa? Was it possible for Che Guevara in the jungles? The common people should rise as one man, then they'll shred your dreams.' He jeered them. Either the beer had got to his head, or his jealousy had got the better of him. Otherwise, he would have noticed that Jagannatha and Margaret were also saying the same thing, more or less.

'My father's Indian, from Gujarat. My mother's British, but I love my father better,' she had said. And added to Chandrashekar, 'I agree with what you said.'

'It's easy for you to say that, sitting here in the pub. If Jagannatha keeps talking this way, he may end up as ambassador in Nehru's government,' he sneered, 'Orators like him rise quickly in India. What else, do you think, is the secret of Nehru's and Krishna Menon's success?' Jagannatha had said the same thing a while ago. They left only after the pub had closed.

'Bye,' said Chandrashekar, trying to be pleasant before leaving.

'I admire your rage,' said Margaret, shaking his hand. Jagannatha was nettled; he could feel an inner vigour in Chandrashekar's sarcasm, in his envy. His bitter talk, his helpless resentment seemed to have stirred the woman in Margaret.

As soon as his friend left, he said, 'He talks big, that's all. He sells pounds in black and is building a double-storey house in Jayanagar in Bangalore.'

He might have reduced Chandrashekar to nothing in Margaret's eyes. He felt uncomfortable.

'Chandrashekar is poor, he's also third-rate. That's why I don't feel the kind of anguish he does.' Hopefully, he would redeem himself by talking to her this way.

'Oh, I know the type,' she said.

Both of them walked all the way to her flat in Bloomsbury.

'I'll fix something for you to eat. Come in,' she said, opening the door stealthily. 'My landlady's very suspicious, climb softly,' she warned him, and, holding him by the hand, led the way upstairs in the darkness.

'Relax,' she said, pointing to the bedsitter, and helped him take off his coat. She put on a record of Ravi Shankar's sitar recital and went towards the kitchen saying, 'I won't be a minute.'

Jagannatha looked around Margaret's studio curiously. She had done up the room in blue. On her table was a picture of Sri Ramakrishna Paramahamsa.[34] On the wall was a Gauguin.[35] In a corner was an

[34] A mystic visionary from Bengal.

[35] A French post-Impressionist painter.

old radiogram. On the dining table were some dirty plates and a few journals—signs of good taste but with a touch of sloppiness. There were a few pop posters too, to say she was not a bourgeois. And a collage of cuttings depicting the horrors of the Vietnam War. Her duffel coat hung on a rack on the door. Simple sofas that seemed soft and soothing. Jagannatha sat warming his hands over the gas stove.

'The whisky's right there. Take it,' said Margaret from the kitchen. He poured himself a whisky from the counter above the bookcase and asked, 'For you?'

'No, thanks,' she replied.

Jagannatha went into the kitchen and helped himself to some ice from the fridge. Margaret was frying sausages.

'Don't trouble yourself,' he said.

'Sit a moment. I'll be done.'

'Do you like Paramahamsa?'

'Yes, I do. Have you read Isherwood? He's my favourite writer,' she said.

'He writes like Forster, doesn't he?'

'Yes. Paramahamsa and Whitman accept everything; they reject nothing. Their personalities can embrace all the complexities of creation,' she said.

'Like hold-alls; you can put anything in them. Like payasa. You know, the Indian sweet dish? Anything goes.'

'I don't agree with you there,' Margaret said, laughing, as she set bread, cheese, and sausages on the table.

After dinner, they had black coffee. He helped her do the dishes even though she said it could wait till the next day.

'My mother has castrated my father. I hate her,' she said out of the blue. And as he was leaving, 'Tomorrow's Sunday. Come for lunch. We could visit my father. He lives close by.'

Jagannatha returned to his flat quite elated. Wow! She was the most honest of all the girls he had loved. Somehow his personality seemed to gain worth and vitality when he was with her.

The next day was Sunday—rainy, slushy, and cold since the morning. Jagannatha took a bus to Margaret's. She had just had a shower. The room was warm and soothing. He sat facing the gas stove.

'Coffee or tea?' asked Margaret.

'I'll make it,' he said and went over to the kitchen with Margaret. She had tidied the room because he was coming; he was happy to see that. He was standing close to her as he poured hot water into the pot. He liked the smell of fresh shampoo in her hair; he found it comforting.

'You know, right now, your hair's long enough to be plaited,' he said, lifting it in his hand. She was wearing a loose skirt with peacocks on the border and a blouse. He was standing close to her, their bodies touching. He put his hand on her shoulder while he told her about his struggle to write his dissertation. While they were having tea, he spoke about his mother, about Bharathipura, about Sripathi Rao making him read Shaw, Ingersoll.

'Who's Ingersoll?' Margaret was curious. She was totally relaxed. They talked on and on, finishing a whole bottle of wine. For lunch, she had made chicken curry and rice.

'Frankly, I prefer vegetarian food,' he said and told her about *upanayana,* the sacred-thread ceremony that made him a twice-born Brahmin.

After lunch, they went to visit her father at Finsbury. Dr Desai looked a bit like his daughter—plump with a round face, chiselled nose, and dull eyes. He spoke to him in Hindi. 'I'm sorry, but I don't know Hindi,' said Jagannatha.

'How's India?' he asked, stroking his bald head, and then, 'I've been to Bangalore.' His accent was thicker than his own.

'Don't you have anyone here to speak to you in Gujarati?' asked Jagannatha.

'Yes, I do,' he said, and fell silent.

Margaret came in with her mother, pushing the tea trolley. Her mother looked stern, blue-eyed, and blonde. She seemed much older that Dr Desai; her face was lined. She grumbled about the dirty habits of the five Indian students she had as paying guests.

'India's a god-ridden country,' she said, in disgust. The mother and daughter argued over this; the father said nothing. Jagannatha too sat silent. Perhaps, this was Mrs Desai's way of showing her discontent with her husband.

'The British are responsible for India's poverty, Mother,' said Margaret.

'Oh, come on,' replied her mother, 'if it hadn't been for the British, they wouldn't have had a scientific attitude at all. They make Indian curries in English homes and stink up the whole place with the smell of spices. They always have their curtains drawn. Anyway, I have work to do,' she added, as she went in. Margaret followed her, perhaps to tell her off in the kitchen.

Dr Desai stood up, sighing. 'I'm very unhappy,' he said, 'Ask my daughter, she'll tell you.' He seemed to be asking for sympathy; Jagannatha felt embarrassed. 'Don't stay here for too long, go back to India. Look at me. If I were to get out of this neighbourhood, who am I? Who'll recognize me as a doctor? Most probably, they'll think I'm an Indian bus conductor,' he grumbled, as he paced the room.

When she came into the room, Margaret's tear-filled eyes looked furious.

'Wretched country, wretched people,' she said, as she took hold of Jagannatha's hand and walked out of the house. He wanted to hug her right there and comfort her. They took a bus to her flat; they did not speak a word.

It was evening. As soon as he closed the door behind him, Jagannatha held Margaret close and kissed her. Her tears flowed as she leaned her head against him, sobbing bitterly.

'Shall I stay the night?' he asked.

She nodded.

That night, Margaret made love to him with a single-minded intensity. Her sad childhood, her wants, her eagerness, the joy hidden in the recesses of her body—Jagannatha received all that she had to offer. Spent, she slept in his arms. Caressing her warm body, he looked at his watch; it was two. Margaret got up early that morning and woke him up with tea.

'You'd better get out of here before the landlady gets to know,' she said. She was in a dressing gown. Jagannatha lifted her up and kissed her, and then he whirled her around. 'I've got to go to school, you better go now,' she said, laughing.

How she had laughed! Much like a naughty girl.

I took root deep inside Margaret, and bloomed.

'Let's get married,' Jagannatha had said.

'I don't believe in marriage. See what my mother has done to my father. She has left him with no dignity at all. She has belittled his identity.'

Even Jagannatha was not all that keen on marriage; it was only his fear of losing Margaret that made him talk to her about it.

He felt vaguely that one day or the other he would have to return to Bharathipura; that was the only way he could become a real person.

But I won't be able to live with Margaret in Bharathipura. I may have to rent a house in Bangalore, become an absentee landlord, talk in English—a radical, throwing parties, living somewhere in the Cantonment with similar rootless people, with an Indianness linked to Ravi Shankar's sitar, the sculptures of Konarak, and folk songs; wearing Lucknow kurtas at parties, in rooms decorated with wickless brass lamps, the dancing Nataraja[36], Kathakali dancing dolls, elegant ash-trays, and women in silk saris with sleeveless blouses and shaved armpits, sisters-in-law of IAS officers or those waiting to get married to military officers, and the usual small talk, 'Won't you have something? Why? Are you dieting?' Margaret was not that type at all, but, if she came to India, would she be able to help becoming that way?

And yet he pestered her about getting married. As the infatuation wore off, their lovemaking seemed to lose its intensity. She would lie in his arms thinking of something else. He would scold her for her indifference, for the dirty cups, for her clothes thrown about everywhere.

'Why do you try so hard to please everyone you meet?' she would ask him, making fun of him. That hurt him badly.

He would be irritated whenever she spoke well of Chandrashekar. And Chandrashekar could be cruel, jealous as he was. But once he guessed Margaret was using Chandrasekhar to arouse him, Jagannatha tried to please him, even to praise him. Margaret was furious. 'You let him say whatever he pleases and get away with it. Are you a man?' she would say to mock him. He would get angry when her body went limp in his arms as if he were there only to gratify her, to get her into a deep sleep; she was using him as a paramour. He too lost interest in her body; it was a bit too responsive, too yielding. He would push her

[36] Another name for Shiva; the presiding deity of dance.

hand away when she caressed him drowsily, as if in an almost-forgotten routine. As for Margaret, she began to treat his moods, his turmoil, and his intensity with indifference.

Early one Sunday morning, it was sunny. She was sunbathing in the garden at the back of the house, lying on a carpet under an apple tree. She had smeared herself with olive oil and was in a bikini. Jagannatha was in shirt and trousers, on an easy-chair. Margaret lay face down to warm her back.

'Jagan, unhook my bra, will you?'

Jagannatha got up, and went to her and unhooked it. He sat by her thinking of something; he could not remember now what it was. The summer sun was soothing, with the quiet of a Sunday morning. Suddenly she said, face still downwards, with no cruelty in her voice, 'Jagan, somehow I feel Chander's spite is more real than your nobility. One can't feel your presence at all ... Your agony over being incomplete seems to be a show; it's Chander who's suffering more. Look, you know the streak of cruelty he has? He'll become a real man with it. Even his meanness .... But you're not enough of a man.'

I remember all that. The apple tree. The sunshine. The green grass. Margaret's back, white under the unhooked bra straps. She spoke, without any feeling. She didn't look at me in the face at all. I lit a cigarette. I don't think I've ever suffered as much as I did at that moment. I sat staring, staring at the grass, staring at the hook of the bra glistening in the sunshine. And as I sat staring I felt I should end my life. But Margaret didn't lift her head. She had wrapped the sun over her tousled black hair, over her bare back; she had thrown her hands and legs about and was sleeping, peacefully. As I sat beside her resting on my arm I didn't want her to see me in this state. After quite some time, she lifted up her head. She saw me. Were there tears in my eyes? My lips, mouth, and throat were dry. She sat up, she hugged me, and she rolled over with me. I didn't say I wanted it; I didn't say I didn't want it. She kissed me, wetting my lips but I was arid inside. She unbuttoned my shirt and kissed me, on my neck, on my chest. My eyes were open, staring. She tried to kiss my eyes shut. All talk had dried up inside me. I sat this way for a long while, not wanting anything, not pushing away anything—the sun, the grass, the woman's body.

The next day I went to my professor. 'I don't have anything beyond ten pages to say about Forster,' I said, 'My article is appearing in *Essays in Criticism*. That's enough for me. I don't think I want a degree.'

He made me sit down. 'You don't have to think this way at all,' he said, 'You're one of my brightest students.'

'Thanks,' I said and came out of his room. Within a week I had packed my bags and headed right back to Bharathipura.

It was two o'clock. There was silence outside. Jagannatha tore up the letter he was writing to Margaret. He would write to her after he became firmer inside. And for him to get firm, the Holeyaru, who lived like animals and birds, had to become brave enough to take just that one step into the temple. Their rebellion alone will bring me to fruition. But first, I must fight their mindset. I must fight with Manjunatha too. Only through this struggle will my inner self get toned up; it will lose its flab. This way, I'll become creative, Margaret. Then I'll write to you.

He turned off the light, drew a shawl over himself, and lay down. He remembered the amulet that Chikki had hidden under his mattress, the amulet of Bhootharaya, Manjunatha's henchman, and smiled. He felt cold and covered himself with a blanket. But he could not sleep. He did not know when he slept. He had a dreadful nightmare. Bhagyamma, Sripathi Rao's wife, was standing before him with dishevelled hair, holding a bunch of areca flowers, the singara of Bhootharaya. She was thrashing her son, Ranganna, with it. He lay there writhing in pain but she did not stop flailing him. Sripathi Rao sat in a daze, looking pale. As Bhagyamma continued to flog him, Ranganna fainted. And then she pounded him shapeless as if she were pounding parboiled rice. Blood spurted from the boy—from his nose and from his mouth. Bhagyamma was trying to carry him as if he were a wrung-out piece of clothing. His neck had snapped. Suddenly, Bhagyamma turned on Sripathi Rao. 'It's entirely your fault,' she wept as she scolded him, shocked to find the singara in her hand.

Jagannatha woke up with a start, perspiring.

FOUR

Action Plan

It was about six months since Jagannatha had returned to Bharathipura from England. Chikki had sent the car to bring him home all the way from the railway station in Shimoga. Budan, the driver, while tucking his bags into the boot, had said, 'I thought you'd bring a new car from England, *Saar*.' He seemed disappointed to see him return empty-handed. 'Since your mother's death, the car hasn't been out of the garage at all. Your aunt stays indoors all the time, Saar.' He was obviously eager to give him all the news on the drive back home.

As they entered Bharathipura, there were festoons of mango leaves to welcome Jagannatha. Seetharamaiah, the chief priest at the temple; Prabhu, the richest merchant in town; Gurappa Gowda, the local MLA; Sripathi Rao; Vishwanatha Shastri, the family accountant and overseer; boys from the local High School, in white shirts and khaki shorts; the headmaster in his baggy pants, with a bright red spot of kumkuma on his forehead; and so many others had assembled, eagerly waiting to welcome him. Jagannatha was highly embarrassed. Even as his eyes looked around for Sripathi Rao, who was standing way back in the crowd, grains of reddened rice fell on him in blessing. A spot of kumkuma was smeared on his forehead and a profusion of mantras gushed forth from Seetharamaiah to bless him. And then, someone thrust Bhootharaya's singara, a sheaf of areca flowers, in his hand; it must have been Seetharamaiah. By the time he could recover from the way Manjunatha had descended on him, Gurappa Gowda had placed a lemon in his hand, garlanded him, and, bringing his palms together, he had even thrown in a speech on how fortunate they were to have a person like Jagannatha in their midst, thanks to Manjunatha's benediction.

Jagannatha felt frightened. My position, my prestige, my duty towards these people has been predetermined. I could easily bloat like a raw chickpea in water. Probably, the only way I can make an impact on them is by rejecting Manjunatha first, by hurting them where they trust him. He had had this vague feeling from the moment the grains of sanctified rice fell on his head.

Sripathi Rao stood somewhere at the back of the crowd smiling at him, chewing a mixture of betel leaves, areca nuts, and sunna, and holding a corner of his dhothi in his hand. Jagannatha knew why he was smirking. His eyes, under his bushy eyebrows, seemed to say: 'As you're the chief trustee of the temple, swallow your atheism and survive. Can you see the way I'm living? That way. Remember, to each his own faith.' He spat out the betel leaves and, with arms outstretched, came towards Jagannatha, hugged him, and patted him on his back. Together with Gurappa Gowda, he made casual conversation with him, 'You must be tired ...'

Look at the way a man becomes a liberal as he grows older, by making compromises to make his life more tolerable! Will this be my predicament too as I grow older and weaker? Will I become a liberal too, like Rayaru? Jagannatha was alarmed, but then, he had a way of seeing himself mirrored in everyone's eye. No doubt there is an acceptance of defeat in Rayaru's smile, but is there a fire at all, still smouldering beneath it? From that day to this, Jagannatha has been searching for an answer to this question in Sripathi Rao.

In the Revolt of 1942, Sripathi Rao had gone on a lone hunger strike in front of the taluk office; he had earlier burnt all the fabric in his store when Gandhi had called for a boycott of foreign goods. And now did he have to become the man with a benign smile, this bushy-browed man? Jagannatha became pensive thinking deeply about the mellowing effect of the Indian ethos.

He had got rid of all the others and come home with Sripathi Rao. Chikki had not shown her face to him as she was a *sakeshi*[37]; a few girls from neighbouring families had sprinkled some sacred reddened water on him before he had crossed the threshold and poured the rest of it outside the main doorstep. He went into the drawing room and sat chatting with Rayaru. He knew Chikki was waiting for him to first prostrate himself before their household god before taking a glass of cold milk from her. It was said that this black stone *saligrama*[38] of Narasimha had been worshipped in this family for a thousand years. Vishwanatha Shastri, the shanbogh, with a big, bright red kumkuma on his forehead and with his black cap folded and tucked under his arm, kept walking to and fro, in and out of the house; no one had the courage to ask Jagannatha to worship the family god. 'Chikki,' he called out to his aunt. She came into the drawing room and gave him the glass of milk. He looked at her with love; there was no need for words. But if she had asked him, he would have had to say: 'Forgive me. If I believe in God I'm afraid I'll become too much of an insider and lose my identity. Without becoming an outsider with things of God, I can't begin to do the things I want to do in this place. Look, Chikki, this is why I've come back, to begin the things I want to do, to become real, to firm up myself.' But he had drunk the milk she had offered him without speaking a word to her, just staring at her with all his love for her. *She is so much like Amma. Only, her hair is thinner and her forehead narrower, but the way she speaks with her head turned slightly sideways is so like Amma.* In white sari and white blouse ever since she had become a child-widow, she had grown up in Jagannatha's family, bringing all her assets to them. She had brought him up. Even though to an outsider the people of Bharathipura looked similar, like one large household of Manjunatha, if you looked at them closely enough you could see they were distinct.

[37] A widow who has not shaved her head.

[38] Stones of the ammonite fossil recovered from the Gandaki river bed in Nepal. They are considered very sacred by conservative Brahmin families.

Then what was it that Manjunatha ruled over? Was it their ignorance? Or … ? It was too much for Jagannatha to dwell on.

Sripathi Rao started talking animatedly about the local political situation. He loved talking politics; it was like munching the spicy roasted gram, *hurigaalu*. 'How do you think this Gurappa won the elections, Jaganna? He was in the pro-British Justice Party, wasn't he? But in '47, he joined the Congress. And before the present elections, he went round to every house in the village with a plate of kumkuma as blessing from Manjunatha. He asked each adult to lay his hand on it and vow, "I will vote for you." After all, most of these people are Gowdas too, aren't they? Also … '

Jagannatha was tired after the journey. He got up to have his bath. He wanted to say: 'Don't talk about the elections, Rayare. Forget the petty politics. Let's think up some action that'll bring about a real change here in Bharathipura.'

But he only said politely, 'Come on, let's have our bath and … '

'I've had mine,' said Rayaru.

'Stay for lunch,' invited Chikki.

Rayaru got talking again—about why he had not stood for the municipal elections this time and how he would have lost anyway, as always. Jagannatha felt disappointed; these were the men who had, once upon a time, followed Gandhi. But then, it was not fair to measure Rayaru against the Marxist discussions he used to have in the relaxed ambience of the cosy London pubs. He went to the bathroom for a bath.

He had got so used to bathing in a tub, he had quite forgotten what it was to soap his face and blindly grope for the *chombu*, to fill it with water, pour it over his head, and feel the gush of warm water washing him down. He was happy. The little copper chombu, bright and shiny; the gooey mash from the maththi tree in a bowl; the homemade soapnut powder and the smell of sandalwood soap—all of them evoked tender memories of his childhood. He had a refreshing bath; he was sweating even after he had towelled himself many times over. He sat down for lunch with Rayaru.

'Anyway, Prabhu has been the chief trustee in my place. Let him continue,' he ventured.

'How can that be?' protested Chikki.

Rayaru looked at him meaningfully and smiled.

From the very next day, Jagannatha was all set to forge a new relationship with Bharathipura. During the celebrations at the High School grounds to welcome him, he had talked about Russell's ideas but knew he had made no impact whatsoever; the audience had nodded a bit too readily, willing to appreciate anything he said. Nagaraja Shastri had even praised him for his erudition. 'But is any of this new to us?' he had also said, 'It has come and gone as a part of our tradition, hasn't it?'

Jagannatha pondered: 'Which path do I take in such a context, to become a real person, to make this town fecund? How do I go about it?' His felt his priority should be to get to know how these people lived. This problem had bothered him the other day on his drive back home from Shimoga: 'Having been born and brought up as a Brahmin with a wealthy ancestry, I hardly know the land to which I belong. Of course, I can make out some three or four types of fruit trees; perhaps, name a few familiar birds; why, I can even remember a few pathways that lead to my farmlands and to the surrounding villages where the tenant farmers live. But beyond that, I know nothing. Because I happen to be their landlord, the farmhands move aside when I walk among them; they lower their gaze respectfully; they act as if it's wrong even to be seen. But I'm not real to any of them. As soon as I turn my back, they're a different people, these very Shudras who act so servile before me. Even if you blindfold them and let them lose, they can wander through the forests in and around Bharathipura with just their sense of smell and touch. And to be accepted, I'll have to hunt, get drunk on toddy, chew tobacco, and be crafty like them. But there may never be an end to such a change.'

He was no longer young enough to think he would be attractive if he were to act noble and pursue his ideals. He was past thirty. If he did not become real now ... But how? Jagannatha mulled this over. Of one thing he was certain; he would never find an answer to this question by merely thinking it over because that kind of thinking was like sinking into a bottomless tunnel slowly, while all around him life continued to shape itself silently, totally indifferent to him. Providing loans for weddings, loans for farming, loans for medicines—that was the only contact he could ever have with these people; only when they were in trouble. By their reverence for him they were protected from ever knowing him as a person. And then there was Manjunatha's protection as well, and that of his minion, Bhootharaya, of whom they were very frightened. He would possess one of them, making him dance and shriek and tremble in a trance and ask, 'Is everything being done according to dharma in this place?' And the chief trustee of the temple was supposed to reply, 'Yes, it is done.' And then, one by one, each man in the queue came forward, with palms pressed together in reverence, to present his petition. 'All right, put down five rupees, take the prasada; you put down ten rupees, take the prasada …' From this kind of a divine dispensation, a few like Jagannatha were exempted. Prabhu had been substituting as chief trustee for Jagannatha while he was away in England and Prabhu had been confirmed in it. With great courage Jagannatha had resigned when the President of the country had visited the temple. Unless he broke out of the bonds of such privileges, Jagannatha knew he would never have a personal identity in the town. Manjunatha was a formless entity; he, Jagannatha, was one such formless entity too. Was at least Bhootharaya real?

Jagannatha remembered his time in England and the unrestrained discussions he used to have there in the pubs with long-haired friends on issues like, life has no meaning; man is independent only in his mind; no socio-political change can alter Man's existential reality. Such discussions seemed like a big joke here in Bharathipura, Manjunatha's hellhole. What with the big bell booming every afternoon, Time had stood still and, from birth to death, life had drifted on as if in a preordained pattern. What would it mean to understand these people, to get involved with their lives? Already he had one kind of a connection with them—that ordained by his wealth and status. He had begun to realize it would be impossible for him to bring about even the slightest change in that relationship, try as he might.

Soon after his return to Bharathipura, he had begun to wear a white shirt and dhothi like any of them. They were impressed. 'What a simple man!' they said among themselves, 'Why, that shanbogh, who manages his estate, looks more like the landlord.' Was there any way he could make an impact on them? Jagannatha felt he might commit suicide if he could not find some way of making a real connection. Getting up in the morning; checking the accounts; lending money; having lunch;

discussing the going price for areca nut; getting saplings planted ... What a pointless life! He felt he was becoming hollow, more false. He trembled. The more impotent he became by being nobody's enemy and smiling sweetly at everyone, the more he would be respected—as long as he did not rock the boat. Of one thing he was sure; rotting slowly from within, he would become manure for Manjunatha's glory.

The way Shanbogh Vishwanatha Shastri is lulling me into complacency; the way I allow him to exploit me is a good instance of my sickening situation, clear and distilled.

After clerk Krishnaiah had died, Vishwanatha Shastri had taken over the management of the household. When Jagannatha was in England, he had thrived like a bandicoot, first under Jagannatha's mother and then, after her death, under Chikki, his mother's sister. He had moved into the very house in which Krishnaiah had lived. He had converted the north wing of the house into his office, the Estate Office, as he called it. Beside it was his house where he lived with his six little children, his wife, and his widowed mother-in-law. Krishnaiah, the clerk, had been a widower when he died, and so Jagannatha was supporting his only son Gopala's education. That had been his mother's wish. But everything that Krishnaiah had been using—the house and the furniture, like the chair and the table covered with a black oilcloth—had inevitably gone to Vishwanatha Shastri.

Jagannatha was reminded of a slimy lizard sticking to a wall every time he looked at Shastri, the light-eyed, fair-skinned man. While everyone had just a small spot of Manjunatha's sanctified kumkuma between his eyebrows, Shastri sported a conspicuous dot on his forehead, much like the large red spot that adorns the brow of old-fashioned married women. Jagannatha had even teased him about it once when Sripathirayaru was around, that it flaunted Manjunatha's glory flagrantly; it was that large. And as the fame of Manjunatha's kumkuma had spread from the brow of the President's wife to that of any vegetable vendor in Bangalore, it announced loud and clear even on Mahatma Gandhi Road in Bangalore that this man was from Bharathipura. It was that big. As if that was not enough, just because he had stepped into Krishnaiah's shoes, Shastri had taken to wearing, besides the oversized kumkuma, the *kachche panche*. He tucked his shirt in, wore a tie, a gabardine coat, and a black cap, and a gold-laced turban whenever he had to go to Shimoga. He would never let anyone see him without any of these. The only time Jagannatha had seen him without his cap and tie was one day at dusk when he was flourishing a five-rupee note before labourer Venkappa's wife and making lewd signs to entice her. There he stood, with one foot slightly raised, trying to get a foothold on a low mud wall to get closer to her, looking around furtively to see if anyone was around, and clambering over and grabbing hold of her, unwilling as she was, before anyone could shout, '*Igo*! Hey!' That was the only time Shastri had not worn a cap or a tie.

He was a smooth-talker, that Shanbogh Shastri. Jagannatha had never seen him flounder for words. He could be so ingratiating, so courteous, and yet so smart and subtle that no one could ever find out whether he meant, 'Yes, it can be done' or 'No, it can't'. Tightening his hold here, loosening it a bit there; being a teasing cat sometimes or a hapless mouse at some other; withholding just when they thought he was giving ... only those who went to him begging for loans knew very well the web he wove around them with the magic of his words. The only day Jagannatha could not bear to see Shastri's face was on Ekadashi,[39] a day of fasting and penance. Without the resplendent kumkuma to proclaim Manjunatha's bounty, his brow looked bare, barren. Obviously, the presence or the absence of the kumkuma on his forehead had made a great impact on the people; they had an appropriate name for him, Kumkuma Shastri.

He had even built a fort of smooth buttery talk around Jagannatha, enough to make him feel powerless. When he had returned from England, the only way Jagannatha could interact with the people was through his wealth. But Shastri had made sure that Jagannatha could never bypass him and forge his own connections with them. He would praise him to them, loud enough for Jagannatha to hear every word; the very flattery debilitated him, bit by bit. He could see that Shastri was so much like him; he wanted everyone to love him, no one to hate him. That made Jagannatha even more disgusted with himself. He felt sick to think Shastri might know of this weakness, possibly even cashing in on it to make himself more real to the people. Jagannatha trembled to see the way he tried to mesmerize them, just to make

[39] The eleventh day of the lunar cycle.

them feel secure with him; Shastri seemed another version of his own deformed self. If only he could hurt this smooth, slimy creature, why, he might even begin to overcome his own weakness.

He did not quite know why, but from the day he had seen Shastri with Venkappa's wife, somehow Jagannatha had the courage to feel he was not that invulnerable, after all. When he saw the way he was trying to grab that unwilling woman, he felt, 'Hey, isn't that the way he's trying to overpower me with his talk?' He felt so sickened at the thought that he went directly to the office. He sat there waiting for Shastri. He came with the eye-catching kumkuma on his forehead and the usual ingratiating smile on his lips. He lit the gaslight. He had no tie but he did have his cap on.

'Shastri, I've been meaning to ask you about something. I'd like to see which of the tenants owe me money this time. Will you get me the account book, please?'

Jagannatha had suspected that Shastri had been faking the entries. So he raised his voice a little, thinking that might cow him down. He might stop overpowering him.

'*Ayyo*, poor you! Why do you have to spoil your eyes poring over the book at this time of night? I myself will read it to you tomorrow morning. But really, you don't have to bother yourself with all this,' he said, craning forward solicitously.

'No!' said Jagannatha firmly, 'I'd like to see for myself how much we make and how much we spend. Get me that book now. I'm taking it to my room.'

Shastri had lost his nerve but he did not show it. He handed over the ledger, but not before making a great show of blowing off the dust and handing it to him regretfully as if to say, 'Oh, come on, you're a person of some stature. Do you have to get so worked up about such a petty thing?' Jagannatha suddenly felt insecure and then he got furious that he felt vulnerable. And he was apprehensive too: 'What if I can't nail him now?' But then he remembered the scene at the farm and drew strength from it.

The next morning he sent for him and said, 'What is this, Shastri? It looks as if some thirty people have yet to pay their dues for the areca crop. I think we should talk to them about it. Ask Budan to get the car. Let's go together.'

Shastri was not flummoxed.

'We could send for them, can't we? Why should we go all the way to their doorstep? They'll feel embarrassed. They'll think, "Did the landlord have to come to us himself, for such a small thing at that?"'

'Oh, that doesn't matter, Shastri. Let's go.'

'Then, let me go. But not today, tomorrow. Today I've asked Janardhana Shetty to get some people to come and spray the crops.'

'I don't want to put this off, Shastri. Come, let's go now.' And to a servant standing by, he said, 'Hey, run along and ask Budan to get the car.'

Shastri blanched; Jagannatha looked at his face and took courage. He felt a sudden burst of energy surging through him.

Shastri closed the door, closed his eyes, folded his palms together, and pleaded, 'I'm a family man, please spare me. There've been a few mistakes in the entries. They did settle all their dues but after a delay. It's just that I haven't entered them in this book, that's all. You can ask for the other ledger from the store and take a look at it if you'd like to. You can check that book to see if I haven't entered the areca crop due to you.'

Shastri might have been battered but, surely, he was not beaten.

'Shastri,' said Jagannatha bluntly, 'Your salary here is two hundred and fifty rupees, isn't it? It's much too little. From today, I shall raise it to four hundred rupees. Give back the areca you've entered into your account, and stop cheating me this way, please. You can go now and do what I've asked you to do.'

For the very first time Shastri was at a loss for words. Jagannatha was pleased. He thought: 'Shastri could be seething with hate, couldn't he?' 'Go!' he said again. Shastri walked out mechanically. Staring at him walking out with his cap tucked under his arm, Jagannatha felt pity for the man. But he did not show it.

After this incident, Jagannatha somehow felt he had gained ground. The vague longing to become one with the people grew stronger. He began to wake up early in the morning, and dressed in his white shirt and white dhothi, he went where the labourers were at work. What do these people think? What are their dreams? What hurts them? What makes them happy? He tried to find answers to such questions that bothered him. He was sure these people who seemed so servile did not really respect him at all. If he tried to get friendly with them, they would suspect his motives; if he tried to work with them, they would talk among themselves, 'Rayaru is greedy for the profit, he's making sure we don't cheat him on the job'; if he was generous with them, they would say, patronizingly, 'He's green; he's still young, after all'. Jagannatha did not know what to do. He had suspected all along that banana, pepper, and areca were being stolen from the farm. One day he stayed on after dark, hiding in the farm without letting anyone know. The very thought of himself sitting there in hiding, all on his own, gave him intense pleasure. And then he began to worry, 'What if the thieves don't show up tonight?' But, anyway, he sat on like a besotted lover, lying in wait for the thief. Around midnight he heard a faint footfall; his hair stood on end. Even in the pitch-darkness, his eyes could make out two figures: one was elderly, the other, younger. They were walking towards him; he waited breathlessly. They came closer, not knowing he was there. But just that feeling of being there as a witness to the theft gave him a sense of unbounded power; just as the sight of the older man cutting bunches of banana and areca from his farm and handing them down to the younger one made him feel he had satisfied his innermost need. As the older man climbed the areca palm, Jagannatha watched the unfolding drama with eager anticipation, holding his breath as if he himself was doing the climbing and hoping the man would not fall from the height. He prayed that the thud of the areca bunches as they fell to the ground would not wake up the watchman. After the younger one had stuffed the bunches of fruit and nut into bags, the two started walking away, carrying the loads on their heads. They had barely gone some distance when Jagannatha felt he would like to find out who they could be, and so he followed them, treading softly. He did not know there was a secret path leading from his farm to the hill beyond. He was curious to know all the byways that only these Holeyaru knew. He followed them stealthily, like a cat, until they reached the crest of the hill. They were barely there when he ran towards them and grabbed hold of the older man.

And then he turned on the torchlight.

They were his farmhands. The older man was Sheenappa, who used to behave like a very decent person. He was around forty-five, stocky, and well built. Looking at him here with his younger son, Gangappa,

Jagannatha felt a new surge of confidence, of power. To Sheenappa, who was groveling at his feet, he said, 'Get up!' And to Gangappa, who was trying to run away, he said, 'Stop!' And then he said gently, 'Don't do this again. I'll let you go this once.' In his voice, there was an 'Am I not one of you?' kind of warmth.

'I'll pay a penalty to Bhootharaya, *Odeyare*! Please let me go,' pleaded Sheenappa. Obviously, he must have found it difficult to believe what his master had said. Feeling happy that to Sheenappa he was at last a person to reckon with, Jagannatha said, 'You can take a bunch of bananas and bring the rest to my house. If you need any money, ask me; I'll give you.' And he started homewards.

'Let me walk you home, Odeyare,' said the trembling Sheenappa. And he walked along telling him about the others who were stealing from the farm, promising to get them to him. Jagannatha walked on, listening to everything he had to say without responding, to show him it was his cunning more than his humility that had made him substantial, a man of some worth.

As news of the incident spread, Jagannatha noticed his stature increasing among the farmhands. It was clear that he could get work done only by instilling fear in them. This led him into another labyrinth of introspection; now, his mind would become preoccupied solely with augmenting his assets, wouldn't it? Though he was not interested in becoming richer, it alarmed him to think it was only his affluence that could get all his abilities to work for him. As long as his wealth stood between him and his people, no personal relationship would be possible with them, but, then, without his assets and status, no relationship would be possible at all, at any level. Even if he planned to share his wealth among them equally, he might not be able to resolve this problem of making a personal connection with them. Because in Bharathipura, every relationship was based solely on prosperity. One had to be either a landlord, or a labourer, or a merchant, or Manjunatha's middleman, or an ascetic renouncing everything. Except for the last category, for every other, bonding was possible only through possessions. As a landlord, one had to lose his humaneness; as a tenant farmer, one would have to be half-dead; as a merchant, devious. Every link was based on wealth and standing—and Manjunatha's henchman, who maintained these connections, was Bhootharaya. Was there no way out of this maze? Jagannatha decided he should probe deeper into this problem.

He wanted to learn about their inner lives, their mindset: Look at Sheenappa, for instance. He seemed so decent and yet he could rob. And even after getting caught, he didn't seem unnerved at all; deep inside, he wasn't flustered. These Holeyaru have a way of getting away with anything; they're nocturnal and there're secret pathways known only to them. True, they fear Bhootharaya, but they know how not to get caught, how to work around the rules, to find secret byways of escape. This awareness added a whole new dimension to his way of thinking. Their servility is just a front; they have a resilience that helps them survive. I must get to know more about it. Beyond Manjunatha, beyond Bhoothraya, beyond the landlord, the merchant, the ascetic, they have the power to live in a secret inner world that no one else can enter; perhaps they're not even aware that they do. Their world has its own shrewd structures to help them cope with our mores. I'd be foolish to generalize idealistically about 'the common people', without reckoning with their world.

There was an overseer among the labourers, a young man called Janardhana Shetty.

He was handsome and he wore a watch on his right wrist to establish that, as a sort of a foreman, he did not have to work with his hands. In khaki trousers and glossy terylene shirt; his neatly-parted hair; the pen, cigarette pack, and matchbox in his pocket; the flourish with which he talked about Bombay; and the rivalry to please him that he encouraged among the women labourers—with all these he had a made a name for himself as an efficient overseer. However much he might try to pass off as a city-bred gentleman with the way he dressed and the way he spoke, the indelible tattoo on his forehead announced brazenly that he was a villager from one of the Kannada-speaking districts.

One day when Shetty was allotting duties to the workers, Jagannatha felt like talking to the young man; they were around the same age.

'Come here, please,' he said. Shetty heard his master call him. And so, he furtively put out his cigarette and came up to him.

'Sit down,' said Jagannatha, pointing to a fallen stump of a tree close to the one on which he was sitting.

'Oh, no, Saar,' said Shetty. He continued to stand respectfully. Jagannatha, not knowing how else to break the barrier between them, persisted, 'It's okay. Sit down.' But Shetty would not sit.

'You know that Sheenappa to whom you were allotting some work? How many children does he have?'

Shetty must have known that the landlord had ticked off Sheenappa. He must have got scared that one of his team had been caught stealing. Jagannatha felt his question was not proper, but before he could change it, Shetty said, 'Please don't use the respectful plural to talk to me, Saar, the singular should do.'

'What have you studied?'

'I've done my Middle School.'

Jagannatha was quiet; he did not know how to proceed. Shetty ventured, 'I too have warned Sheenappa, Saar. You asked me how many children he has—three daughters and three sons. The eldest is working here; she has left her husband and is now living with her parents. The second, the one who takes the greens to the farm every day, is called Kaveri. Even the third one works here. Apart from Gangappa, the other two boys are still quite young. Poor fellow, he's a family man. If it had been anyone else but you, he'd have lost his job.'

Shetty might have been perplexed by Jagannatha's curiosity. But he warmed up to him only after he had misconstrued his intention in asking about Sheenappa's family. Though Jagannatha was embarrassed by the reason behind Shetty's overtures of friendliness, he let him carry on; that seemed the only way to get this man to open up. Shetty began to gossip, giving him colourful details of Sheenappa's family.

'Forget about this Sheenappa, Saar, his elder brother had a eye on his own daughter-in-law and sent her packing home when she didn't comply. Not that she was any better; she's the type who'll spread her legs for any man.'

Jagannatha did not want to show that he was embarrassed, so he added his own bit. 'Oh, there're so many of that kind,' he said, breezily.

Now, Shetty was full of fire. 'This is nothing, Saar. You surely won't believe what I'm going to tell you about Sheenappa. He is keeping his own eldest daughter. Did you know that? Why else would he bother to get her away from the clutches of her husband's family, you tell me.'

Now Shetty lit a cigarette. 'Why don't you smoke, Saar?' he asked.

Jagannatha wanted to show Shetty he was not at all perturbed by what he had heard. And so, he got talking, saying things he never meant to say.

'That second daughter, Kaveri, why hasn't Sheenappa got her married yet?'

Shetty smiled. 'Sheenappa's very greedy, Saar,' he said, 'Nothing less than five hundred rupees as bride-price, he says. Anyway, she's earning. And she's good-looking too, in the bargain. He's arrogant, that bastard. That's what he is.'

Shetty seemed to be thriving on this kind of familiarity.

'All in all, these people have no morals, Saar,' he said, 'You know the saying, the distant hill is smooth. It's true, Saar. You must get close enough to them to know them. These illiterate sons of widows have no scruples at all, whatsoever. They keep their own daughters, their daughters-in-law. No sense of *dharmic*[40] responsibility that she belongs to another man.' Shetty must have surely heard of the way he had humiliated Vishwanatha Shastri. Jagannatha wondered how news travelled from ear to ear in Bharathipura. One of the farmhands might have eavesdropped, standing outside the office door, the day he was taking Shastri to task. Shetty became chatty. 'You really gave it to that Shastri. You should've seen how high-handed he used to be before you returned. Do you think he's any better, Saar? That woman is his wife in name only; he's keeping his mother-in-law. It's the talk of the town. The eldest son was born to the mother-in-law. Her daughter suffers everything silently. What else can she do, tell me?'

Jagannatha somehow endured everything patiently until he made it back to the house, and, then, he sank into a chair. Whew! What a tangle these lives are if we look at them from the inside! How many are conceived and survive in Manjunatha's womb! And how many the secret byways, like so many loopholes, that help to bring their lives to fruition!

And now Jagannatha was caught in another predicament, thanks to his intimacy with Shetty. The very next day after the conversation, instead of the usual maid, Thimmi, Sheenappa's second daughter,

[40] Dharma/*dharmic*: duty, righteousness.

Kaveri, came to sweep his room. A buxom wench, she had tucked her sari high enough to display her shapely thighs, and tied her hair into a bun and stuck a rose in it. She bent forward provocatively to sweep under the bed. When she was working on the farm, Jagannatha had seen her stand around sometimes, talking to the other women, unnecessarily arranging and rearranging the top end of her sari that covered her breasts.

He had all along been attracted to her but he did not seem to know the moves he had to make to show his interest in a woman of her class, so different from the ones he would use with someone of his own kind. After all, it was impossible to have anything more than a few moments of sleeping with her. Beyond using her as an object to satiate his lust, he could not expect any other kind of bonding to arise out of such an intimacy; no personal involvement of any sort. He was amazed to see how much desire her body could arouse in him and how unreachable it was, all because of a class difference. And yet his body warmed to her every time she came in to sweep his room. He felt nervous.

One day when Kaveri came into his room, Jagannatha was on a chair in front of a mirror, shaving. On a suitcase behind him was a ten-rupee note. He could see it in the mirror. He could see Kaveri too, sweeping with zest, noticing the note, standing by it twice over, and then sweeping the floor around the suitcase over and over again. Jagannatha lathered his face, lost in wondering what she would do next. Kaveri bent to sweep a third time. She looked into the mirror. Did she guess at his hidden consent when she saw his face in the mirror; that he wanted her to take the bait? Surely she should know he could see everything; she could clearly see that, while his hand was lathering his face, his eyes were transfixed, watching her hand. She picked up the note and tucked it slowly into the folds of the sari at her waist. And as she was tucking it in, she let fall the top end of her sari, revealing her breasts. And, trailing that bit of the sari on the floor, she slowly made her way to him, still sweeping. Under the pretext of sweeping around his chair, she pressed her left breast to his thigh. And then, under the pretence of dusting the windowsill on which the mirror was, she stood behind him and bent towards him, pressing her body against his. A firm breast pressed against his cheek.

Jagannatha sat still. The possible bloom of an auspicious present could end in a future of emptiness; the very awareness made him impotent. There's a chasm between us that a burst of lust cannot bridge. Forgive me, he wanted to say but he could not. He just sat there, perspiring. Once again he felt as he had felt with Margaret under the apple tree—totally lost. He felt he was not real. Kaveri swayed out of the room, seductively. Jagannatha recovered, stood up, and walked to the bathroom and washed his face.

From the next day Jagannatha was not in the room when Kaveri came in to sweep it. And also, he tried to keep his distance with Shetty whenever he came to talk to him. If you want to get to know these people, it looks as if you had to get entangled in their warped relationships as well. If you try to get to know them better, it's like looking at the skin under a microscope; you get to see so many unwanted details, losing your grip on the essentials. When you know them from a distance, you feel fired to become a political activist on their behalf, but when you get close enough, you feel such action is impossible, even pointless—and then you get confused. A father who keeps his daughter, a father-in-law who keeps his daughter-in-law, a son-in-law who sleeps with his mother-in-law, a husband who beats his wife; the vulnerability, the rage, the pettiness, the daily grind of joy and sorrow—when you look at all these, you get the feeling that historical changes are only superficial events that scratch the surface; that nothing ever alters profoundly. If our daily share of pain and pleasure has to remain this way forever, if the cycle of night and day spins on without change, what can we hope to achieve, whatever we may do? Why should I think I could improve, through change, the life of someone like Kaveri who could arouse me and leave me loathing myself?

For many days after that, Jagannatha was once again lost in conflicting thoughts, not making any headway. He had lost interest in improving his farm. He could see that his interest in the inner lives of these people was steering him towards forbidden ground, and he was afraid. He felt even more anxious to see himself reverting to his apathetic attitude that, by and large, life is, after all, meaningless and all we can do is to try and understand its pointlessness. Of one thing he was sure—if as an insider he did not engage in action that would make a radical difference to society, it would not matter whether he lived or died.

Once he had been sitting on one of the huge boulders behind the temple. It was evening. The President of the country had come on a visit to the temple and left. Suddenly, he heard the temple bells calling for evening worship. At that very moment, an idea struck him: 'I must take the Holeyaru into the temple. I must change the tradition of centuries with that one step. I must break Manjunatha. I must make these people feel the anguish of becoming responsible for their lives.'

He had got up and headed back home. He had selected ten young men from among the Holeyaru and had begun to talk to them. From that day onwards, every evening, shadows would form in the distance and those shadows would move nearer and say, 'Odeyare!'

'Come!' Jagannatha would say. They would come only to the edge of the front porch. Jagannatha would talk to them. He would say, 'Think for yourselves, take decisions, and act responsibly.' But those words did not seem real, at least not yet. Jagannatha would ponder over this sense of emptiness night and day, *How can I make my words make sense to them? How can I make them accept what I'm telling them and make my words real by turning them into action? How can I slit the womb of Manjunatha and walk out? Bring them out.*

FIVE

Nagamani

As usual, Jagannatha got up before dawn and walked out through the backdoor of his house. The house was on top of a hill. Behind it was another elevation with a grove of cashew trees that belonged to him. He knew that about half the cashew crop was being stolen. He loved to walk right up to the crest of the cashew hillock early in the morning and look at Bharathipura, to see the groves that covered the hillside—jackfruit with dense, dark green foliage; mango, laden with blossoms even after the season; areca, swaying in the breeze down in the valley—and the red-tiled houses that dotted the green landscape. A town that was neither village nor city. To the east, a stream meandering like a serpent; next to it, the dome of Shri Manjunatha's temple seen from any vantage point in town. Weathered by sun and rain, it had aged as a home for birds. Right next to the temple was Bhootharaya's mound—no woman who had not reached menopause was permitted to climb this little knoll and enter Bhootharaya's temple.

The festival fair of the New Moon was about a month away. We should be ready by then, the Holeyaru and I. Pilgrims will be here from all over the country. By tomorrow or the day after, my letters will be in the papers; I must tell Rayaru about my plan today.

Jagannatha paced the hilltop for a while. It was cold and he was wearing a dark polo-necked sweater; Margaret had bought it for him. The mist that had covered all of Bharathipura was clearing in the warmth of the morning sun. From the brow of the cashew hill, the town in the distance looked beautiful with shimmering tiled houses; the greenery; the river twinkling like bits of mirror wherever the sunlight fell on it; the dewdrops on the tiny cobwebs woven across the grass, with some of them sparkling like diamonds whenever the sun cut them at an angle. It was only as you came downhill and walked the streets that you got to see the emaciated people with nothing to show but a pot belly, thanks to Shri Manjunatha's bounty of a daily free lunch, the well-fed street dogs that lazed around, not stirring even when buses come hurtling down the road, and the monkeys on the peepul[41] tree near the temple that brazenly snatched bananas from pilgrims. It was only in the sky that you saw birds, forever healthy, freewheeling. What you saw from the top of the hill was one thing but what you got to see when you walked the streets that reeked with the stench of urine was something else. As Jagannatha came downhill, he saw the first bus leaving for Shimoga; it was one of the buses from Prabhu's Shri Manjunatha Bus Service. He had run all the way downhill and now he was hot. He bathed and entered the dining room. There were around twenty people sitting down for breakfast, each with a banana leaf in front of him, waiting to be served. Some of them were familiar, some, not. These people would have come from wherever, to make a visit to Manjunatha. The poor came to his house or they went to the choultry his ancestors had built. The Brahmins waylaid the rich and booked them into their homes as paying guests.

Jagannatha had spiced puffed rice for breakfast and headed into town, determined to meet Rayaru and tell him about his plan: 'You seem depressed; this might pick you up. It may even put some new life into the town. Or else we'll continue to sink into Manjunatha's

[41] A tree scared to Hindus. Often, a platform is built around it and people circumambulate it in reverence or to petition or to fulfil a vow.

hell-hole this way. Don't you feel this town has been rotting for centuries, Rayare? I can't really convince you in an argument how Manjunatha's responsible for this; only action can prove it. Life in such a society seems pointless because there's no scope for any action here except eating, mating, dying. Let's put our hand to the wheel and turn it, right on the day of the Chariot Festival. In the one new step the Holeyaru take, all of us will die and be born anew.'

Jagannatha felt he had recently got into the habit of talking a lot to himself. It might stop if he could get to talk to the Holeyaru. He went on his way, mechanically bringing his palms together to wish those who wished him. He saw Nagaraja Jois seated on his front porch but sped past as if he had not seen him. He was on his way to Rayaru's house on Chariot Street.

As you turned into Chariot Street, there was a shop selling vegetables; that is, vegetables like coloured cucumber, pumpkin, sweet gourd, coconut, small cucumbers, varieties of banana eaten as fruit, small ones, dark ones, and a variety of raw bananas meant to be cooked as a vegetable. Since his return from England, Jagannatha had felt no one had ever tried to see if anything else could be grown. When the price of areca rose, even paddy fields had been converted to areca groves. The health, the essence of the soil became areca nuts. On the one hand, it was Manjunatha, and on the other, it was areca; nothing else flourished in this soil. And so, Jagannatha was surprised to see a withering cauliflower in the shop. Curious, he asked Byari, the vegetable vendor, 'Where was this grown?'

Byari, with a coloured lungi wrapped around his waist, stood up respectfully, spat out the betel leaf and nuts he had been chewing, undid the strip of cloth he had wrapped around his head as a turban and hung it on his shoulder, and stared, perplexed. He was wondering if it would be proper to ask his visitor to sit on the bench when Jagannatha smiled and said, 'I just asked how this cauliflower had managed to come to Bharathipura.'

'I get them from Shimoga once in a while, Dhanigale. This, peas, carrots—just for the Puraniks; nobody else eats them.' Jagannatha's face brightened with a grin. 'Very good!' he said and walked on.

On the floor above Byari's shop was a sign that said, 'Shri Manjunatha Prasanna, Brahmin Youth Association'. When he had just returned from England, Jagannatha had been curious to see what kind of a club it was. Unemployed sons of the fairly rich got together there right after breakfast to while away their time playing cards. There was a carom board but nobody played the game. There was a pile of novels too, some twenty-five of them with their cover pages in tatters. That was it. The books were in a box made of nutmeg wood; the carom board was on top of it. In the middle of the room, on the unswept floor, was a mat of woven palm leaves. On it sat the young men, playing cards. The walls, as usual, were decked with a picture of Shri Manjunatha with the crown; a picture of Bharath Matha, Mother India, with her flowing tresses spread out as the Himalayas in the map of India in the background, and of Gandhi spinning on the wheel.

Even though the gutters reeked, women sprinkled watered-down cow-dung every morning and evening only on Chariot Street and decorated it with beautiful rangoli designs. The reason? Occasionally, the idol of Manjunathaswami arrived in procession, on a chariot. Some homes were decked in fronds of areca and sheaves of paddy. As the New Moon Festival neared, walls were whitewashed, the black stone floors of the verandas were scrubbed clean, and rangoli drawn on them with a sticky white flour paste, to preserve the festive look for many days. Some homes seemed to have school-going children for they had hung pictures of Nehru and Kennedy together, or of a laughing, chubby-faced Kennedy alone. Usually, in the room next to the front veranda where the eldest son of the family slept, you could see, beside the Kennedy picture, calendars of Madhubala, the Hindi film actress, or of some woman scantily clad in wet clothes. Some old men sat on a bench in an Ayurvedic pundit's clinic that smelt of medicinal herbs and powders. Shyam Pundit, the doctor, stood up and brought his palms together to wish him. Suddenly an advertisement for family planning. 'A son for fame; a daughter for blessing,' it said. And then rows and rows of small packets of the contraceptive, Nirodh, in a pan-shop selling cone shaped *beeda*. The irony of it all was there was no electricity in Bharathipura. And in broad-faced Jinendra's store, copper-cooking-pots neatly stacked one on top of the other and stainless steel plates and tumblers. He was the only Jain merchant in town. Every time Jagannatha walked down this street he looked around hoping to see something new. And now, the only thing that caught his eye in every store was prints of the President on art-paper, bare-bodied and worshipping Manjunathaswami, priced at seventy paise. The Temple Committee had got it printed in Bangalore.

Eager to meet Sripathi Rao, Jagannatha hurried down the street that led to the river and stopped in front of the house. Rayaru may not have left for his Khadi store yet; it was not yet nine. He stepped into the dim central hall and called, 'Rayare!' They had not started cooking yet; there was no smoke. Someone came out of the dining room wiping his mouth with a handkerchief. Not Rayaru but a stocky middle-aged man with cropped hair. The strip of cloth he had over his shoulder was gold-laced. With him was a young girl in a nylon sari. She did not look like a local; her blouse was short, revealing her midriff. They went out with Rao's son, Raganna, without noticing him. Bhagyamma shouted after them to Ranganna, even as she was coming out of the kitchen, 'If you don't get Udupa, tell Rama Jois I sent them. He'll see to everything—the oblations at the river, the ritual bath, and the visit to the temple.'

And then she saw Jagannatha and stood, shocked.

'Sit down,' she said, and went in to get him some coffee in a copper tumbler. Neither spoke for a moment. And then she started, 'He took the morning bus to Shimoga. He should be back by tomorrow evening.' Jagannatha sat on a wooden plank sipping coffee sweetened with jaggery, and said nothing. Bhagyamma continued, 'He feels she could teach in Shimoga for a year. He went to make arrangements for her stay at his friend's place. Now tell me, can she stay with them without paying for her board? How much can she send us to meet our expenses? If I ask him that, he doesn't even bother to reply. And if I say, "What'll you lose if you put in a word with the DEO?" he pounces on me. He himself says the man who's the education minister had been to prison with him during the freedom struggle. But what's the use, tell me? I'm tired of dancing to his tunes, Jaganna. Had your mother been alive she would've told you everything. When he set fire to his cloth store protesting against foreign goods, didn't I listen to him and burn the four silk saris I'd got from my mother's house? Ask anyone. And now our daughter is sitting at home without a salary. And I have to run the house somehow, haven't I? What else can I do, tell me? I keep telling him every day, "At least get me a buffalo. I'll sell the milk and run the house. If we think of status and dignity, we'll have to cover our bellies with a wet cloth." But will he listen to me? I'm just so tired of living, Jaganna. You must save our self-respect somehow. I've known you since you were a child, haven't I? That's why I can forget my embarrassment and ask this of you. You know these people who had come today? They're from Chikkamagaluru, friends of my mother's younger brother. That's why they've come to our house as paying guests. I may make ten rupees at the most. I didn't send Ranganna to get them from the bus stop, I swear on your head, Jaganna. I wouldn't dream of cheating him but what else can I do, tell me?'

Jagannatha felt very uncomfortable to see Bhagyamma squatting on the floor, resting her head on her left hand, hoping to gain his sympathy. He noticed Savithri behind the door, feeling embarrassed, making frantic signs to her mother, and, to change the topic, he said, 'You know why I came here, Bhagyamma? We need a boy in our office to write the accounts. Anyway your son Ranganna has finished school and is staying at home, why shouldn't he come and work for us? That's why I came here, to talk to you about it. Send him right from tomorrow. I can give you two hundred rupees as an advance on the salary. And I too need someone reliable, you see.' And he stood up, saying, 'I've got to be going now. It's getting quite late.' He felt embarrassed to see Bhagyamma's face glow with gratitude. 'Send him soon, I need someone urgently,' he said brusquely, trying to keep his tone business-like.

As he walked away, Jagannatha thought of Bhagyamma sitting in a corner, demeaning herself to work on his sympathy. Her words were insufferable, dripping with a false humility; she was ingratiating herself with him though she was also trying vainly to maintain a semblance of self-respect. His heart was heavy with the tragedy of her situation. What a shame that she was forced into deceit! She almost said, 'Don't tell him about this.' All the while that he had sat with her, Jagannatha had been dreading that she might put her plea into words. And now, he sighed with relief.

Suddenly, Jagannatha felt depressed. How we wear out our dreams in the mere act of living! Perhaps everything continues the way it is, whatever we may do to change it. Perhaps this land is barren; perhaps nothing can blossom here. He saw a group of Deevas coming down the hillock with small sprigs of areca flowers stuck behind their ears, Bhootharaya's prasada. Only the areca seems to blossom, in the hands, on the ears, on the heads, on the tall swaying areca palms. These men of the toddy-tapping community have come all spruced up to worship in the temple; they're beaming. They'll never think of Manjunatha the way I see Him. Their concerns are different. They may talk about rainfall, drought, a buffalo calving, or their debts. They may forget these things too. They may quarrel, take a vow. But that's not enough; there's more to their lives than all this. I've put my hand to the wheel with anguish, with anxiety that they may become aware. Will the dark-skinned people too put their hands to the wheel with me, those who carry baskets of human shit on their heads? I'm waiting.

Jagannatha warmed to the thought and walked briskly, swinging his arms. On reaching the town square, he took a short cut towards home along the narrow alleyways. On the way, he had to pass Nagaraja Jois's house again. He had come out to spit out the betel leaves he had been chewing and, adjusting the wrap around his shoulders, he asked Jagannatha in.

'I have to be going,' said Jagannatha, climbing the steps to the porch.

'Come in for a minute,' said Jois, spreading a mat and getting him to sit down. He sat at the other edge and put a tray of betel leaves, nuts, and sunna between them. He pulled out a chain of rudrakshi beads strung with gold that hung around his neck and let it hang outside the wrap. He prepared the betel leaf, clipping the tips and smoothing it as he began to talk.

'The other day, you talked of Russell at the High School. I've been thinking about it. I don't think we had these temples and these superstitions during the Vedic times. To put it in a nutshell, in a tradition in which an individual turns towards the east and prays to the sun god to bless everyone with mental power, surely there can be no place for temples, worship, or vows. You've resigned from the trusteeship of the temple; you'll get what I'm saying. That's the reason I'm telling you this, we don't say, "Manifest the power in me." We say, "Manifest the power in *us*." We mean the whole family of mankind. And what is this intellectual power we're asking for? It is scientific temper, the same thing your Russell is talking about.'

Preoccupied as he was with his own thoughts like a brooding hen, Jagannatha thought, 'This man talks so much, let me tell him of my plan, and see how violently he reacts.' 'If we think superstition is wrong, what're people like us doing to oppose it as intellectuals, *Joisare*? What we need is action, not mere words.'

Jois remembered something else, suddenly. 'What a shame! Yesterday, I sent you away without even a cup of coffee. "Nagamani, Nagamani!"'

There was a soft tinkle of bangles in the hall.

'The landlord's here. Yesterday, we had sent him away without offering him anything,' he said to her, and turning towards Jagannatha, said, 'Nagamani is my daughter-in-law. You know my elder son who's a lawyer in Shimoga? His wife. The rents are pretty high in Shimoga; he doesn't earn enough. And here, after my wife died, I don't have anyone to see to the guests. My daughter's just ten. And so Nagamani stays here with me. What can be done, tell me? People look for our house and come here because we're a well-known orthodox Vedic Brahmin family. Sometimes, there are around fifteen to twenty pilgrims in the house. I let my elder son live a secular life but I'm training the younger one to be a Vedic priest. Shankara knows everything: astrology, the Vedas, the rituals of worship, everything. You know we can't let go of what's come to us from ancient times. When I get him married during the next wedding season, I'll send Nagamani to Shimoga to her husband.'

Jagannatha stifled a yawn with great difficulty. No point in talking to Jois. It was possible to plough such unyielding places only through action. Jois had taken out the day's paper and was looking for something to show him. He has me sitting with him on the front porch only to let passers-by know the landlord is a frequent visitor. My weakness is hidden in my need to be civil to such people. I can make them aware of my real self only through action.

Nagamani stooped down to lay two bits of plantain leaves as plates before him and her father-in-law. His attention was riveted on the girl who had bent before him. It's hard to imagine such a robust young woman in this house. A chiselled figure with a checked blouse covering her full breasts and a plain dun-coloured sari; slender waist; dusky complexion; hair, parted in the middle, combed back, and plaited tight; a longish stroke of kumkuma on her forehead. Except for the chain with the thali to show she's married, she wears no other jewellery. As she bent down to put some *chakkuli* as a snack on the plantain leaves and stood up, her breasts filled her blouse and jiggled a bit. She isn't wearing a bra. But it's obvious she isn't aware of how provocative she is. Her every pose is innocent; the way she bends, walks, looks about, or stands against the door waiting—these are but the movements of her daily grind, not postures to flaunt her beauty. Now Kaveri would manipulate even a simple act like carrying a basket of greens on her head to draw attention to the seductive sway of her hips. When Margaret talked seriously, the way she drew on her cigarette with eyes half-closed, or raised her head while pushing back a profusion of hair, had another kind of charm. But the way Nagamani stands like a dancer against a door facing me is only for some respite from blowing into the wood fire in the kitchen or drawing water from the well, that's all. And she's leaning against the door, perhaps in a dancer's stance, only because it isn't proper for her to sit when there are men around. Nagamani is so engrossed in her chores in the kitchen, she's not aware of the beauty blossoming in her body. These women live only to cook and serve delicious meals; those Holeyaru live only to carry away the shit that this food becomes; and between these are the men of Bharathipura, whiling away their time on their verandas, digesting the food they've eaten—Jagannatha trembled with rage.

He looked at Nagamani's face as she stood by the door, holding the box of chakkuli. She had translucent skin, so smooth, so soft; full lips; ears, a bit too large for her face. When his eyes searched her big ones, there was no expression other than waiting to serve him more of the snack after he had eaten what was on his leaf. He stared at her, hoping to fathom the grief in the innermost recesses of her heart. But she just stood staring at him as if she was staring at emptiness. Nagaraja Jois looked up from the paper. 'Look, someone's written that growing cardamom is bad for the areca,' he said. Jagannatha nodded and looked at Nagamani as if to worship her beauty that hoped for nothing, wanting somehow to share in her sorrow. But she stood like a statue that could blink. He felt his anguish for her would never reach her. Even with his dispassionate love for her that asked for nothing in return, he would not be able to refresh her life force, deadened beyond revival.

Jagannatha suddenly felt depressed. If people like her could not bloom, then his plan of action would be fruitless. But, then, why has her body blossomed with such maddening beauty?

'Perhaps, the heady scent of the cardamom sucks out the goodness of the soil. Perhaps, that's why it's not good for the areca palms. What do you say?' asked Jois.

'I don't know,' replied Jagannatha.

'I don't want any more chakkuli,' he said, staring at Nagamani, trying to be friendly.

'Let her serve you at least one more,' pressed Jois. Nagamani went in to get coffee. Jagannatha felt it was impossible to make someone else's sorrow your own, however hard you tried. She brought the coffee and bent again to put the glass on the floor. I can never ever be anyone to her. If the whole town can be renewed, then she might burst forth with life; this is all I can hope for, all I can dream about. Nagamani went in. Jois would not let him go; he talked on, boring him.

Again, it was about the temple; a Brahmin who faces the sun god in worship should not worship idols as well. Jois and the current chief priest of the temple, Seetharamaiah, were of the same family. Jois's grandfather and Seetharamaiah's foster father's father were brothers. Though Seetharamaiah was adopted, Jois had records to prove that the adoption had not been done according to the rules. And so, he felt only he had the right to officiate at Manjunatha's worship, not Seetharamaiah. Also, Seetharamaiah's son, Ganesha, did not conform to ritual ablutions. And besides, he had had a nervous breakdown once. Now *his* son, Shankara, was different; he had memorized the whole of the Vedas. Jois was planning to sue the trustees of the temple for installing Seetharamaiah as the chief priest.

There was the sound of a ladder toppling in the attic.

In the hall, Jois's daughter was playing dice with a friend. Jois's son came running in from the street. 'All of them will eat at the temple today and will come to our house in the evening,' he said, 'I got them to bathe in the river and worship at the temple. Now, I'll show them around the town and get back.' And he walked away with a group of pilgrims waiting for him. Jois would not let go of Jagannatha. Resting his left hand on the floor, clenching and releasing his right fist as if he were under great stress, he edged closer to him and said, 'Had you been the chief trustee of the temple, we could've settled the issue somehow. But you are not. What can I do now, tell me? They say the people of Bharathipura should not go to court; that Manjunatha decides everything. But can I sit back trusting this belief? I said to my son, "Find out what the law says about this; we'll file a case." All I ask is, in such a famous temple, shouldn't the rituals be done according to proper rules of worship? Prabhu, the current chief trustee, turns a deaf ear to me. What does he care? After all, he's a Konkan; he doesn't belong here. I've written a letter to the President of the country. You must translate it into English, please.'

Jagannatha did not say, 'Yes', he did not say, 'No'. He had waited for a chance to tell Jois bluntly what he thought of him. But it is impossible to plant anything in the slush of Jois's mind. Nagamani cannot bloom. Probably, no one can bloom. Listening to him, even I may weaken in my resolve. Slowly, Manjunatha may overcome me too. How is it that Nagamani doesn't have secret ways of fulfilling herself like Kaveri? She stared at me with no feelings whatsoever. Wasn't she even aware that she was a woman? She had just stared vacantly, waiting to serve the chakkuli; my stares didn't spark off anything in her. There was a vacant look in her large eyes. Her long-lashed eyelids opened and closed. Even when she did look at me, she wasn't aware of me. In this way, a hundred pilgrims come to eat in this house and go their way. They see her. And she waits on them. She stands staring at their heads, their hands, and their eyes satiated with eating, as she eases her tired limbs with the poses of a dancer. I'm but one of a hundred who've eaten her chakkulis, that's all. Her well-fleshed-out warm breasts and the warm folds between her legs will never arouse her. She'll go to Shimoga some day to be with her husband, she'll stop having periods, she'll become pregnant, and she'll deliver babies. That's it. After a few deliveries, her tummy will wrinkle and her breasts will sag. That's about it.

He tried to recall something else about Nagamani. *Had someone said something to me about her?* He was disturbed. And then he quite forgot what he was trying to remember. Jois was talking on and on. His daughter's friend finished the game of dice and got up to leave. She skipped down the steps in a skirt and blouse, and a *davani*. This verve would last only until she got married.

'The frauds this Seetharamaiah has committed, are they one or two? You know the gold crown your mother gifted to Shri Manjunatha in your name? If you think all that gold is on his head, you're crazy. Where do you think Seetharamaiah got all that gold for a girdle for his son and ear studs, bangles, and necklaces for his wife and daughter?'

Jois had been moving closer to Jagannatha in his bid to get intimate and now he was sitting right next to him. In fact, he was almost whispering in his ear. Jagannatha stared at his reddish teeth and his ruby ear studs. He felt disgusted; there was no point in telling him his plans.

'It's getting late, I should be going,' he said and stood up. He'll always remember this moment: the midday, the empty street, and the loud gong of the bell announcing the last worship for the day. He was stretching to shake off the boredom when Jois's daughter came clattering down the attic steps screaming, 'Appaiah! Appaiah! Come here! Athige, Athige …' Jois ran in. Jagannatha too ran in and climbed the stairs. And there in the attic, among the coloured cucumbers tied to the rafters with plantain fibre and some clothes hanging to dry, was Nagamani hanging by a rope tied to the main beam.

On the floor lay a ladder.

Jagannatha set up the ladder against the beam and climbed it quickly, held Nagamani against him, lifted her up slightly to slacken the rope, and screamed, 'Get me a knife!' Jois threw off his wrap, ran down, and brought him a knife. Jagannatha cut the rope and gently laid Nagamani on the floor and loosened the noose.

'Run, get the doctor,' he said. Jois ran down again. Jagannatha touched Nagamani. He felt her body was still warm, or was he imagining it? Her neck was broken and blood had streamed through her nose and mouth. Her eyes were stuck upwards. He tried all he knew to revive her; he turned her over, turned her face sideward, and pressed her back; he tried the kiss of life, he rubbed her chest. He closed her eyes that were stuck awry. He got the little girl to fetch him some water and wiped her face clean.

The doctor came on a cycle, examined her, and said, 'She's dead.' Jois sat with his hands on his head. Jagannatha stood about not knowing what to say to Jois who was in a state of shock. The doctor was a young man; he had just qualified. 'Since this is a case of suicide, you'll have to inform the police. We'll be doing a post-mortem. Sorry, but I should be going,' he said and left. Because of all the commotion, a large crowd had gathered in the house.

'Oh, what a good girl she was! She used to do all the work in the house without complaining,' said some women and started crying. Jagannatha got hold of Nagamani's husband's address. Only when he asked for her father's address did he get to know that both her parents were dead. Someone told him her elder brother was a cook in some hotel in Hassan. Jagannatha told Jois he would send a telegram to his son to come immediately and went out. There were crowds of people everywhere, in the house, on the street. He felt sick. Some of them had just had the free lunch at the temple; they had come with their tumblers. He trembled uncontrollably from time to time. His throat was dry but he felt sick even to swallow his spittle. He went to the post office, sent the telegram, and went home. He told Chikki he did not want lunch and went up to his room and fell on his bed. He wanted to cry but could not. He could only keep sighing, unable to understand what was happening. He waited for the evening.

In the distance he could see a group of Holeyaru approaching. Dark bodies in mere loincloth, heads with unkempt hair, eyes that hoped for nothing. He went out to them and said, 'Not today,' and sent them away. Chikki must have known he was in torment because of Nagamani's death. She came in with a cup of coffee, laid it on the table, touched his fevered brow, and went down. She knew that, as a child, he would run a temperature whenever he was upset. And so, now, she had left him to himself. Gratefully, he closed his eyes and slept. When he woke up suddenly sometime in the night, there was moonlight all around. Jagannatha felt irritated; he closed the window. What thought could ever rise from such a vacant mind? For everything, take a decision; push forward, no need to fear because, where action isn't possible … Jagannatha stopped; he did not know how to put the rest of the idea into words. Nagamani had been alive, now she was dead. Jagannatha tried hard to fathom what could have gone on in her mind and failing, slept, exhausted.

SIX

Jagannatha Tells Sripathi Rao about His Plan

To shake off his depression, Jagannatha walked up the cashew-hillock as soon as he left his bed the next morning. Snatches of the letter he had been planning to write to Margaret surfaced in his mind. *Now I'm plunging into action desperately, Margaret. With the dialogue I may possibly have with the Holeyaru, I may bud again; the whole town may put forth new shoots. When I think of how Nagamani had decided her fate while we were chatting on the veranda .... But the implications of what Nagamani has done elude me. In my anguish, am I making a commitment to a pointless action? Am I exposing myself to ridicule? No, it isn't that. What's it, then? She stood, she bent over, she served us, she climbed up the stairs; she stuck her head in the noose, she kicked the ladder, she died. She was smouldering and no one knew. She snuffed out her life and no one knew. The way she decided to put out the fire raging within her makes my plan of action absurd. Is my commitment a farce, then? You've seen me fail; you tell me, Margaret.*

This Manjunatha is slimy, so are Jois and Shastri. Kaveri and Nagamani screamed. The Holeyaru may scream too, probably. The sunshine, the proffered back, the apple tree, the quiet of a summery Sunday afternoon, when these rejected me; and then, yesterday, when Nagamani rejected me ... Jagannatha stopped walking. It was a steep climb to the crest of the hill. '*When I try to find images to fit my thoughts, I become mushy again. I wait like a brooding hen, hoping this gooey stuff will become beak, feathers, wings, and claws. I bear down with birth pangs. While I was trying to bear down yesterday, Nagamani climbed the stairs of the attic. She kicked the ladder and died. She doused the fires of her bothersome youth that had sprouted hair in the warm places, desiring pleasure. Yesterday afternoon, I was rejected all over again. I guess I'll continue to be a slimy, formless mass despite my anguish to firm up unless I take on Manjunatha, unless I find the words that will become seeds to be sown in the minds of the Holeyaru who haven't yet found a voice in history.*

Jagannatha stood on the crest of the hill and looked at Bharathipura. The town looked dreamy, cloaked in mist.

My anguish seems pointless, Margaret; it's like a mother hen sitting on the town hoping to hatch it. I'm telling you all this because you hoped the formless mass that I am would form beak and claws. Most probably, even you may never blossom. Pushing back your hair from your cheek, you sit as if you're ready for an awesome truth; you get as prickly as a bilva tree during an argument—but some day even you'll feel that this is all a farce. I'm scared, Margaret; the sun may reject you too.

Jagannatha came down the hill. He washed his face, had some coffee, and lay down again. But someone was at the door. He went downstairs. It was Ranganna, Rayaru's son. He gave him two hundred rupees and said, 'Give this to your mother. You can start working right away.' Someone else called Ramakrishnaiah was waiting to see him—a skinny man struggling to support eight children. The temple authorities had seized his farmland because he had not made the payments. They had seized his house too.

'Go to court,' said Jagannatha. Ramakrishnaiah sat quietly, a gutless man.

'What can I do?' asked Jagannatha.

'Please talk to Prabhu,' Ramakrishnaiah pleaded. Wrinkled face, ear studs, dishevelled hair, and hoarse voice—Jagannatha was irritated.

'If you go to court, I'll meet the expenses,' he said. Ramakrishnaiah did not respond to that.

'I'm a family-man. Don't let me down, please,' he said.

Jagannatha was angry. 'If you have the guts, you should go to court, Ramakrishnaiah,' he said.

Ramakrishnaiah sighed; he may have to forego even the free lunch at the temple, perhaps.

Jagannatha floundered not knowing how to respond.

'Look, I don't have any farmland to give away,' he said, 'But I have an uncultivated paddy field. I could give it to you. I may be able to help you a bit. Come tomorrow or the day after. A letter of mine will be in the papers one of these days. Please read it before you come.'

Ramakrishaiah nodded, brought his palms together in gratitude, and was about to go.

'Come back for lunch,' said Jagannatha.

'I will.'

Jagannatha went upstairs to his room and wondered, now, why did I tell Ramakrishnaiah about the paper? Is there anything I can do to rouse the man's temper?

We live in apathy, Margaret. All our dreams are but heaps of areca nut, ready to be bagged and sent to the market. Sometimes, the crop decays and our dreams come to nothing. A man like Ramakrishnaiah would long to own a farm, even if it was only old arecanut palms.

He felt it was impossible to hurt a man like Ramakrishnaiah or to enrage him. The only people who never dreamed of cultivating areca farms in these parts were the Holeyaru. People who never planted anything for themselves, who swept out shit, and carried it away from the town—these were just the people to reject Manjunatha. Jagannatha was exhilarated.

He sat at his table, ready to write.

In the afternoon he had lunch with a few pilgrims, some people who had come to town to buy their medicines, Ramakrishnaiah, and some others. Under his bed he found a fresh sprig of areca flowers, Bhootharaya's singara, his amulet, and a small packet of Manjunatha's bright red kumkuma powder. This was Chikki's way of fortifying him against evil; she was worried to see him every evening with the young Holeyaru, trying to teach them to write the alphabet on sand. Jagannatha smiled. He left them under the bed untouched to show Chikki that God had no power over him. He had not yet told the Holeyaru about their entry into the temple. They were not yet real to him as persons. He was trying to make friends with them while teaching them the alphabet. They traced the alphabet with their forefingers on a spread of sand on the ground. They were petrified, so they obeyed their master's instructions. That was all there was to it. And if this scares Chikki, how would she react when she knows what my intentions are? Jagannatha began to worry.

The Holeyaru came in the late afternoon. I keep forgetting the names of these. Who's Pilla? Who's Kariya? Who's Mada? On the sand he wrote the letters that made the *cha*, *ja*, and *ta* sounds and asked them to go over them again and again. These men can chop wood deftly with ease and yet, look at the way they perspire writing the letters as they sit in front of a spread of sand and bend over to write on it! As they pronounced each letter and went over it with their forefingers, their rippling muscles contorted with tension; the nerves on the back of their necks stuck out. After a while, their legs would go to sleep and, after the lesson was over, they would clump away as if they had sand-bags tied to their legs. Jagannatha felt terribly dispirited sometimes when he saw the fear in their eyes as they traced the letters. And when his farmhands stood around at a respectable distance, curious to see what he was doing, he was greatly embarrassed. He felt as if he were performing some esoteric ritual of magic and sorcery.

The one hour of class must seem like an age to the Holeyaru. He decided he would tell them about the plan of action he had in mind from the next day, bit by bit. They stood up on leaden legs. Jagannatha also stood up, hoping for some kind of a rapport between them. Kaveri walked by with a basket of greens, swaying her hips, jiggling her buttocks, and glancing at them sideways and smiling.

'Give us something to chew, Odeya,' asked one of the Holeyaru.

Jagannatha shared among them the betel leaves, nuts, tobacco, and sunna he had in a bag. He thought it would be good to give them the betel leaves to chew even as they sat down to do the lesson; it might help them unwind. Then they might not be so tense while tracing the letters. They might learn better when they are relaxed. Slowly, they might even open up to him. As he crossed the yard after the Holeyaru had left, he saw Chikki waiting for the cattle to go into the shed. She looked at him accusingly and went on to call the cows into the barn, 'Kattu Bai! Kattu Bai!' Shastri was standing by the office talking to Ranganna. Jagannatha guessed Shastri was not happy to have the boy in the office.

The servants were lighting the lamps in the house. He was about to go in when he saw Sripathi Rao walking towards him and waited. Rao seemed to have headed towards Jagannatha's house as soon as he returned from Shimoga.

As soon as he sat down, Rayaru said, 'Jaganna, my son Ranganna knows nothing about business. Why have you hired him?'

'Oh, he'll learn. I need someone reliable.'

'That's a lie. I've just had a quarrel with my wife about this. She must've pestered you to take him on.'

'No, Rayare, it wasn't like that at all. Anyway, you leave Ranganna to me. I've something else to tell you.'

It was getting dark. Jagannatha took Rao up to his room and closed the door behind them. They sat facing each other under the gaslight. Rao, who was sitting cross-legged on a cane chair, took out his bag of betel leaves and said, 'What is it?'

Jagannatha lost his nerve, yet he babbled on. 'During the New Moon Festival, I plan to enter the temple with some of the Holeyaru. I've written about it to the papers; it should be out tomorrow.'

His throat was dry.

Rao blanched. He seemed stunned, unable to talk. Looking at him, Jagannatha was happy. So, my action must have some meaning if it can shock a person like Rayaru! Rao was fumbling for words; he was trying to hide his fear with an artificial smile. Jagannatha braced himself for a discussion.

'It won't help, Jagannatha. The health minister is a Harijan. The DC in Shimoga is a Harijan. What good, do you think, has come of it?'

'Tell me why you're scared, Rayare. Why am I scared?' he asked bluntly.

'It's not a question of fear, Jagannatha. People live by their faith. What right do we have to destroy it, tell me? Can we ask them to forget their faith in God and live by their trust in a cabinet of ministers?'

'You're a loser, Rayare. And so you're talking like a liberal. Unless we destroy the power of Manjunatha, this town cannot become creative. And only the Holeyaru can do this. See how frightened you are.'

He wanted to be more aggressive. In the very fear Rayaru was experiencing, Jagannatha could see that his action would bear some fruit. And so, with great enthusiasm, he spelt out his plans in detail. Rayaru said in a tired voice, 'Gandhiji used to say, we should have no hatred in our hearts; our minds should be pure. When we start a revolution, we should be free from selfish motives.' Jagannatha felt Rao was finding it difficult to face his own fear. He said gently, 'We don't have a sense of history, Rayare. You're talking like a tired man now. But there was a time when you set fire to all the goods in your cloth store to boycott foreign goods and you carried out a solitary fast in front of the Taluk Office in protest. That's the reason why I'm planning this course of action now. You've shaped me this way. I might get just as scared as you and step aside some day. But history will make us slog for it; relentlessly make us work for it.'

Rao smeared a bit of sunna on the betel leaf and began to talk; he had recovered his poise. Jagannatha thought, 'Oh, both of us are becoming punier in all this big talk.'

'All that these Holeyaru need is booze, not God,' said Rao, 'They're obeying you only because they happen to be your slaves. You're tormenting them, that's all.'

Jagannatha did not reply. He was disgusted that Rao was sidetracking the issue now. Rao continued, 'People will say you're tainting the reputation of the town. Why do you want to take the blame? Politics is filthy, Jaganna. Why should you dirty your hands, tell me? In this country, no good will come out of anything we do. And besides, you've also made the mistake of being born a Brahmin. Sometimes I feel these people need a military dictatorship to straighten them out.'

Jagannatha asked him out of the blue, 'Do you know Nagamani committed suicide?'

Even before Rao could reply, he walked to the window and stood looking out with his back to him. 'Whether I win or lose, that's not the point, Rayare,' he said, 'If I don't do anything for a radical change, I'll have to commit suicide too. That's it.'

After he had said that, Jagannatha felt he was being melodramatic; he was embarrassed. But when he returned to his chair, he was relieved to see that Rao had taken him seriously. In recognizing the intensity of his feelings, Rao had legitimized his plan of action. Jagannatha felt grateful.

'You know there's been no difference though Harijans have entered countless temples,' Rao said, 'But your intention is different; I know it. My only fear is, the Holeyaru will enter the temple, the papers will make much of it, and then, all the excitement will die down.'

Jagannatha was irritated again. He felt Rao was not looking intensely enough to see what lay deep within him. He was not as real when he argued as he was when he was scared. Jagannatha sat quietly.

'You've become slithery, Rayare,' he wanted to say.

Rao stood up and said, 'You need guts to have integrity, Jagannatha. A loser like me can't even become ethical.'

Jagannatha was startled to hear him. Somehow he felt assured again that something would bloom from this. He walked down the hill to the road with Rao and then walked back home. He spent the night hoping to see his letter in the next day's paper.

SEVEN

Rejected

Jagannatha waited for the first bus from the city to bring in the day's newspapers and anxiously scanned the pages. His letter was front-page news. He felt fear as soon as he saw it, but he was also glad; now, there was no turning back. Hoping Chikki too would read the news, he left the paper in the hall and walked up the cashew-hill. Striding briskly, he reached the top. By now, the people of Bharathipura would have read the news. He felt hot under the sweater; a cool breeze blew over his warm face. The mist had cleared and the town was bathed in sunlight.

Just fifteen days to the New Moon Festival! I must get the Holeyaru ready by then, working on it every single moment, staying focused all the time.

As he looked at the pinnacle of the temple he remembered: Thousands of pilgrims bathed in the river during the new moon day and the next day was the Chariot Festival. As a boy, I'd be up at the break of dawn to walk down to the river with Amma to bathe. I'd be skipping about her to fight the chill. Despite all that pushing and shoving, people would still make way for us. Shivering in the cold, I'd pull off my shirt and shorts and stand chubby and naked, staring at the water. Amma would take her first dip and surface with dripping hair on her back and chest. "Come now, take a dip," she'd say, laughing.

'"No! No! It's cold!" I'd say, staring at the steaming water, in fascination and fear.

'"The water's warm. Come on," Amma would say. She'd pull me by the hand. She'd dip me into the water, laughing. I'd feel a thrill engulf me with that first dip in the warm water and, thrashing my hands and legs about, I'd cause a spray of water around her. Once she got me in, it would be quite a task for her to get me out. Then she'd wipe my hair dry to keep me from catching a cold. But water would still be dripping from her thick flowing tresses. And from there we'd go straight towards the temple, to walk round the peepul tree in front of it. By the time Amma went round it thrice, I would've circled it ten times and my body would be warm. There were monkeys on the peepul tree. They'd grin boldly while picking lice from their babies. If they were teased, they'd come down chasing, and snatching bananas from our hands, they'd gobble them up. We'd go past the outer wall, plastered with red mud and clay, to the banyan tree. Usually, under the tree sat the barber, Rama. He would shave the heads of children by holding them firmly between his knees, scolding them if they moved. But with the elders, he was always respectful; sitting behind them and shaving the back of their heads. The rest had to sit obeying his instructions, bending the neck until it hurt; bending and twisting in one angle or the other while he deftly moved his razor to shave the head. But no, on the new moon day, he wouldn't there. There would be snake-charmers, opening their bundles of used-clothes or tying their turbans; or photographers who would print photos by exposing them to sunlight—coloured photos that stayed fresh until about the next New Moon Fair, and then faded. Chariot Street would be lined with stalls that were set up for the festival. The chariot would be ready, all decked up. Around the dome of the chariot were the ram, the bull, the twins, the crab, and the rest—signs of the zodiac. In front of the chariot lay dew-drenched cords of thick rope, like pythons. I'd follow Amma along the ropes zigzagging to avoid treading on them.

'Coming to think of it, all my profound memories were centred in Amma and Manjunatha and, whenever I'd be scared to turn the dark corners of the stairway, Bhootharaya. Amma, with her thick black hair and her forehead bereft of kumkuma, in a white sari and blouse. Manjunatha, with the gold crown as a reminder of saving my life, returning to the temple after going round the town in his chariot every evening.'

Jagannatha leaned against a jackfruit tree, shocked at becoming sentimental; fearful of losing his will to act. 'Unless I stop being emotional, I can't reject Manjunatha,' he said to himself as he walked down the hill. He walked slowly, preparing himself to face Chikki who would have read the paper by now.

He headed straight to his room, took off his sweater, and, as he was coming down the stairs for his bath, he saw Chikki coming towards him. Her face was ashen, like that of a corpse. She just stood there. Her lips trembled but no words seemed to come forth. His heart began to beat faster. Chikki was leaning against one of the pillars in the hall. Jagannatha stared at her, sharing her fears. Poised as he was to take a step into the unknown, he felt something new would be born out of this dread. That he was alive was true, what he was doing was real. He felt this was the first step in doing away with falsehood. Chikki did not speak a word. Her face was contorted as if she was about to cry. Jagannatha felt there was no use talking to her at this point and was about to walk on when he stopped as something occurred to him. He stared at the plank on the shelf; it was a solid piece of wood on which he used to sit while playing indoor games with his mother. It was made of some heavy wood.

Chikki climbed the stairs. Jagannatha had his bath, put on a fresh white dhothi and shirt, and went out to Sripathi Rao's Khadi Store in the town square. He was afraid to see familiar faces. Kini, the owner of a bookshop, saw him and pretended as if he hadn't. Jagannatha was upset. 'Henceforth, I'll have to become the person no one will want to acknowledge. I've begun to be rejected since this morning. I used to feel great seeing myself mirrored in the eyes of other people, but now I'll have to bide my time like a seed fallen to the ground. I must split open in anguish. And I must strain to push forth a shoot from the darkness of the earth into the light.'

Krishnappa, the manager of the restaurant, who was looking out into the street, bent his head. His withered face, pitted by smallpox, looked like a tortoise shell. The faces on the street had sightless eyes; no one wished him except the tailor, Shyama, who had borrowed money from him. 'I've been rejected by the whole street since the morning,' thought Jagannatha. Someone in a black cap stood aside respectfully and, bringing his palms together, wished him; perhaps he was an illiterate. He moved only after Jagannatha had walked past him.

The houses and shops were freshly whitewashed; the facades were spruced up for the New Moon Festival, to hide the filth of the backyards. Bharathipura with a smiling face but a stinking backside; the Holeyaru clear her shit, carrying it in baskets, walking through the back-alleys. They are never seen on the streets. 'I haven't yet caught the eyes of these people; these who have never sown anything on this land, but who have nothing else but this land. But some day I will; and then I'll become a new man.'

Jagannatha gathered courage and walked into Rao's khadi store. There was a soiled cushion on a mat. He sat down, leaning against it. He looked at the photo of a smiling, toothless Gandhi, and stared curiously at a rare picture of Nehru in a waistcoat and a kachche panche. Sripathi Rao was alone. He was opening his bag of betel leaves and nuts. He smiled at Jagannatha fondly and said, 'Would you like some coffee?'

'Yes.'

Rao stood up and clapped his hands but no one from Govindaiah's restaurant opposite the cloth store could have heard him; the Hindi song from a battery operated radio was much too loud. And added to that was the cook's clatter of the ladle on the griddle to signal that dosés were ready to be served.

'Don't bother, please,' said Jagannatha. But Rao himself went across, ordered coffee, came back, and sat down.

'I don't know why but Raghava Puranik has sent for me. Will you come along with me?'

'Sure.'

'Have you met him?'

'I remember going to his house as a boy with my mother. I hear he doesn't see anyone these days.'

Rao smiled.

In a bid to carry on the conversation, Jagannatha said, 'I've heard his story. He married a widow in 1920, didn't he?'

'I was one of those who went to his wedding,' said Rao, 'Something happened on the eve. Some people were coming in a lorry to the wedding. One among them, who was sitting at the edge, dozed off, fell down, and died. And you know what people said? "A widow's marriage brings three hundred hindrances." Almost the whole town ostracized the Puraniks. Since then, Puranik has changed completely. See for yourself how they live. You won't believe me if I tell you; you must see with your own eyes.'

Rao seemed embarrassed to talk of the topic of the day. Jagannatha guessed as much. He said, 'I can well believe you. If we confront society, it's quite likely that, once in a way, we'll feel we've lost our roots in it. I've seen the plight of inter-caste marriages in Bangalore. They live in the Cantonment; talking in English, throwing parties, admiring paintings from Ajanta and Ellora, collecting folk art, and sending their children to convent schools.'

Jagannatha wondered why he was talking non-stop. Hadn't he been terrified that that would have been his plight had he married Margaret and brought her down? Rao did not say anything. Even as he was hoping Rao would say something about what was foremost in their minds, Venkataraya Prabhu walked into the shop and wished him, 'Namaskara!'

From his grocery store in the town square, Prabhu had seen Jagannatha walking into Rao's Khadi store. He was the biggest merchant in town; besides Jagannatha, Prabhu was said to be the wealthiest man in the neighbourhood. He had taken over as chief trustee of the temple after Jagannatha had resigned from the post.

Prabhu had a hold on every business in Bharathipura; his eldest son worked with him in the grocery store, the second one had a cloth store, the third owned the Manjunatha Rice Mills, and the fourth ran the Manjunatha Lorry Service. Prabhu owned the six Manjunatha Bus Service buses that plied between Bharathipura and Shimoga. He also had his sons-in-law working in the various family businesses; one was running the Manjunatha Soda Factory, another had a cycle shop, and yet another was the owner of the biggest hotel in town. Each one's business helped the other and not one of them did anything without consulting the others.

Prabhu was known all over Shimoga for his business acumen. There was a rumour that he had made money by selling rice, sugar, and kerosene in the black market during the Second World War; Prabhu had heard it too. But he had not lost his nerve, not even after the police had searched his warehouses. And since Independence, he had worn only homespun clothes.

This was Prabhu's policy: You can lose honour and self-respect to make money; honour and respect will come with the wealth you've made, anyway. He would often say this to his customers as he weighed their groceries for them. He commanded a lot of respect too as his clients would have run up an account in one or the other of his stores. Also, he had the catering contract for the free midday meal at the temple. He had even become the president of the municipality during the previous term.

As Prabhu walked towards Rao's cloth store, Jagannatha guessed he was coming to see him. He would naturally be interested in the worship of Manjunatha as most of the business that came to Bharathipura was from the tourists and the pilgrims to the temple.

Prabhu was a smooth-talker. He grieved over Nagamani's death even as he came in. 'I heard she had just served you some coffee and eats. Wonder what came over her!' he said to Jagannatha. He praised him for his timely help during the crisis. He sat beside him on the mat, refusing the chair Rao had offered him. Rao ordered another round of coffee from the restaurant across the street. 'One without sugar for me,' said Prabhu, taking out a sachet of saccharin from his pocket. And he started talking as if he were addressing only Rao, though he did glance at Jagannatha from time to time.

'Do you know, Rayare? My younger son, Sanjay, has great regard for Jagannatha. He's very fond of him. Just to tell you how smart youngsters are these days: the other day someone said, and I don't want to mention names—I don't have to tell you how spiteful some people can be, do I? They can't bear to see you prosper. Well, where was I? Ah, yes, someone said some English girl had corrupted Jagannatha's mind and that's why he's running around with Harijans. Poor fellow! He doesn't know what Mahatma Gandhi has said about them—or, perhaps he does. He's seething because he couldn't acquire Jagannatha's lands in Padubidre. Anyway, my son was in the shop at that time and, do you know what he said? After all, he's still doing his SSLC; he'll be taking the Board exam this year. Like Jagannatha, he hopes to study in England some day, Rayare. Why shouldn't it be possible with Jagannatharaya's help? Now, what was I saying? Yes, yes, do you know what my son said? "Aren't the Holeyaru too human beings, like us?" he asks. Now, how do you reply to such a question? Tell me.'

A waiter came with cups of coffee. Prabhu added saccharin to his, stirred it, closed his eyes, took a few sips, put the cup down, and said to Jagannatha, 'I'm telling you this to show you how times are changing. Even Sripathi Rao knows; ask him. Now, Satyaprakash, the deputy commissioner posted in Shimoga, I hear he's a Harijan. The other day, Srinivasa Prabhu, my son-in-law's father who's the director of the Areca Society, was telling me how learned the DC is. He has read all the Vedas and the Upanishads. He knows astrology and the Puranas[42] so well that he could easily put our Nagaraja Jois to shame. I hear he can also speak very well though he does fumble a bit with *sha* and *sa* sounds.'

Prabhu lowered his voice suddenly and, leaning towards Rao, said in conspiratorial whisper, 'Now, let's say the DC comes to this town. Say, he even comes to my house. Won't I ask him in? Won't I offer him coffee? Then, can I give it to him in a coconut shell? I'll serve it in a silver tumbler,[43] won't I? It is said that we have to bow to changing times, *kaalaaya thasmai namah*![44] That's why I thought, "*Besh*! *Well said*!" when I heard my son speak that way.'

Jagannatha was surprised; he waited. He felt as if he had had his fill of a watery payasa of sugary words. After saying so much in favour of the Holeyaru, how will Prabhu be able to turn his argument around? Jagannatha was sure that was his intention. He wanted to prick Prabhu's balloon.

[42] Sacred stories from Hindu myths and legends.

[43] There is great irony here. One throws away a coconut shell. But, according to Brahminism, silver, gold, and silk are the only materials that cannot be polluted.

[44] Literally, we bow to Time. The usage is a philosophical way of saying, Time is supreme.

'Then, Prabhugale, will you be willing to walk the Holeyaru into the temple with me?'

'Sure.'

Jagannatha was stunned. Prabhu did not stop at that. 'I told you earlier, didn't I? We have to change with the times, 'kaalaaya thasmai namah'! Everything will be fulfilled in its time. That's why I told those who were finding fault with you, "What! Do you think our Jagannatharaya doesn't know what he's doing? How much have *you* studied? How much has *he* studied? You think you can teach this young man who has returned from England what's right and what's wrong, don't you? What will he get out of destroying the glory of Manjunatha? The crown on Manjunatha's head is his; the big bell of the temple that resounds through the whole town was given by his forefathers; his family built the choultry for pilgrims. His father was such a pious man he wouldn't eat a meal without sipping some holy water first. Do you really think a peace-loving person belonging to such a family wouldn't think deeply enough about what he's doing?" This is what I told them, really. Ask anyone. And I asked them straightaway, "Now the High School in Bharathipura is being run with funds from the temple. Almost half the revenue of the town is from the tourists who visit the temple. How else, do you think, we could sustain the hundreds of families that live here? If ever there's any threat to Manjunatha's fame, what would happen to hundreds like us who live trusting in his bounty? Let's say our children can afford to go to Shimoga to study but if we don't have a High School funded by the temple here, where can the children of the poor be educated? Okay, take the areca farming, for instance. I don't have to tell you how much the pilferage has increased. Now, if people don't have to fear Bhootharaya at all, do you think we would get even a single nut? Do you think Jagannatharaya wouldn't have thought of all this?" I asked them straightaway. You know me, don't you? I'm not the kind who'll say one thing to your face and something else behind your back.'

Sripathi Rao sat staring at the street. The priest's son, Ganesha, came by with a bottle of medicine.

'Who's ill, Ganesha?' he asked him.

'My stepmother,' said the young man.

'Send your wife to my house. My wife wanted to see her.'

'I-I w-w-will,' stammered Ganesha. He stood watching Jagannatha with great interest. A few others too who had seen Prabhu talking to Jagannatha had gathered in front of Rao's khadi store—those who had gone to the grocery store, some of the pilgrims, and some villagers who were shopping for clothes. Jagannatha guessed that, most probably, they would know of his plan of action. He felt his burden lift. He knew there was no point in talking to Prabhu and yet he said, bitterly, 'Prabhugale, this is my reply to the latter part of your argument. Ours is still a medieval economy. And Manjunatha is at its centre. It's natural for you to fear your business will turn topsy-turvy if there's any threat to his fame. But then, look at it this way; because of Manjunatha, our lifestyle has stagnated. We're rotting. Once we destroy Manjunatha, we'll have to become responsible for our lives. We'll have to look for newer pathways. Let's have a tile factory in this town. I've heard there's copper ore in this soil; let's mine it. Now we've been growing only areca. Let's experiment and see what else we can grow on it. We've become barren now. Let's say the Holeyaru enter the temple. Then, there's sure to be at least some change in the minds of all those in the country who fear Bhootharaya and worship Manjunatha. What may be a slight crack in the system today will loosen it tomorrow. We'll become independent. What's important right now is to prepare the Holeyaru for it. We'll have to make them take their first step in history. Their first step across the threshold of the temple may change the reality of centuries. Through the Holeyaru, all of us may come alive again. Without some shock treatment, nothing can happen, you see.'

Jagannatha was carried away. Sripathi Rao was staring at him as if to say, 'Why are you wasting your breath on him?' The crowd that had gathered in front of the shop stared at Jagannatha, unable to understand the discussion.

Prabhu took some tobacco from Rao, added a bit of sunna to it, and rubbing them together, said, 'Oh, don't get me wrong, please. I didn't say all this because I'll lose my business. As you know, I came here from Kundapura with nothing but my weighing scales. I believe all the wealth I have today is through Manjunatha's blessings; not through my endeavour, honestly. Even to this day, I'm quite content with my two bowls of gruel. My children too are like me. The only bad habit I have is chewing on tobacco, you know. Now why am I talking about all this?

It's because I do see your point. Whatever you're saying is right but then again, to have a copper mine or a tile factory, don't we need electricity? Won't we need a railroad from Shimoga to Bharathipura? Don't we need to do up these damned mud roads with cement concrete? Not just that, we'll need a port in Mangalore and a railroad from here to Mangalore as well. Yes or no, tell me?'

Jagannatha could see how crafty Prabhu was. With a look of appreciation, he glanced at Rao. He had a naughty smile on his face. Groping for the right way to tackle Prabhu's challenge, Jagannatha said, 'I agree with you there. Let's campaign for electricity. Let's fight for railroads. Let's look at all the ways in which we can radically change the lives of our people. But the very need to look elsewhere will rise in us only if we suffer a blow to our faith in Manjunatha. And for that to happen, only the Holeyaru, who don't have a stake here, can start the revolt.'

Prabhu seemed to be enjoying the debate. Jagannatha was irritated; the dialogue was heading nowhere, it was just a lot of glib talk. And yet he sat quiet; he was too polite to be rude. Prabhu spat out the tobacco and said, 'Let's suppose the people say, "First, let's get electricity, then the glory of Manjunatha will wane eventually." What will you say to that? Pardon me, but I'm just saying this for the sake of argument. These days, it's only people like us who fret over things like God, family, compassion, or karma. Do you think people in places like Calcutta or Bombay bother about such things?'

Prabhu saw his son's lorry cruising to a halt in front of his grocery store. 'Just a minute,' he said and went across to say something to his son in Konkani and returned. Seeing Jagannatha getting up to go, he said, 'I've told you right from the beginning, Jagannatharayare, I'm with you in this. Write out an application for electricity for this town. You and I can go to the Vidhana Soudha to hand it in. Let's take Gurappa Gowda with us. Sripathi Rao too can come. Weren't he and the chief minister in jail together during the freedom struggle? The chief minister can't discard petitions from educated young men like you. First let's get electricity and the railway to this town. Now that the President has visited this place, the whole of India knows about Bharathipura. I'm sure the minister won't reject your letter. With progressive-minded young men like you, we can change this town into a garden. Well, I should be going now. We'll talk this over again.'

As Prabhu walked out, the crowd scattered. Jagannatha thought, 'What a cunning merchant! Today he's profiting from Manjunatha; tomorrow, the same fellow will cash in on the electricity he'll bring into the town using me. Why, he might've even started thinking about the twin projects, the tile factory and the copper mines.' Jagannatha smiled as he looked at Sripathi Rao. It looked as if Rao had read his thoughts.

Jagannatha said to him, 'When we do get electricity, I think the real beneficiary will be Prabhu. Then, we may have to mount a protest against him too.'

Rao stood up and walked out of the shop, smiling. When Jagannatha asked, 'Aren't you going to lock up the place?' Rao said with a guffaw, 'What have I got in there that should be locked up?'

While they were walking down the street, he said, 'Jaganna, it's true that I'm apprehensive. But I also feel that nothing will come out of your taking the Holeyaru into the temple. But don't go by what I say. For ought I know, I might've gone to jail during the freedom struggle just to get away from a nagging wife. It's just that I don't want you to take a false step and incur the wrath of the people. I may be wrong about it. But it's true that I'm nervous.'

'I'm scared too, Rayare, but there's no other go.' Jagannatha did not know what else to say. He was upset that Rao could be so calm while talking to him.

'I've been rejected at this momentous moment; I've jumped into a bottomless netherworld. If Rayaru asks me now if I have absolute faith in what I've set out to do, I'll have to say, "I don't know." But I'll also add, "My life will have no meaning if I don't take this on myself."' He felt like asking Rao, 'Isn't our social life becoming pointless only because there hasn't been a radical change in our society, Rayare?' But he held back, thinking that any talk before the action is a lot of noise. He trembled with disgust to think there were some people in Bharathipura who could glibly say the very things he was saying but with a different intention. But he was also glad he had to prepare himself for the anguish of standing alone, without any mirrors to boost his image.

EIGHT

Is Change the Only Solution?

If you walked towards the east, you would reach Seebinakere. Beyond it was the new subdivision, Tashkentpura; the education minister had inaugurated it. Short of the layout was a bye-lane across a paddy field behind the Manjunatha Rice Mills, a short cut to Raghava Puranik's house. A brisk walk would take you there in about half an hour.

Rao walked with Jagannatha, greeting the people he met on the way and asking after their well-being, making Jagannatha feel, *Rayaru is the person who's put down real roots in this place, not I.* To a farmer walking by with his umbrella tucked under his arm, Rao said, 'Did you give the petition I wrote out for you to the *amaldhar*? What did he say?' And then, 'Why does he want you to go again? Nothing gets done without a bribe.' He asked a young man wearing ear studs, 'How's your father? Take him to Dr Anthony's house.' And to another who took off his slippers, stood barefoot, and brought his palms together to greet him, 'Come and see me later. I'll give you a letter to a lawyer in Shimoga.'

And added laughing, 'Don't you know your petition to Manjunatha won't work with Muslims?'

Rao knew everyone, even children and women. He knew them by name, he knew their lineage, their secret illnesses, their family problems, everything. Perhaps he had come to the decision that any change was pointless because he was so deeply involved in every aspect of their lives.

As they walked through the lane where the Muslims lived, Jagannatha felt he had come to another town. Men in chequered lungis who sat in their front yard tinning brass vessels or rolling beedis stood up respectfully and said, 'Salaam, Saab,' to greet them. There were hens foraging in the drain and eggs in wire-baskets hanging in front of some of the houses.

'Even our boys eat eggs on the sly these days,' said Rao, laughing. 'Jaganna, you said you were teaching the alphabet to some Holeyaru. Tell me, have you or they ever touched each other at least once, even accidentally?'

'No.'

'That's what I'm saying. Whether you touch them or don't is not the point here. What's important is whether *they* would touch you willingly, if they have any desire to touch you at all. It's natural for you to want to touch them; you're an educated man. Your awareness has grown. You're heir to every good fortune in life; you want to reach out for this new ideal. To you, it's a luxury, but to them?'

Jagannatha was happy Rao was talking to him seriously. 'That's true, Rayare,' he said, 'The day they really feel that way, I'll truly feel I've won. I'm trying to make such an awareness burst upon them. Because the day the Holeyaru are brave enough to take that one step ...'

'That's not possible through just your efforts, Jaganna.'

Jagannatha said nothing.

Walking on enthusiastically, Rao said, 'It was Raghava Puranik who first gave me books by Ingersoll.'

Walking in the wintry sunlight, Jagannatha too felt exhilarated. His mind cleared. Wherever he turned, he could see fresh blooms, on mango trees, coconut trees. A chieftain's wife crossed them wearing fragrant kedage flowers from some tree in some deep corner of the forest—a beauty with tattooed hands and heavy dangling earrings held up with short chains hooked to her hair. She was briskly walking barefoot towards the temple. In the gardens of some wealthy farmers, there were flowering trees, parijatha, and sampige. Jagannatha thought, isn't it possible for a keen eye to see something new every day even in a way of life that has continued to be the same for centuries? A baby might be born in some house; someone might've died in another; a baby could be kicking in some pregnant woman's womb. Here, a delicate rose swaying on a strong stalk. There, a dog on its back sunning itself with all its legs up in the air; a child pretending to drive a car by trailing a stick between his legs; and a harassed mother scolding her son who was fussing about coming in to eat. Bees swarming around the mango blossoms. Beehives hanging on trees in the verdant forest yet uncleared for areca plantations. In the hidden corners of the forest, animals with eager eyes sniffing the ground and prancing about.

Sripathi Rao walked silently.

I'm looking for fruition in life only through change, but I mustn't forget what may bloom in the routine of everyday life. But, then, how would action be possible? Women take daily offerings of bananas and coconut in well-scrubbed shining plates to Manjunatha, who wears a gold crown because of a blind belief that he saved my life. Are they the real beneficiaries of this permanence? Or are they mere foetuses in the womb of Manjunatha?

'Look, that's Raghava Puranik's house,' said Sripathi Rao.

NINE

Raghava Puranik

When there are so many inner bye-ways for every class of people to fulfil their lives; when the very act of putting down root, blossoming, and bearing fruit happens so quietly in the warmth of the sun, is it mere arrogance to believe in human endeavour? Is this action only for me, to satisfy my ego? Does the town also need it?

While continuing to be plagued by such questions, Jagannatha looked at the house. A compound wall over ten feet high, an iron gate, a sign warning, 'Beware of dogs'.

'There was a time when they were the richest landlords in town, next to your family. But most of their wealth has dwindled now. Puranik's shanbogh will become wealthier than him one of these days. Already, he owns a lorry,' said Sripathi Rao, pressing the bell on the gate.

Jagannatha looked surprised.

'You're in for more surprises, wait and see! He has a generator and electric bulbs to light up the house,' said Rao, and pointing to the aerial atop the four-storey building, he added, winking, 'Puranik is in touch with every corner of the world.'

As the house was quite a distance from the garden wall, they were not sure if the bell was working. Rao pressed it again. 'Puranik was a great revolutionary, at one time. He belongs to the time when Aurobindo[45] was making bombs,' he said.

After the second bell, a Gurkha watchman in a khaki uniform brought the keys.

'This is one of the surprises. Wait till you see more,' said Rao. The Gurkha saluted them and led them to a spacious foyer with teak panels covering the ceiling.

In one corner of the hall was a hat-stand. On it were an evening hat, an ordinary sun hat, a Kashmir cap of fine fur, and a variety of walking sticks. In another corner were three rifles mounted on a wooden stand. The walls were decked with prints of some of the finest paintings by Western artists, all of them tastefully framed: Brueghel's *Icarus*; Constable's *The Cornfield* with its sunny village and fields of wheat, and the play of light and shade on the winding country lane; John Sell Cotman's watercolour, *Greta Bridge*, in delicate shades of blue, black, and ash-grey; Hogarth's painting of the happy *Shrimp Girl*; and Sir Joshua Reynolds's *Age of Innocence*. Jagannatha noticed with curiosity that most of the paintings were by British artists. Even the chairs they were sitting on were Victorian, with their delicate legs and straight backs. The Gurkha brought them a slip of paper and Rao wrote down their names on it. He took it upstairs on a carved tray.

Jagannatha stared at Rao, astonished. In the hall was a large brass urn with a plant that looked like aspidistra. And there was a variety of cacti, all along the walls. Out in the garden were English roses, probably from Ooty. 'These days, people don't grow aspidistra inside the house,' said Jagannatha, smiling mischievously.

Soon they heard the muffled footsteps of someone coming down the stairs. Jagannatha guessed the stairs were carpeted. He awaited the host with rising curiosity.

'How do you do?' said a man of about sixty, walking briskly into the lobby and extending his arm. He shook hands with Rao and included

[45] A freedom fighter and visionary who became a mystic and established an ashram at Pondicherry.

Jagannatha in a gesture of welcome. He was in a pair of rather loose old-fashioned black pants, waistcoat, and tie. His chin was clean-shaven and shiny.

'Jagannatha, Anand Rao's son,' said Rao in Kannada, introducing him. Though Puranik looked frail, his handshake was firm and warm.

'Pleased to meet you,' he said, 'I've heard such a lot about you from Sripathi, my only friend in this blessed place. I used to know your mother, a beautiful, cultured lady. She used to play sweetly on the veena. Come in, please come in,' he said, pointing towards the living room. 'After you,' he said to Jagannatha, urging him to go in. His British accent sounded stilted, reminding Jagannatha of BBC's Dimbleby's pronunciation.

Just as he had guessed, the stairway was carpeted, in red—a wooden staircase with a well-polished brass banister and prints of paintings by reputed artists at every landing. Puranik's study was on the third floor. He pushed the door open and said, 'Please come in.'

As soon as he entered, Jagannatha stood stunned.

'Please sit down,' said Puranik, smoothing away a mass of white hair from his forehead. There was a circle of sofas on a Kashmiri carpet. In a corner stood a beautifully carved rosewood writing table with a well-padded swivel chair in front of it. Bookcases with glass shutters lined two walls facing each other, stocked with books. In the middle of a wall was a fireplace; embers from a fire lit that morning were dying. On the mantelpiece above the fireplace were small models of animals in glass, a few Japanese dolls, and a framed caricature of Churchill chewing on a cigar. A furry dog slept peacefully under one of the sofas, neck outstretched. Jagannatha let his eyes roam over the books on the shelves: Reynolds's novels, Russell, Bernard Shaw, Kipling, Churchill, Shakespeare, Tolstoy, and Forster. He pulled out Forster's *Howards End* and flipped through the pages. There were signs that Puranik had read through it. He was drawn to the passage marked in red and ticked:

'Miss Schlegel, the real thing's money, and all the rest is a dream.'

'You're still wrong. You've forgotten Death.'

Leonard could not understand.

There were two strokes beside *You've forgotten Death*. The lines made Jagannatha curious about Puranik's inner life. He walked beyond the books. To the east and west of the study were large glass windows with thick blue drapes, covering three-fourths of the walls. He looked out of a window. Hidden among the trees was Bharathipura, the river, and the ash-coloured peak of Manjunatha's temple. He noticed a large radio on a table. Puranik must have observed his curiosity. He came over and said, proudly, 'I can get almost all the major short-wave stations in the world on that radio.'

He was quiet for a while and then stood before the fireplace. Lighting his pipe, he said with laughter in his eyes, 'I'm in total retreat. Sripathi may have told you.'

Jagannatha sat on a sofa near the table. The radio might have taught him English.

'This is more comfortable. Come,' said Puranik, pointing to a sofa closer to him; it had silk-cotton cushions in red.

Jagannatha noted that not just his hair but even his eyebrows were white. And as he also had hair sticking out of his ears, his pointed features and twinkling eyes gave the impression of an animal peering out of its lair. A wan face, thin lips, long nose—but his liveliness was in his eyes and in his ears sprouting hair. As if he were reading slowly from a book, he said again, 'Yes, I am living here in exile with my books, a few friends like Sripathi, and my ailing wife. Excuse me. I have been in a monologue mode without offering you anything. What will you have to drink?'

Puranik slid open the glass shutter of a side-table. In it was a variety of foreign liquor—brandy, whisky, gin, wine, and sherry. He took out two cut-glass tumblers and looked at Jagannatha questioningly. As he had given up drinking since his return from England, 'I'm not particular about any. Thanks,' Jagannatha said.

He was also embarrassed as Rao was with them.

'Have some whisky. I can assure you it is not adulterated. My friend, Avadhani, brings it from Bombay for me. It is awfully cold these days, you see, although we do have a bright day today,' he said, as he poured out whisky into the lovely cut-glass tumblers. Adding soda from Prabhu's Soda Factory, he said, 'Tell me when to stop. You must excuse this awful soda, and sorry, there's no ice.'

He handed Jagannatha's glass to him and turning towards Sripathi Rao, he said, 'The teetotaller will have a fresh lime as usual.' And he pressed the bell. A butler came in, dressed in white. 'Nair, get him a fresh lime,' said Puranik. That was the first sentence in Kannada that Jagannatha had heard him speak. His Kannada was more stilted than his English.

'What have you been doing in this medieval town?' asked Puranik. He had left his pipe on the radio and was standing by the hearth, sipping his whisky. Curious to know what Puranik would say about his plan of action, Jagannatha asked, 'Did you see today's paper?' He looked at Rao as if to ask him to elaborate. But Puranik had remembered something else. Drawing on his pipe, he said, 'Excuse me. I have a problem that only Mr Jagannath can solve. As you perhaps know, I have never been abroad. A cold climate would kill me as my lungs are weak. For nearly forty years now I have lived in this room amidst these books and my pictures. Early in the morning and in the evening I walk around my garden.' He waved a hand towards it. 'This is my world and I meet nobody. Yet I inhabit a large world, thanks to my radio. Yesterday midnight, I heard *Swan Lake,* God knows from which station, and it was not a bad performance. It was perhaps midday where it was played. Doesn't it fill you with wonder?'

Puranik paced about the room, talking to himself. Jagannatha saw that he stooped a bit and his woolen trousers were frayed at the seat.

'I have never stepped out of my compound but have mentally reconstructed all the famous places in London. Look, I was about to ask you for a clarification and I began to wander.'

Puranik called Jagannatha to his writing table and drew a sketch of some streets on a sheet of paper and asked him, 'If you enter Fleet Street from this end, you can see the dome of St Paul's, can't you? Now, where would you find the pub that the great Dr Johnson inhabited? To our right or left?'

'Right, perhaps,' said Jagannatha, 'If you go this way, you'll reach Gough Square. There you'll find the house in which he lived while compiling his dictionary. It's the Johnson Museum now,' he added, adding the street to the sheet.

'I know that. Thanks a lot. Do you know how many books I have read trying to locate some of these famous historical places? The book I read was vague about this pub. And on many nights I've lost sleep trying to figure out whether it was to the right or left.'

Puranik's eyes were gleaming with excitement. 'To the right then. Good,' he said to himself, engrossed in thought. And then, smiling, he turned towards Jagannatha, 'You must be tired of listening only to me. You must meet my friend. I shall bring him here.' And from his study, he went into another room.

Jagannatha looked at Sripathi Rao. He sat cross-legged on the sofa in his khadi dhothi and short-sleeved shirt. Not just that, he was smearing some sunna on a betel leaf. His smile seemed to be provoking Jagannatha. But his mirth turned to concern as he said, 'Puranik's lands are disappearing bit by bit. For many years now, not a single tenant has seen his face nor has he seen any of theirs. He deals with them through the shanbogh who's thriving like a fattened bandicoot. And this friend of his is another bandicoot. In a few years from now Puranik's suits will be in tatters. He has already started taking overdrafts.'

'My friend, Avadhani,' said Puranik, introducing a man in a polo-necked pullover and a pair of baggy trousers. Avadhani staggered to a sofa and sat down. From the smell of it, Jagannatha guessed the fluid in his glass must be liquor. He looked about forty. Watching Avadhani in Puranik's beautiful study that could pass for any flat in England, Jagannatha wondered why he was sensing some incongruity. And then it struck him, Avadhani's face was scarred; the left side of his forehead carried the sign of a branding done to fulfil a vow to Bhootharaya. His unwashed face with a four-day stubble of peppered bristles and the dirt in his eyes were in sharp contrast to Puranik's clean-shaven face and refined demeanour. He probably had not washed his face at all that morning.

'Drink is the only consolation of a lonely life, you see,' said Puranik, to cover the embarrassment of his friend's condition. 'He does all my shopping for me. Hence you can guess how well-travelled he must be within the country.'

Jagannatha could see Puranik was trying to get Avadhani to talk. He downed his drink in one gulp, put down the glass, and wiping his mouth with his hand, said, 'Mr Puranik is a great gentleman. He is my refuge. I run away from my home to this place every day. My house is infested, you understand, with pilgrims.'

Avadhani was slurring his words. Puranik was embarrassed with the compliments and so, to change the topic, he said, 'Mr Avadhani is an agnostic but he claims he has psychic powers. Perhaps he does. For myself, I don't believe in any of that kind of stuff. Mr Avadhani claims he was a medium once and Bhootharaya used to speak through him. I have always laughed at this kind of nonsense, yet I would like to do some research, you know, in this area.'

Avadhani perked up. Still slurring, he argued that psychic powers were real, that he had the spirit of Bhootharaya through being branded. 'Now, look into my eyes. Don't you feel compelled to keep staring? I've saved Puranik from many evils with my psychic powers, you know,' he boasted. He complained about the pilgrims, he complained about the shrew of a wife who had turned him out by getting her relatives to live with them. He was melodramatic; he was drunk. He said Puranik and Puttamma would never let him down and he began to weep. 'I suspect my wife. Her mother's brother has tried black magic to get hold of my property. It has not been effective only because of my psychic powers. See if I don't finish him off by the next New Moon. I've already told Bhootharaya everything,' he ranted. He had started in English but switched to Kannada as he snivelled and raged. Puranik looked at his friend seriously, took him by the hand, gently but firmly, and led him out of the room. He returned after a while and said with some concern, 'You must pardon my friend's misbehaviour. For Mr Jagannath, who has seen cocktail parties, this may not be an unusual sight. Mr Avadhani needs to read more of Russell. He is very sensible and helpful, but breaks down when he drinks. He is very unhappy, you see.'

Puranik had not lost his poise.

'Let me fill your glass,' he said.

'No, thanks,' said Jagannatha. He felt it was time to leave and stood up. But he could not get Puranik's attention; he seemed engrossed in some train of thought.

'The only way is to Westernize ourselves. Look at Avadhani's tragedy. This country grabs you by the neck when you are weak.'

Rao, who had been quiet all this while, seeing Jagannatha getting restless, asked Puranik, 'Did you see today's paper?'

'No. It is ages since I have looked at newspapers. Does anything new ever happen in this country?'

Jagannatha was surprised. Before he could even point to the radio and ask him, Puranik responded, 'I abhor news. I listen only to music and, occasionally, to serious talk and poetry.'

Jagannatha was astonished; *wouldn't some barber come at least once a month to cut his white hair? Would he go away without sharing some news about Bharathipura?* He felt it was ridiculous for Sripathi Rao to be explaining his plan of action to Puranik. And he was even more embarrassed to hear Rao mouthing his own expressions; he probably looked like a fool in Puranik's eyes. But Puranik listened seriously to everything Rao was telling him and then he said, 'I wish you luck, Mr Jagannath. I was also a rebel once, you see.' He was quiet for a while and then, sighing deeply, he said, 'I am sorry to say so, but I think it is utterly futile in India. We live in the womb of God. Perhaps you can save yourself and a few others who are like you. But collective action is impossible. Therefore I say: Westernize yourself. Stay sane. But don't attempt to change this country. She is amorphous.'

Puranik spoke as if he were delivering a lecture. Jagannatha shuddered to hear him say, 'womb of God'; that was his expression.

'Shall we go, Rayare?' he said.

'My young friend, you must excuse my pessimism, I admire your impatience; it is healthy. I too once took an interest in this town. Then I did some research on Bhootharaya, who, according to me, is the god of passion and psychic energy unlike Manjunatha who represents the intellectual and religious aspect of Indian thinking, which is hypocritical, I needn't add that. I wrote down all the fascinating songs and tales about Bhootharaya that I collected from the peasants. I was a very young man then and very impatient, like Mr Jagannath now. In those days of bomb-throwing, Bhootharaya fascinated me and I wondered why and how he came to be … er … to be …'

'Subjugated,' added Jagannatha.

'Yes, subjugated to the *Nirguna* Brahman,[46] the god of the hypocritical Indian liberal. The material is still with me. I shall search for it and give it to you. You can make use of it if you like.'

'Shouldn't we be going?' asked Jagannatha as he took a step but Rao just stood there, without any hurry, without getting worked up.

[46] The Creator, an abstraction beyond any specific qualities.

Puranik's shiny shoes, his clean-shaven chin, his stance, with a slight stoop, his hands clasped behind him, a neatness that exuded self-confidence—Jagannatha was astounded by it all. His pants were wearing out; his English still had traces of a Kannada style of speaking; his close friend, Avadhani, had faith in the power of demons—going over all this, Jagannatha tried to see him with humour, with compassion. But the thoughtful expression in Puranik's eyes had a look of understanding, of irony, of a sense of the tragic. It was possible to live in a place like Bharathipura and skip a few centuries like Puranik, wasn't it? But when and how would he know such a jump was only an illusion? When he became a pauper, perhaps.

Another doubt surfaced in Jagannatha's mind, something that had not occurred to him before. Though I've been with Puranik for so long now, and though he's been engaging me in serious discussion, why haven't I said bluntly, 'Mr Puranik, you've created an unreal world to live in?' Without being aware of it, am I just indulgent, as I would be in humouring a child? Does Rayaru also have this kind of a compassionate relationship with him? Isn't Puranik aware that he arouses such feelings in people? Jagannatha felt he should come again and probe deeper. What a shame my action will never touch him in any way! Can any canker worm enter the fortress to destroy this Parikshithraja?[47] How will it?

Jagannatha had a strange uneasy feeling beyond all thought.

'Shall we go?' he said again to Sripathi Rao.

'Sorry if I have bored you. It is the silence of the place which makes me unpleasant to meet, you see,' said Puranik, stretching out his arm and looking affectionately at Jagannatha. Jagannatha felt ashamed of himself as he shook Puranik's soft hand.

Rao said, 'I'd like to meet your wife.'

'Oh, yes!' said Puranik, as if he had awakened suddenly, 'You must see her. You have a soothing effect on her.' And turning towards Jagannatha, he said, 'Sorry, she can't come up. If you don't mind the trouble, please come down with us.'

[47] Son of Abhimanyu and Uttara. It was prophesied that he would die of snake-bite and was sealed up in a castle, but was killed by a worm in a fruit he was about to eat.

'Not at all,' said Jagannatha, and felt he was entering another world as he walked across the hallway to the inner rooms. He had not reckoned that this house too would have doorways where you duck your head; dark rooms; small shelves; rangoli on the threshold drawn with a white sticky paste to make it last; Krishna and Radha painted on a mirror; festoons of leaves no longer fresh.

'Sorry, you have to walk carefully. This is an ancestral part of the house, you see. My eccentricity made me build the other parts of this house,' said Puranik as he led him by the hand with needless courtesy. He entered a room and called gently, 'Savithri.'

Pale-faced Savithri tried to sit up on hearing her husband's voice. 'Please don't bother. Lie down. Sripathi has come to see you,' said Puranik with great concern and love. Savithri's face brightened to see Rao. You could make out the withered face was that of a youngish woman. Rao moved closer and said, 'Jagannatha. Do you recognize him?'

'How're you? When did you return from England?' she asked, very politely. And turning again towards Rao, she said, 'Poor thing! I heard Jois's daughter-in-law died. I had heard she was a very pretty girl.' And then, 'Why are you standing? Please sit down,' she said to them and looked at her husband as if to ask him at least to help her sit up.

'You sleep now,' he said, caressing her brow, 'Don't bother about us.'

What surprised Jagannatha more than the love the couple shared was the picture of Manjunatha in the room, adorned with roses. Beside her bed was a copy of the *Udupi Krishna Almanac*.

'The New Moon Chariot Festival is almost here again,' said Savithri, looking at Rao.

'Yes,' he replied.

The three men left the room so as not to tire her. Standing in the hallway, Puranik shook Rao's hand. 'Thanks for cheering up my wife,' he said. And to Jagannatha, 'I admire you but I am also sorry for you,' he said as he shook his hand with sadness and affection. 'Come again when you want to relax.'

Jagannatha left the place with Rao in great haste.

The Gurkha saluted them and locked the gate.

TEN

Bye-lanes

'Manjunatha is the canker creeping in to eat away this Parikshithraja. He is omnipresent,' said Jagannatha, arguing with Rao, 'The very earth is giving way beneath the shiny shoes of this man, Puranik, who can skip centuries while living in the present. Prabhu is far better. At least I can fight him; he's not a fake like Puranik. He's grappling with reality even if it be to cheat others. Just as those who live in the womb of God are inactive, Puranik, who thinks he's outside it, is also inert. And even you, Rayare; the more liberal you become, the more quiescent you get. Unless all of Bharathipura labours in the throes of change, life cannot become creative here.'

'That's all very well, Jaganna,' shot back Rao, 'But in the midst of this, we also have to bear babies, rear them, get all excited about festivals—Ramanavami, Krishnashtami, Gouri Puja—and also get medicine from Dr Anthony, haven't we? You're still egoistic; you trust in your ability to do things. Fine. We need people like you too.'

There was no point in arguing with Rao when he was speaking for the pure pleasure of talking.

As they walked into Seebinakere, Rao said, 'If you put your hand to a drastic revolution straightaway, you may end up like Puranik.'

They reached the town square.

In one of the lanes, an umbrella repairer had set up business in front of a shop. He had been there since Jagannatha was a boy. He knew all the intricacies of his trade: patching holes in the cloth, tying the broken metal rods with fresh bits of wire to hold the cloth in place, fixing the catch that kept the umbrella from collapsing. His name was Rangappa. In black cap and a pair of glasses on his nose, he would work there all alone. There he was now, in the same place, still with a faded black cap. On a pole nearby, hung a sign. The lopsided letters on it had always seemed funny to Jagannatha because it said: UMBRELLARE PAIR RANGAPPA. The same sign with the same misspelling still hung there.

Surprising! Jagannatha told Rao about the sign. 'One of his daughters passed out of the High School here. She eloped with some lorry driver to Bombay. Poor Rangappa lives alone now,' said Rao. Reaching the end of a trend of thought, he added, 'Of course, I admit there's no real action involved in washing people's bums. We have to dig canals; we have to teach them to wash their own bottoms.'

Jagannatha laughed.

As they walked through Seebinakere, he remembered someone. 'How's Kamala?'

'Who? You mean, Seebinakere Kamala? The one who was in your class? I heard she's in Bombay now,' said Rao, and added, 'Come on, I'll come to your house for lunch. Chikki has been asking me for some time now.'

'You know Rayare, how uneasy I was watching Puranik! Perhaps because it's so easy for me too to live like him. Anyway, it's possible for people like us to skip centuries like him. But it's never possible for people like these,' said Jagannatha, pointing towards a few Shudra women who were bustling about the shops.

'Yes, perhaps what you say is true.'

'Makes it worthwhile to fight with Manjunatha,' argued Jagannatha vehemently, hoping to convince Rao.

'Like wrestling with air,' retaliated Rao, winking at him.

It was impossible to make this man understand all his thoughts and feelings. It would be more worthwhile to spend time with those Holeyaru instead of arguing with this man.

Jagannatha thought of Kamala again. She would have put on weight, most probably.

Out of the blue, he remembered Subbaraya Adiga. It's ages since I met him. I must see him. He'll surely come to see me as soon as he reads the paper.

The town of my childhood; the people I've known since I was a boy; the god I've grown up with; the awareness I have because of my Western education; Nagamani, Kaveri, Margaret, the youthful Holeyaru, this Rayaru; my weakness to see myself puffed up in the mirror of other people's eyes; my longing to put down roots here, to put forth shoot, and to blossom—everything has teased me into a tangle again. It's going to make me gooey again and again. I have to sort myself out through action; I must firm up. There's no other way. Margaret, I'm desperate. Because Nagamani died, I have to act. I just can't sit back. Will the Holeyaru be prepared to touch me? That's the most important question.

By the time they reached home, he was pleasurably hungry after the exercise. Lunch was at one. It was just twelve. Chikki was waiting in the hall. Her eyes were swollen with weeping. Because Rao was with him, Jagannatha had the nerve to ask, 'What happened, Chikki?'

Chikki replied with great difficulty, 'No one seems to be coming today.'

Perhaps this had never happened before in his house. At least twenty people had to come for lunch every day. But today, after the news of his letter, not a soul had ventured this way. Jagannatha did not know what to say. He was afraid. He was upset.

'Rayaru's eating with us,' he said to Chikki and was happy to see her face brighten. He signalled to Rao with his eyes that he should comfort her and went into the courtyard as if he had to see to something else.

He was happy: Subbaraya Adiga was there right before him, with a bundle of dried banana leaves on his head, and stacks of cups made of dried banana leaves strung together and hanging from his shoulders. His face was bathed in sweat. On his neck and back were some kind of patches that they used to make fun of when they were younger, calling them Manjunatha's sacred ash; only, they seemed to have spread much more. His teeth were as strong as ever, though he looked older.

Jagannatha stood speechless; he was so happy.

'I'll deliver these to the temple and get back, Jaganna. Tell Chikki I'll be here for lunch. Even I have lots to tell you.'

Adiga's eyes seemed tranquil. Surely he must have heard the news; he had come through the town square. And yet he did not look alarmed.

'Do come back. Of course, we'll talk,' Jagannatha said as he went in to tell Chikki.

She was still in deep conversation with Rao. She could not believe Adiga would be coming for lunch.

'He knows. Yet he said he'll come,' said Jagannatha.

Chikki went into the kitchen in a hurry. Jagannatha went upstairs with Rao.

'I'll tell you a story. Listen,' he said, sipping coffee. He had suddenly felt guilty in Chikki's eyes.

He wanted to talk to forget everything else.

ELEVEN

The Five-rupee Note

Rayaru finished his coffee and sat rubbing a pinch of sunna with his thumb into some bits of tobacco on the palm of his hand. Jagannatha started on a story from his childhood.

'Between me and asceticism there's a hurdle of five rupees, Rayare. Did you know that? The day I return the five rupees I had stolen from Subbaraya Adiga, that day I'll become an ascetic and clap my hands and dance before Manjunatha, I guess.' Jagannatha's tone was light, but the memory had agitated him. Even Rao, who was not particularly interested in such sensitive issues, listened patiently, seeing him so earnest.

When Jagannatha was in high school, he was very fond of Subbaraya Adiga who was such a restive spirit that pretty soon after his wedding he had renounced the world and travelled across the country. He could speak and write in both English and Hindi. Jagannatha's mother was very fond of him too. He would sing Meera bhajans,[48] Amma would

[48] Verses by the fifteenth-century Bhakti poet Meera, in praise of her Lord-beloved Giridhara Gopala.

accompany him on the veena, and Krishnaiah, the manager of the household, would enjoy the recital. And he would tell them stories of his adventure, of climbing the Himalaya, of visiting Rishikesh and Badri. Jagannatha would be mesmerized by his graphic description of nature's pristine beauty in these places.

'Jaganna, do you know? When you stand on top of the mountain on a bright day and look down a ravine, the air is so thin, so clear, you can toss a coin into it and see it glistening all the way down as it falls thousands of feet below,' he would say as he slowly sniffed a pinch of snuff and talked on, reliving his fantastic experiences through the awe-filled eyes of the boy.

Adiga used to come home every day to teach Sanskrit. He was so crazy that Jagannatha has seen him pulling up a vishnukranthi flower from the ground, tenderly separating it from the grass that had surrounded it, holding it up, and meditating on Neelameghashyama[49], weeping in sheer ecstasy. Once he had taken Jagannatha far away from Bharathipura into the depth of the forest and made him sit on the bank of a pond near the ruins of a Jain temple. Not a soul was in sight. It was quite late in the evening. As he got talking about the incarnations of Vishnu, he seemed to forget himself and danced in utter abandon. They could hear a cowherd playing a flute somewhere and Adiga started singing softly, 'Krishna, come to me soon.' Jagannatha was embarrassed. And he began to feel a little uneasy when he realized Adiga was singing to him, as if *he* were Shri Krishna. But Adiga's devotion pervaded the boy's heart slowly and tears began to flow from his eyes. 'You're not an ordinary boy, Jaganna. Like Shukamuni,[50] you are a great devotee,' Adiga had said then, making him feel ashamed of his childish craze for the spicy snack, kodubale.

Adiga's lifestyle was pure, heady with his love for God. He made his living by cutting banana leaves, drying them out to make them into plates and cups; spinning the sacred thread on a spindle for Brahmins; getting the sacred kusa grass from the banks of the river; and selling these things. He officiated as a priest wherever he was invited, tucking whatever money he was offered for his services into the folds of his

[49] A reference to Shri Krishna who was dark-skinned.

[50] An ardent devotee of Vishnu who narrated the story of Shri Krishna's life to King Parikshit.

dhothi at the waist and using it as added income to run his house. And he was a gracious host; everyone who visited had to be served a meal or a cup of coffee or, at least, a glass of limejuice sweetened with jaggery. He had many children, one born every year; one would be crying, another would have wet himself and be splashing it about, yet another with a runny nose would be sucking on a fruit, and in the midst of all this would be Adiga, spinning yarn for the sacred thread and singing the glory of God. Or he would lose himself in praising some stupid godman or some devout widow or in discussing some comment by Shankara,[51] Ramanuja[52] or Madhava[53] in the light of the Upanishads.

Subbaraya Adiga would not fault anyone. His theory was that, while you can see the presence of God clearly in some hearts, in some others it is blurred, being clouded by the person's ego.

A houseful of children—some had died, some were alive. To run the house, he would walk all the way from the village to the market every day, to sell his wares and to get some medicines from Dr Anthony on the way back, counting the distance in terms of the number of times he could utter one of the names of Vishnu, 'Achyuthaanantha Govinda'. His wife, who had known how many children were born, how many had died, whose birthday was when, had died in childbirth. She was blessed. But the house had to be run. How could he attend to the little ones when he had to be out earning for the family? So he married his dead wife's sister. And he had a few more children by her. How many? And why?

'I don't know how many more times I have to be born to work out this weakness of my flesh.' he would say, laughing sadly. 'Manjunatha is not only the god of the celibate, he is also the god of the sensual—and I've vowed to be a family man.'

And in the midst of all this, he did have a spell of renunciation. 'I have the mark of the wheel on the sole of my feet and so I'm destined

[51] The great eighth-century Vedantic philosopher who preached nondualism. He founded the sect of Smartha Brahmins.

[52] He lived in the eleventh century and is the foremost name in Indian philosophy after Shankara. He maintained a modified dualism. His influence led to the worship of a personalized deity in India.

[53] A celebrated Vaishnava teacher of the thirteenth century who maintained that the Divine Being and the soul of man are distinct entities.

to travel,' he said, justifying his wanderlust. He wandered the length and breadth of the country, meeting saints and ascetics. That was when he had attended one of Gandhi's prayer meetings at the ashram at Wardha, when Gandhi was engaged in attaining liberation of his spirit by Karmayoga, doing his duty. He had found favour with him by donating his ear studs to the Harijan Fund, and one of the rings hanging from his sacred thread.

As the fires of renunciation cooled, his feet dragged him back home. And what did he see? His younger sister, a child-widow, was pregnant. He did not ask her who's baby she was carrying and why? He did not scold her. He turned a deaf ear to his wife's nagging. His sister's belly filled out, people talked, and so she got someone to abort the baby. What can anyone do? She was working out her karma.

Nevertheless, there was no way out but to do the *ghatashraaddha*.[54] He had to earn a living as a priest to feed his children, hadn't he? He had to suffer the consequences of his karma. And so, he excommunicated his sister. Yet he let her live in his house; she slept on the veranda, she ate on the veranda, she cut the banana leaves for him, and had shaved her head as was becoming of a widow. Adiga praised her detachment as greater than his own. Who would do the temple chores as well as she did? She did not enter the house; she did not pollute anything. She combed and plaited his children's hair. She swept the courtyard and sprinkled watered-down cow-dung over it. Somehow she had been living like a drop of water on a lotus leaf, working out her destiny. She had not lost her love for her brother; neither had he lost his affection for his sister. 'Let us leave the decision about who's right and who's wrong to Manjunatha,' he said. Everyone in the village accepted Adiga's decision. After all, as the saying goes, is there any home where dosés don't have holes in them? Subbaraya Adiga was very fond of Jagannatha. And Jagannatha respected him even more because his mother liked him. He was amazed that this man who wore no shirt knew English. In his pilgrimage across the country he had collected a number of books on Hinduism in English. Swami Shivananda of Rishikesh had even autographed his books and given them to Adiga, blessing him.

[54] Funeral rites performed for a living person as if (s)he were dead.

Adiga would lend his books to Jagannatha. He would sit before him and sing. Once he gave him a book entitled *Celibacy is Life, Ejaculation is Death,* saying, 'This path has been too difficult for me; see if you can walk it. When I could have wet dreams right there in Rishikesh, I realized there was no escape for me from the desires of the flesh—not in this life.' And Jagannatha, who had barely begun to discover the possibilities of pleasure in his body, felt most embarrassed reading it.

This crazy man who could think the grey fungal patches on his body were the sacred ash; who could be moved to tears while singing hymns, would weep while laughing, and laugh while weeping; would dance in lonely places; would spend all his savings on feeding Brahmins during the month of Karthika; whose mind was elsewhere while he was here—this man really went mad one day, raving mad. He threw stones, bit anyone who went near him, spat on people, woke up in the middle of the night and wailed; flew into a rage on seeing his wife—that was the news that did the rounds. When Jagannatha gathered courage and visited him, Adiga wept on seeing him. Jagannatha expected him to turn into an ascetic, but he became withdrawn when the madness left him. Jagannatha put it down to a state of contemplation.

In a bid to follow Adiga, Jagannatha changed his ways and his mother was alarmed. Seeing the impact it had on his mother, he made a greater show of renunciation; he gave up his breakfast and ate tulsi leaves instead. And he developed certain mannerisms while talking; at times, he would close his eyes, at other times, he would open them wide and stop talking; he would giggle, he would raise both his hands, and, tilting his head, would talk of shocking things—all this in imitation of Adiga.

In those days, Seebinakere Kamala—the one who later went to Bombay—was in High School with Jagannatha. The boys in their class would translate the English words—leaf, lotus, pearl, umbrella—into Kannada in that order and giggle because together they meant, 'Hey, Kamala, give me a kiss!' but Jagannatha, Adiga's disciple, would not join them in teasing her; he would erase the words as they appeared as graffiti on a wall day after day. Jagannatha had been greatly influenced by Sharatchandra's novels, *Debdas* and *Shesh Prashna*, and so, in his sight, this daughter of a prostitute was an ideal girl. And as the other boys respected him as the son of a landlord, Jagannatha's solemnity increased further. Wrapped in Adiga's mysticism, the adulation of his teachers, the wealth of his family, his mother's support, and the romantic novels of Sharatchandra, Jagannatha could not see the ground he was treading.

But he was seething within. Though his love for the goddess of his heart was pure, he was very upset ever since he heard that one of his classmates, Rangaiah—a small-time lawyer's son who had grown as uncouth as the bison in a swamp—accompanied Kamala on the tabla as she sang, had gifted her a hanky, and been spending days with her on the pretext of studying together. And, thanks to the magazine, *Kaliyuga*,[55] which he had accidentally found in Krishnaiah's room, he could well imagine Rangaiah slowly undressing her and then stripping himself. Jagannatha felt helpless, in a turmoil; he could not control his fantasies, he could not talk to anyone about them. He could neither eat nor sleep nor study. All his efforts to surrender to Adiga's mysticism seemed to be in vain.

At that time, something happened that changed the course of Jagannatha's life completely, something that he could remember distinctly even to this day. Adiga had lent him a book. It was a book by Shivananda on the lives of some saints. It was wrapped in an old issue of the newspaper, *Thayinaadu*. Eager to read a bit of stale news further, he removed the wrapper and out fell a five-rupee note—a crisp new note at that. Why had Adiga hidden this note in the wrapper of this book? From whom was he hiding it? And why? Had Shivananda given him the money? Had he saved it for a rainy day? Countless questions sprang to his mind; he was surprised that a man as unworldly as Adiga had hidden money in this way.

Even now Jagannatha could not understand why he had not put the five-rupee note back into the wrapper, why he had pocketed it. He did not want for anything. Though his mother never gave him any money, she bought him everything he wanted. But from the moment he had slipped the five-rupee note into his pocket without any qualms, he seemed to change gradually. And yet, he could not quite understand the significance of the incident that opened up many chinks in his world.

[55] A weekly devoted to sex education.

He could only talk of what had happened. Until then, he had never kept anything from his mother, but now that he had pocketed the five rupees, he would move it from pocket to pocket without her knowledge every time he changed his clothes. To do that, he discovered isolated nooks in the house. Somehow the hidden note also prevented him from enjoying his mother's tenderness whether it was the back-rub she gave him during his bath or the way she ran her fingers through his hair or the way she talked to him intimately. And because he was disgusted with himself for having a secret from Chikki who called him 'Jaganna' so lovingly and from Krishnaiah, the manager of the household, there were subtle changes in his behaviour too. He felt alienated from everyone; perhaps he was fascinated by the awareness of a dark corner in his consciousness of which the elders knew nothing. And that fear might have brought a new flavour into his life. If anyone dear to him had asked him at that point what he would do with the money, he would have said he would put it back into the wrapper, and meant it too.

But, surprisingly, he did nothing of that sort. Jagannatha had reached a state in which he had to face the consequences of his guilt.

One Sunday morning, Adiga visited him. He might have been up before dawn and had his bath and smeared his body with sandalwood paste. He might have walked all the way from his village in a great hurry; he was sweating but his eyes were twinkling with joy. Seeing Jagannatha on the porch, he said, 'Jaganna, what do you think happened today? I came past the graveyard. It was still dark. A Holeya was digging a pit, to bury a dead calf perhaps. His black body, matted hair, the rippling muscles on his shoulders, his concentration on the digging—everything about him suddenly reminded me of Shri Neelakantaswami.[56] As I walked along mulling over it, I remembered what a yogi had said at a pilgrimage centre in Kanyakumari, "Before anything else, this body needs to be purified so much that we should not have to wash ourselves after going to the toilet. And to be able to do that, do you know how much we'll have to control our appetite and to eat only as much as we need? Then, Man will really get close to birds and animals." Oh, as

[56] A name for Shiva, meaning, the blue-throated Lord. Legend has it that when Shiva swallowed a deadly poison that would have destroyed the world, his wife gripped his throat and it turned blue.

usual, I started on something and I've wandered off. To get back to it, why can't that Holeya be Parameshwara[57] who lives in graveyards? I'm just imagining it here,' he said, pointing to his head. And then, putting his hand on his heart, he said, 'If I can feel it here, then my shackles will be loosened,' holding up his sacred thread in contempt.

'By the way, where's Amma?' he asked, walking into the house.

Jagannatha felt a quiver of panic run through his body. Amma served *uppittu* and coffee to the guest. Adiga said to her, 'In Orissa, they sing the hymns of Jayadeva[58] so beautifully. After all, that's where he was born, wasn't he? I'll sing his songs and you play the veena tomorrow, shall we?' Jagannatha escaped from there as if he had something to see to and went towards the cowshed. Ganga stared at him as if ready to butt him; she had just calved and had been tethered. With trembling hands, Jagannatha hurriedly took the five-rupee note from his pocket and stuffed it into his vest and tucked the vest into the folds of his dhothi at the waist and came out of the shed. The note was beginning to look soiled with sweat; it had been moved from pocket to pocket in fear, too many times. He saw Adiga coming into the bathroom to wash his hands and said calmly, 'Ganga has calved. You should see how she tries to butt.'

And then he went upstairs and sat reading something.

Adiga was the priest officiating at the Neelakanteshwara temple that was supported by Jagannatha's family. He received a sack of rice and sixty rupees per year as payment for his services. Jagannatha heard his mother tell Adiga she would be sending the rice to his house in a cart. Adiga used to take off on a pilgrimage as soon as he got the sixty rupees as a lump sum. 'Where're you off to this time?' asked Amma. Both of them were climbing up the stairs.

'I'd like to visit Kaladi and travel a bit around Kerala,' replied Subbaraya Adiga. They were on the landing. It looked as if they were coming towards his room. Jagannatha started perspiring. He felt that, if he wanted, he could even now shove that five-rupee note into the wrapper of the book. But he did not budge from his seat; he did not know why. His body was damp with sweat. He stared blankly at the

[57] Shiva.

[58] He wrote the *Gita Govinda*, an erotic poem in *ashtapadi* metre.

book; the words were blurred. He pretended he had not seen them even when his mother and Adiga stood right before him. 'If your power of concentration is this great, even God will manifest Himself before you,' said Adiga laughing, and asked, 'Jaganna, if you've finished reading Shivananda's book, can you return it?' Jagannatha jumped up as if he were startled, opened a box, and made a show of rummaging through it, stalling for time. He checked the folds of the wrapper to see if he had wrapped the book exactly as Adiga had done, but he could not quite remember how Adiga had done it. He stood there reading a snippet on the wrapper about a strike somewhere, not knowing what to do. Jagannatha was caught in a double bind; returning the five-rupee note to Adiga was as difficult as retaining it.

'If you haven't finished it yet, don't worry. You can return it later,' said Adiga, walking out of the room. Amma was arranging his books neatly on the table. Neither of them suspected anything. He could have easily kept back the book and returned it later, with the five-rupee note back in the wrapper. But he heard himself saying, 'I'm done with it. Here it is!'

He handed over the book to Adiga. Perhaps even to this day, Adiga may not know that he had stolen the money. It won't be surprising if Adiga did not even remember tucking the note into the wrapper of the book. Whatever it be, when he returned the book to Adiga, Jagannatha felt exultant; he had acquired a strange new sense of liberation.

Amma also went down the stairs with Adiga. All this had happened in the same room as he was sitting in right now.

He shut the door and bolted it from inside. He felt he could do anything now. He put his hand inside his vest; it was damp, so were the five-rupee note and his sacred thread. He took out the note and put it into his pocket. He felt like removing the sacred thread. He did not know why. If he were to remove it according to ritual, he would have had to slide it down to his feet, slip it out, and put on a new one. But he pulled it through the right sleeve of his shirt and took it off his neck. In the mirror, he saw a smile mingled with a look of fear because he had removed the sacred thread in the forbidden way. He put away the thread in a box. Since his initiation ceremony, Jagannatha had never ever, even for a moment, been without the sacred caste thread. His mother may not know of his new nakedness as he had the shirt to cover his body, bereft of the thread. Was it safe to go about without the protection of the sacred thread? To check it out secretly, he came down the stairs slowly. He stood for a while in front of the room where the family gods were installed. The family priest was making sandalwood paste. He went out into the yard and walked about in the barn. He had heard that there was an old serpent in the barn. Wondering if he would be polluting the place by walking around without his sacred thread, Jagannatha inspected every snake pit and every hole in the trees in the gentle sunlight. He whistled a hymn, '*Watch over us, Shri Gauri, Thou billow of compassion!*' Snakes were supposed to be attracted to the sound of whistling and so he stood under a tree whistling. And, then, he virtually ran all the way downhill towards the main street in town. The second bus to Shimoga was puffing its way up the hill. He stood staring at it for a while and then, whistling softly to himself, he took the short cut to Seebinakere. Kamala's house was in an alley. Would Rangaiah be there? Would he have stayed there for the night and got up late? Would he be sipping the coffee Kamala would have given him, without brushing his teeth? Would they have got dosés for breakfast from a restaurant? Rangaiah's father had no regard for social norms, neither did his son. Someone was singing in Kamala's house; he could hear someone playing the harmonium and singing an invocation to Sri Ganesha together with the notes, *Lambodhara Lakumikara*, *sa, ri, maa, ga, ri, sa, ri, ga, ri, sa.* He was very sure Rangaiah was on the bed with his head resting on his hand, listening to Kamala singing. He was in anguish. No one was on the street and yet he walked purposefully as if he were on a mission, his body damp with sweat. He noticed a grocery store; a store selling cooking oils; an old man getting a back-rub from his grandson; a naked boy running away from his mother, his body gleaming with oil before a bath; and a farmhand who asked, 'How come, Ayyavare, you're here so early?'—but he walked on with bold strides to give the impression that he had not walked that way hoping to see Kamala. He came to the town square, and walking through the main street and Chariot Street, he went straight to the temple. He remembered that, as a Brahmin, he was not supposed to enter a temple without his sacred thread, and yet he crossed the threshold and went in.

Everyone made way for the landlord's son. The door to the sanctum sanctorum was not yet opened. He could see the two oil-lamps, ever burning, through the grill. Through sheer habit, he brought his palms together in prayer. The typical temple scents of sesame oil, incense sticks, frankincense, and red champak flowers mingled in his nostrils. He raised his prayerful hands, he did not know why. One hand reached for the big bell meant to be rung only in the afternoon, the one his forefathers had gifted. He was thrilled to remember that this bell could be heard all over the town. His fingers felt the smooth surface of the tongue. The very next minute, he was jumping up and ringing the bell.

Everyone stood transfixed, staring at him. Someone screamed in alarm from a corner, 'It's meant to be rung only during the final worship!' But Jagannatha kept jumping up and ringing the bell, trembling like one possessed. He was mesmerized by the metallic sound. He felt a heady sense of power knowing that the sound of the bell would be reverberating throughout the hill-town of Bharathipura, shocking the people, and so he rang it on and on, he did not know for how long.

Someone caught hold of him and rubbed his back saying he could be possessed by a spirit. They soothed him down. They gave him some holy water to drink and sprinkled a little on his head. Someone said Bhootharaya was angry and so had sent a demon to possess him; everyone nodded. They smeared kumkuma on his forehead in reverence and thanked Bhootharaya for warning them in this way.

Jagannatha left the temple, a hero in everyone's sight. He walked home quietly. His face was red and his ears were warm. The sound of the bell was still echoing in his ears; he walked in its hum. He met many familiar faces and gloated that no one knew his secret.

Suddenly, he turned again towards Seebinakere because he knew that someone concerned about him had been following him right from the temple. After losing sight of the man, he turned into the lane where Kamala lived. At the corner was a small shop. Subba, Hotel Sunderayya's illegitimate son born to a prostitute, was selling *beeda*s with the betel leaf twisted into a cone and stuffed with areca nuts and sunna and secured with a clove. He was sticking them on a wire-rack shaped like a tree. He needed to make two more to load the rack. Jagannatha stood watching him. But he moved away and walked on when a policeman with a baton saluted him. Along the way, he passed a barber with a box tucked under his arm. From a house to the right came the sounds of dosés being fried, and the delicious aroma filled the air. Someone came out to the porch, spat, and went back into the house, talking animatedly. The morning sun was getting hotter. Jagannatha stood in front of Kamala's house. No sound of the harmonium. Through a window he could see an inner door, festooned with bits of glass bangles. A picture of Ravi Varma's *Damayanthi*[59] hung beside the door. Not a soul in sight—just a crow and a dog in the drain. He climbed the steps to the porch of Kamala's house and thrust the five-rupee note through the window. And then he jumped down and ran away. He felt the eyes of the whole town behind him. But when he turned back he saw no one. Only the dog barked a bit because it was expected to, and then stopped.

His mother looked at him anxiously as he reached home running. Someone from the temple might have told her that the spirit of Bhootharaya had manifested itself through him. But she did not talk to him about it. Jagannatha went straight up to his room and put on the sacred thread in a hurry and came down. Without speaking a word, his mother cracked her knuckles to ward off the evil spirit from him.

[59] A princess of Vidharbha who was married to Nala, a prince.

TWELVE

Subbaraya Adiga

After Jagannatha finished his story about the five-rupee note, Rao said, 'Come, let's go and see what Chikki's doing,' and stood up. After listening to the story, he had only laughed. Now he sat on a low wooden seat Chikki had given him.

'Lunch will be ready in half an hour. Would you like a snack?' Chikki said.

'I'll wait,' said Rao.

Chikki busied herself making *jilebis* for Adiga as that was his favourite sweet. Jagannatha was amused at Chikki's excitement that Adiga was staying for lunch. It looked as if she had got over her sadness that the cauldrons of rice and curry meant to feed twenty to twenty-five Brahmins every day would go waste as none of the pilgrims had turned up. She might have pacified herself that the farmhands were always there to eat the food. There was also the Holathi who cleaned out the cowshed.

Chikki loved the Holathi. Jagannatha had heard her tease the woman that she littered like a sow. Quite often, before she went for her purificatory bath, Chikki would tease her with, 'So, how many children do you have now?' And that would lead to talk about her husband's debauchery, her eldest son's alcoholism, her younger daughter's elopement with a Holeya from Thirthahalli; about one of the sons who went to work in the coffee plantations in Chikkamagaluru and had not come home even once; about the baby being possessed by a demon—they would keep chatting on and on until it was time for Chikki's bath.

As she was kneading the dough, Chikki said to Sripathi Rao, 'Tell me now, when they have something to sleep on and to cover themselves, what do they have to achieve by entering the temple?'

Jagannatha was happy that Chikki was addressing the issue directly.

'Not that way, Chikki. Our lives will get some meaning in this country only when these lowly people rise in revolt. Look at the poor farmers in Vietnam. Haven't they taken on a country like America? That's the amazing news these days, much like the Black American struggle in America. When such people stand up for their rights, not only will their lives blossom, but ours will too. Unless the Holeyaru become like us and feel human, we'll remain incomplete beings.'

Chikki looked resentful and Jagannatha felt embarrassed; he might have sounded like an orator.

'I don't understand what you're saying, Jaganna. I hear the Holeya is paid an incentive to send his children to school. Do you know what they do with the money? They squander it on drink. Unless they feel the need to improve, everything you do is like doing *homa*[60] in water, an unproductive activity.' Chikki sighed.

'It isn't like that, Chikki. If we help them, they won't improve. True. They have to rise in protest against us. Then they too will begin to feel they are human. We've made them believe they're lower. This is awful. That's why I ...'

'Whatever you do, Jaganna, don't forget our family's honour. It's like Hanumantha[61] trying to eat the sun and getting burnt in the face. Ask Rarayu, he'll tell you ... You were still a baby. You had been unconscious

[60] An act of oblation by casting clarified butter into fire.

[61] Also known as Hanuman, the Monkey God; devotee of Rama. His temple is usually outside the village. The proverb is based on the story that he had as a baby tried to eat the sun.

for three days. Adiga had you on his lap, saying the Mruthyunjaya prayer for your life. Your mother sat in front of the prayer room, praying with tears in her eyes, "He's my only son, spare him!" I can still see it all. All of us were fasting. However much we branded you with spots, you didn't regain consciousness. At last your mother made a vow to offer a gold crown to Manjunathaswami and immediately you opened your eyes. Is it proper for you to forget all that now?'

Rao was looking at Chikki with great compassion. Chikki was very upset. Jagannatha did not reply; it did not seem proper to say anything to her.

'Don't worry. Don't think Jaganna will act rashly,' said Rayaru to comfort her.

Both of them left the place quietly and went upstairs. It was around one o'clock. Soon Subbaraya Adiga joined them.

'We've half an hour before lunch. Adigare, you don't have any objections to playing a game of cards in the meantime, do you?' asked Rayaru, laughing.

'We're three hands. Let's play Twenty-Eight then,' said Adiga, sitting down. Though he was not interested, Jagannatha joined them.

'What shall we do for a deck of cards?' he asked.

'It should be in that niche in the wall,' said Rayaru to him. And to Adiga, 'I would've gone crazy in prison if I didn't know any card-games, Maharayare.'

'What else do you think we do during the monsoons? Spinning yarn on the spindle or frying wafers of raw jackfruit, eating them, and playing cards,' said Subbaraya Adiga, laughing.

'These people are ready for anything. Why am I not like them?' wondered Jagannatha looking for the pack of cards. 'But that wasn't quite true. Hadn't Rayaru burnt the machine-made cloth in his store? Isn't Adiga passionate about God? People who adapt themselves easily to their situation are a different sort. Probably, only Amma was like that. Whether she was being hospitable to guests, or celebrating festivals, or giving gifts to family and friends or singing—whatever it be, Amma could put her soul into it. Adiga says there are many stages of preparation before launching a project: meditation, contemplation, recollection, comprehension, study, experiment, and achievement. Wonder at which level I am.

'The pack of cards was not in the niche. Margaret loved so many things: politics, visits to museums, good clothes, heady chatter, wandering the streets window-shopping.

'But I'm bound to a single purpose.

'Adiga says a man's destiny is unfulfilled if his very act of living is not centred in his inner being. He quotes a Sanskrit proverb that says "Yoga stills the wandering mind". My mind also revolves around a single point, but, in its still centre, I don't yet see the Holeyaru as human beings; I see them as the lengthening shadows of the evening, as dark bodies that listen to me from afar and then go back to their homes. What do they talk about when they're drunk? How do they sleep with their women at night? What do they think about? How do they pet their children? How do they weep? I don't know. I even keep forgetting their names. Who's Pilla? Who's Kariya? Who's Madha ... ?'

He went to his mother's room to see if there was a pack of cards in a trunk of his High School days. It was an old-fashioned brass trunk, dented in places. It had been with him until he had left Shimoga. He lifted the lid. The notebooks he had used in High School. It was writer Krishnaiah's job to buy wrapping paper from Shenoy's stationery store and wrap the books. 'In those days, I had an *uttaramukhi* pen, and then a Blackbird. How Margaret used to laugh at the shawl Amma had given me—well-worn and patched in places. Amma had got it from Kashmir; even now I cover myself with it at night.'

Jagannatha turned the pages of a notebook. There was something about Robert Clive. He had written, 'Shri Manjunatha Prasanna' at the top of the page. He had scribbled 'Shri Manjunatha Prasanna' even on the cover page of another book, and on all the other pages too. 'In those days, I used to remember Manjunatha every time my left eye quivered or my left leg tripped[62] or even when I stretched out my hand for a question paper in the examination hall. And the funny thing is that I remember him even now; only, the way I do it is different. There, in a corner, was a pack of cards, old and dog-eared.'

'They're not smooth enough, they're very old,' he called out to Rayaru.

'They'll do, don't worry,' he called back.

[62] Considered as bad omens.

Rao dealt the cards among the three of them.

Adiga's stomach rumbled.

'You must be hungry,' said Jagannatha.

'I can wait half an hour,' said Adiga.

Rao made a bid.

Jagannatha raised it by one.

'No,' said Adiga, and then, 'Trump?'

'Diamond,' said Jagannatha.

'Dip?' asked Rao.

'Yes,' said Jagannatha, picked up the dip and frowned.

'Your turn,' he said to Adiga.

'What's your eldest son doing, Adigare?'

'Oh, that's another story, Jaganna. My wife and the daughter-in-law are like oil and soap-nut powder; they can't get along. They squabbled all the time. Also, my son doesn't like being a priest. "Do what you please," I said to him. He's moved to Shimoga; he's working in a restaurant. Remember I'd given my second daughter to someone in Sagar? He died and she's back home with her three daughters. Now I'll have to get them married. The wife can't get along even with the daughter. Life moves on, somehow.' Adiga spoke sadly, yet there was a smile on his face. He played a diamond and said, 'Even I haven't been well these days, Jaganna. I can't travel around as I used to.'

It was Jagannatha who lost the game.

'Come for lunch,' said Chikki. They went to the dining room. They were the only ones; the others had finished theirs—the family priest, the cook, and his children. The three of them were really hungry.

Adiga ate the rice and curry with great relish, talking about this and that.

And then he said, 'Jagannatha, is it true, what I heard?'

'It's true,' said Jagannatha, happy Adiga had come to the point.

'Look, Jagannatha, you're a knowledgeable person. Unless we've rid ourselves of our ego, it isn't proper for us to put our hand to such a task; it's a question involving the future of the whole town.'

Chikki was eager to listen, so she came in to serve them some *bondas*. Everyone had a generous helping of Adiga's favourite ridge-gourd bondas; they were too engrossed to say 'enough, enough' to Chikki. Knowing it would be an insult to take Adiga's comment lightly,

Jagannatha said, 'I know your line of argument, Adigare. You're saying only an ascetic has the right to defy social norms, aren't you?'

Adiga mixed curry with rice, broke some bits of bonda into it, and said with conviction, 'Yes. To the ascetic, the food we offer to God and what we excrete are one and the same. Ramakrishna Paramahamsa cast off his sacred thread when he found he took pride in wearing it. He could see as his guru the beggar who scours garbage with dogs and crows for food. For such a person, who's a Brahmin? Who's a Holeya?'

These were familiar arguments; Jagannatha was not provoked. But, respecting Adiga's earnestness, he wondered what would be the right thing to say.

'If you say a man can do nothing worthwhile if he's not detached, doesn't it mean a man of the world is incapable of any earth-shaking action? Then you're saying there's no meaning in society; that all meaning comes only when one transcends it.'

Rao was listening to him eagerly. Chikki served the jilebis. Even when Adiga spread the palm of his hand over his leaf to say he had had enough, she served him two in the space the palm of his hand had not covered and said, 'You're fond of them, aren't you?'

It seemed as if Adiga had not heard Jagannatha in the transactions that were happening between him and Chikki. As he enjoyed the jilebis, he said, 'See, Jaganna, I wear this caste thread. It's a symbol of my livelihood. Because I wear it, people ask me to serve as a priest in their homes, to sing the *Samaveda*[63] in the temple, even you've appointed me as temple priest at the Neelakanteshwara temple. However, if I'm trapped in its divine power, I'll burn out like the camphor we use at worship. As long as I'm attached to my karma, as long as I'm a man of this world, I need the rituals. Once I'm out of it I won't need anything.'

Adiga had started to make a point but had veered off. That was so typical of him; his words scurried wherever his fancy blew them. Jagannatha tried to be sarcastic to draw his attention since an earnest discussion seemed to melt in his deceitful mind like the delicious jilebis in his mouth.

'See what the Puranas say,' said Jagannatha, 'Brahmarishi Vashishta, was the son of a devadasi, Urvashi. He married a Holathi called

[63] One of the four Vedas. It is said that Indian classical music has its roots in it.

Arundhati who was transformed into a star. And every bridal couple has to worship it. Ours is such a revolutionary religion, isn't it?'

Seeing both Rayaru and Chikki nodding in agreement, Jagannatha got irritated.

'This is what I call deceit. There's no greater danger than cunning, Adigare. See what the religion that says such things has done to our country? In a country that has created such revolutionary myths, society has remained the way it is for hundreds of years. What's the reason for this, tell me? With their manipulative ways, these Puranas, these beliefs only serve to keep the upper castes at the top and the lower castes at the bottom.'

Subbaraya Adiga did not get angry. Rayaru stared at Jagannatha as if he wondered if the discussion was leading anywhere at all; he finished the main meal and waited. Adiga took with him one of the two jilebis Chikki had forced on him. Jagannatha, who did not care much for sweets, had finished his meagre meal quite some time ago. These days he was trying to eat as little as possible. Unmindful that the others had finished, Adiga took his time breaking bits of jilebi and putting them into his mouth, and said, 'This is all I have to say, Jagannatha. Do you really love the Holeyaru? If you love them unconditionally, you'll be one with bird, beast, and chandala, and become an ascetic. There'll be no question of any conflict whatsoever; no need for a revolution. You'll live in a state of absorption. All that I'm trying to say is that you and I haven't reached that stage.'

Adiga grew fervent. Holding the last jilebi in his hand, he continued, 'Twenty years ago, God stood everywhere, calling out to me. I've felt God calling me for at least a few moments or is it my ego that's persuading me now to say that He did? I'm not quite sure. But now I'm not like that. I'm very short-tempered. Sometimes I beat my wife; I get furious when the children cry. I hate to go back home; I'd rather wander about. And I'm very greedy too; look at the way I'm eating jilebis though I know they'll upset my stomach. Do you know why I'm telling you all this? Oh, I started on something and I've forgotten what it was. All of us are in Manjunatha's womb—the good ones, the bad ones, greedy ones like me, brave ones like you, Rayaru with his selfless action, Chikki with her longing to preserve family traditions—all of us.'

Jagannatha laughed when he heard the last bit. He felt there was no point in saying anything. Adiga had gone off at a tangent. But, even now, some things that Adiga said that day fascinated Jagannatha. True, he was not the Adiga he once was; he was a man lost. He was also weaker. Or, perhaps, he was even then a weak man and I didn't know. I'm not sure.

Chikki came to serve them rice for the final course with curd. Jagannatha did not want any. Rayaru did not want any more; the morsel on his leaf would do, he said. Rayaru's fingers were dry with the waiting. Adiga took a helping.

Jagannatha said, 'I'm looking for a possibility for some positive action, Adigare. Tell me why? Because it's been possible only for ascetics to be revolutionaries in our society. Within the social fabric ...'

Adiga butted in, 'You too will become an ascetic, Jaganna. You'll be rid of all desire, you wait and see. It'll have to be so. Or else nothing works in this country. What did Gandhiji become eventually? I have a story. I'll tell you later. I heard it in Orissa. It's a great one.'

With something else on his mind, Adiga mixed his rice and curd. Jagannatha noticed how much he relished his food; looking at him even a sated person could feel hungry again.

Chikki was standing in a corner, a copper pot in hand ready to fill their glasses with water. She said, 'So what are you saying, Jaganna? That the saying—if you worship, he is God; if you nourish, they're children; if you protect, they're citizens—is wrong?'

Jagannatha did not know how to respond, there seemed to be no connection between what he was trying to say and how Chikki was seeing it. She continued, 'Get married; everything will be fine. If your mother had been alive, there wouldn't have been any need for all this.' She served them water and went in to get some vermicelli *kheer*. She served it to them in little banana-leaf cups despite their protests. 'Jaganna doesn't eat well these days,' she complained.

Rayaru, who had been quiet all this while, said, 'There's some truth in what Chikki says. Manjunatha's fame has spread because he has listened to the joys and sorrows of crores of people for hundreds of years. Not that I say he has heard them, it's because people believe he hears them. I don't have the faith.'

'Only when such faith is destroyed ...'

'Such faith is essential. As long as human nature exists …'

'When copper ore is mined, when the town receives electricity, when the hospital gets an X-ray machine, when scientific outlook begins to spread, surely, this faith will automatically …'

'It won't go, Jaganna, it won't! They destroyed God in Russia. What happened? Stalin became God, didn't he?'

'This kind of a discussion is like a school debate, that's all. It's like saying, anyway we'll have to die some day or the other, so what's the use of doing anything at all.'

Their fingers were drying. There were about to get up to rinse their hands when Adiga started talking, 'Finally, this is all I have to say, if we can't live intensely, there's no point in living at all. When Paramahamsa touched him with his feet, I believe Vivekananada[64] was terrified as if the very ground beneath his feet was sinking. That's the way we feel when we're caught in the hands of God; we're shaken up as if we're burning. If we don't feel such a terror at least once, then life is a waste. True, it's a terrifying fear as if we're losing our hold on everything, makes the hair stand on end. In this way, when we merge with the rest of creation, we have to lose the feeling that *I* am a separate identity, don't we? That's very difficult. A guru called Govinda from the Badarika ashram told me the same thing, "I go thus far, Adiga, but then I'm afraid. I find myself tossed on this shore and struggling." If Jaganna has any fervour now, even if Manjunatha covers his mind with hate, he's lucky. That's what I'd say. Accepting or rejecting Manjunatha is not the point here. Even Jaganna will surely suffer that terror, that anguish. He'll have to lose his ego.

One is born a Shudra,
One's karma makes him a Dwija,[65]
One's reading of the Vedas makes him a Vipra,
One's knowledge of the Brahman[66] *makes him a Brahmana.*

[64] Vivekananda (1863–1902), born Narendranath Dutta, was the chief disciple of Sri Ramakrishna Paramahamsa and the founder of the Ramakrishna Mission. He was a major force in the revival of Hinduism. He introduced Hinduism to the Western world at the Parliament of World Religions at Chicago in 1893.

[65] Twice-born, born once physically and born again, spiritually.

[66] Ultimate reality, not to be confused with the Brahmin caste.

'Why do they say this? At the most, we're all Dwijas, that's all. Through meditation, selfhood, and knowledge, Jaganna may have reached the third stage of the Vipra. He's set on changing the relationship between Manjunatha and the people. He'll understand everything during that process of change; he'll become clearer. To put it in a nutshell, something in him is struggling to break free from something. Like a baby kicking his way out of his mother's womb, he's kicking Manjunatha. Let him; he's not a dead foetus, after all. Perhaps, even that kind of a service will thrill Manjunatha, won't it?'

Adiga spoke with his eyes closed, as if he were drugged; he was also picking out the cashewnuts and raisins from the kheer and chewing them with great relish. Some of the things he was saying were quite trite coming from a Brahmin, but other things were really scintillating. As he listened to him with love and awe, Jagannatha waited for Adiga's fervour to disappear in a flourish of banality.

'A delusion—what is an illusion? What is real? Jagannatha says, "The people are living in a delusion trusting in Manjunatha, I'll wake them up; they'll wake up through suffering." The dream you had last night seems like an illusion in today's reality; in tomorrow's understanding, today's awareness seems an illusion. When we rise beyond this understanding to a vision; then, who is God? Who is twice-born? Who is a Holeya?'

To change the topic, Rayaru said, 'Don't dismiss what Chikki said, Jaganna, wife and children give you a sense of responsibility. Your plan of action gains credibility only when you can carry it out while being responsible for your family. Without knowing what it is to live with a wife or to raise children, it's no use talking about revolution. When you know neither joy nor sorrow, who are you fighting for, and why. Tell me. See what rotten people have come to power, thanks to Gandhiji's revolt.'

Jagannatha got up, fearing the discussion would turn into a game if allowed to drift this way. The three of them went to the bathroom to rinse their hands. He gave Adiga a small pot filled with water. Adiga rinsed his hands, wiped them on a towel, stepped out of the bathroom, and waited. The look of fervour on his face had increased. Jagannatha knew Adiga was waiting for him to come out. Looking forward to what he might have to say, he stepped out. Rayaru went upstairs, eager for his betel leaves and areca nuts. Jagannatha stood beside Adiga, who said nothing but whose face mirrored an inner joy as he stared at him with half-closed eyes. Jagannatha felt a shiver remembering what he had done long ago, seating him on a stone near the ruins of a temple in the forest.

'Jaganna, you're a secret devotee.'

Jagannatha laughed. *How cunning*, he *thought*. Adiga caressed his back familiarly. His bare body, besmeared with sandalwood paste pressed against his shirt. His hand stretched along his back in a hug—grey patches of a skin infection on his neck and his eyes glistening in a trance. Jagannatha tried to laugh, to cover both his embarrassment and his irritation.

'Come, let's go up,' he said.

Rayaru was lying on a mat on the floor, eyes closed; he looked tired. Adiga, chewing on his betel leaves and nuts, got excited about the story he had wanted to tell.

'Yoga controls the wayward mind,' he started, quoting a Sanskrit sloka. 'This is about the power of being focused. A mendicant in Orissa told me this story. I didn't tell you then because Chikki was with us.

'Once upon a time there was a Holeya. His job was to clean the toilets in the palace. I don't have to describe those toilets to you; elaborate ones with raised platforms. One day, when he went to one of the toilets to clean it, he found the queen using it. While he stood outside waiting, he bent down and looked in; he saw her private parts and was stunned. In his entire life, he had never seen them so fair. And so, now, he was obsessed by them day and night. Dwelling on the queen's fair-skinned body, he gave up his food, drink, sleep, and bath. His face grew gaunt, his eyes became sunken, he grew a beard, and his hair became matted. His wife was worried; she did not know why her husband was getting so emaciated. She nagged him, she begged him. And one day he told her what had happened. She thought over it; she knew she had to save her husband's life at all cost and she felt brave. Somehow she managed to come before the queen's presence. The queen laughed to hear her story. "All right," she said, "Bring your husband to me. Tell him he can see me wholly naked."

'The Holeya came, he stood, he saw. The queen stood before him naked. But the surprising thing was, he had been fantasizing about the queen's naked body for so long that, when at last he got the chance, he had been freed from his desire to see it. He had become a yogi. The queen saw the Holeya with his beard and matted hair. The Holeya saw the naked queen. He bent low, touched her feet, and prostrated before her. And she touched his feet and prostrated before him.

'The gist of all that I've been saying is here. Its meaning will occur to you gradually.'

THIRTEEN

Educating Pilla and His Friends

Adiga and Rao rested awhile and left after a cup of coffee. Expecting to cater to hundreds of pilgrims who might come home during the New Moon Festival, Chikki had bought all the rolls of dried banana leaves and cups Adiga had brought. But she had also felt sad wondering if anyone would ever come to their house again; she had pleaded with Adiga to advise Jaganna. To pacify her, Adiga had quoted the Sanskrit proverb, 'kaalaaya thasmai namah!' She had packed a few jilebis in a banana leaf and given them to him saying, 'Give them to your children.'

After the two had left, Jagannatha waited eagerly for the young Holeyaru. 'I must see if they'll touch me today,' he thought, as he sat on a chair on the veranda. How strange, I hadn't thought of it before this! By his side, he had the new slates and pieces of chalk he had bought for these men; so far they had traced the letters on sand. What were the basic letters they would have to know? After they had learnt to read, how many books did he have that were good enough to give them? I must get them to read *Chomana Dhudi*.[67] I must also simplify some writings, about Basavanna,[68] Esur, the French and Russian revolutions, the Cultural Revolution in China. He had already written a few pages; he thought he would go over them the next day. I shouldn't be embarrassed to talk to them about anything. The hard truth was that their reality was the only thing that was real to them. And so I must make whatever's real to me, real to them too. If they can reach a point where they can touch me spontaneously, from that moment everything else will become real to them: from that moment Manjunatha will recede. And things will begin to blossom. He waited eagerly.

He could see them approaching in the distance: reddish dust in their matted black hair; black blankets thrown over their bare bodies; nothing but the loincloth to cover them. And a knife tucked into it at the waist.

They stood beyond the yard.

'Come,' he said. They did not come much closer; they stood in the middle of the yard, hesitant, fearful. They stood there awkwardly, with one leg twisted behind the other and with a slight stoop as if it were wrong for them to be standing there; to be there at all so late in the evening.

'Come closer to the porch,' he said. They came, slowly dragging their feet. Jagannatha did not have the courage to say, 'Climb the steps and come and sit on the veranda.' There was an air of painful coercion.

'Sit down,' he said. They spread their blankets and sat down. To ease the tension, he threw towards them some areca nuts and tobacco that were on a plate beside him. One of them stretched out his hand eagerly, caught them, and shared them with the others. 'Come on ... chew,' he said. He too smeared some sunna on a betel leaf as he chewed a nut; he tried to create an ambience of friendly informality as if whatever they were doing was normal and usual. But the Holeyaru would not blend sunna into the tobacco in his presence. They sat there afraid.

Not knowing how to break the ice, Jagannatha called out the first name that came to his head, 'Pilla.'

'O,' responded one of them.

[67] Shivaram Karanth's classic novel about bonded labour.

[68] Social reformer and mystic of the twelfth century who moved away from Vedic priestly traditions.

'Oh, so this is Pilla,' thought Jagannatha, noticing him particularly. 'How tall and dark and well-built he is!' he said to himself, taking in the thick thatch of black hair, the scraggly moustache, and the stubbly chin. And good-looking too. I must make him the leader.

'Why haven't the other five come?' he asked them.

'They've gone to Besthur, Odeya.'

'Come on, chew some,' he said. Chewing on his betel leaf and nut, Jagannatha waited. They must have relaxed; they put the nuts into their mouths and rubbed some sunna into the tobacco. *How absurd to tell them of my plan now,* he thought, and yet he said simply, 'The day after the New Moon is the Chariot Festival. On that day you must come into the temple with me.'

The Holeyaru sat still; they did not ask him why. 'In which direction were their minds flowing? How can I stall the flow and get my words to capture them?' He did not know. He asked himself why he could not do it; he tried to answer his own question. The Holeyaru sat quiet with the tobacco in their mouths. He started talking, about Gandhiji, Ambedkar, Negro slaves—whatever. They just sat still. He thought, 'How absurd! How ludicrous!'

'From now on, you'll have to learn to write on slates,' he said to change the topic. On one of the slates he wrote the word, *Basava*, and, stretching out his hand from where he sat on the porch, he said, 'Pilla, take this.' Pilla stood up. 'Here, take it,' repeated Jagannatha. Pilla stood ready to catch the slate, expecting Jagannatha to throw it to him.

Jagannatha also stood up and brought the slate close to Pilla's hand, trying to hand it over to him. Pilla quickly lowered his hands. 'If the slate falls, it will break, Pilla,' said Jagannatha, bending further. Suddenly, Pilla's hands went further down. Jagannatha bent further. Pilla could not bend any further. He sat down and put out his hands. It seemed as if he would try to go underground if Jagannatha had bent any further. What a ridiculous game of stretching and bending!

Feeling disgusted, Jagannatha dropped the slate, Pilla caught it deftly.

'Read what I've written there,' said Jagannatha.

Pilla stared at the slate with the nerves on his neck standing out. With great difficulty he said, 'Basava.' On the other slates, Jagannatha wrote the words, *Kamala, Karaga, Ramana, Chapala,* and threw the slates at the others. Two of them stammered out the words with difficulty; the other two did not read at all.

Once again Jagannatha explained to the Holeyaru why they ought to enter the temple. Though he felt he was delivering a monologue he carried on relentlessly, telling them everything on his mind.

'Now ask me questions,' he said.

No one spoke.

'Hey, Pilla! Ask me about something,' said Jagannatha.

He thought, if someone were to see me now, see the way I'm trying to be familiar with these Holeyaru, I'd be most embarrassed, as if I'm doing something deceitful and stealthy.

Pilla scratched his head shyly.

'My father said he has to get me a Holathi. He has to pay fifty rupees as bride-money. He asked me to ask you for it.'

'And who's this Holathi?' asked Jagannatha, teasing Pilla to make them laugh.

Another Holeya explained, laughing, 'She's the bride for Pilla, Odeya. Don't you know his father will have to pay bride-money for her? She'll come here and work for you to pay back the debt.'

A Holathi for Pilla. Who could she be? How is she to look at? Did Pilla love her? He knew that when they came of age, the Holeyara boys pestered their parents to get them married. Jagannatha had gathered this from the stories of joy and sorrow he had heard the elderly Holathiyaru tell Chikki.

'Go and see the accountant tomorrow; I'll tell him about it. So, when's the wedding?' he said.

'In another two months,' said the others. Pilla was beaming; he could not believe he had got the bride-money so easily. That was because Jagannatha had not hassled him as Amma or Chikki would have done. But Jagannatha felt these men may not understand him even though he had come to Pilla's help so easily; perhaps they might distance themselves from him even more.

After the Holeyaru left, Jagannatha thought of a trick; I must get them also to wear a white shirt and a white dhothi like me. Then they might feel they can touch me. Jagannatha was excited with the idea: tomorrow, I'll get short dhothis from Rayaru's store for all the ten of them, and readymade white short-sleeved shirts from Shyam's store.

He got up to go in. Kaveri walked into the yard, carrying firewood and driving the cattle towards the shed. She gave him a sidelong glance and smiled shyly. With a torch in hand, Janardhana Shetty followed her; he might have asked her to walk this way in front of him. He came up excitedly to talk to Jagannatha. He must have read the paper. Trying to act familiar, he said, 'Why do you want to have anything to do with these Holeyaru, Saar?' Jagannatha was furious with his impudence.

'How's the work going?' he said authoritatively, and went in without waiting for a reply.

A servant was in the hall, lighting the gas lamps. Jagannatha told Chikki he was not hungry for dinner as lunch had been late. He went up and lay on the bed, trying to read the book at hand. He felt he should visit Puranik more often. But, then, that too would be a waste of time. Kaveri hung around outside his room under the pretext of folding the clothes she had brought in. She noticed that his table lamp was not bright enough for reading and got a gaslight from downstairs and placed it on the table. Jagannatha, breathing heavily, tried to read on, ignoring her. He felt he was detaching himself from life even in this way; he must write to Margaret.

He was glad when Kaveri left.

The next morning, as soon as he was up, Jagannatha went out and bought ten pairs of short white khadi dhothis from Rao's store and ten pairs of white short-sleeved shirts from Shyam's store and brought them home. Shanbogh Shastri, who was waiting for his return, came into his room, ledger in hand. Ever since he had hired Rao's son, Jagannatha had sensed displeasure in Shastri and so he asked him gently, 'What is it?'

'Krishnaiah's son, Gopala, wants to come home from Mysore for the Chariot Festival and has asked for a hundred rupees. Should I send it to him?'

Jagannatha was furious. Gopala was being brought up as a son of the family since his father's death. How petty of Shastri to ask for his permission to send him the money.

'Do you need to ask me? Send it to him,' he said.

'It's not that. We had sent him a hundred and fifty rupees barely a fortnight ago. That's why I asked if we should send him money again,' replied Shastri, ingratiatingly.

'Doesn't matter, send it,' said Jagannatha, taking up the book he had been reading.

The bus brought the day's mail. Among the letters addressed to him, Jagannatha noticed one from Margaret and he tore it open eagerly. She had scribbled a short, loving letter in a hurry. *You're an unreliable rascal; why haven't you written for so long; the election fever is on in England; I feel the Labour Party shouldn't win, they've cheated the coloured people; the English have no real choice between the two parties. See what a farce democracy has become; Wilson and Heath are really Tweedledum and Tweedledee.* She had scribbled on and then had said she would like to visit India. *I hear there's an International School near Bangalore run on the lines of J. Krishnamurthy's*[69] *philosophy. I could teach English and history there; I've written to the principal about it. Father knows him. Do find out from him and let me know.* She had ended the letter lovingly. *I need you in the cold; I remember the warmth of your body...* She had raked up memories, intimate to both of them. *How many women are you trying to tempt with your expressive eyes? Be careful!* She had teased him.

Jagannatha replied to her immediately. He felt all his burdens become lighter as he wrote about his plan of action to her. *I'll go to Bangalore in a week and fix things for you*; he wrote and mailed the letter himself. And then he sat down to write the history of revolutions in simple Kannada for the Holeyaru.

By lunchtime, Chikki might have been disappointed that there was no one else for lunch except the household staff. Ganapathi Bhatta, the priest of the household, would not even glance at Jagannatha before eating because he would not perform any of the mealtime rituals, like circling his banana leaf with a dribble of water, setting aside a morsel as offering to the gods, and the ritual sipping of a spoonful of water before and after meals. While eating, Bhatta would lean his left hand on the floor, he would lift his glass and pour water into his mouth, and drink it in great noisy gulps—gluck, gluck—he would close his eyes to savour his food. And there were the two sons of the cook, with their

[69] Jiddu Krishnamurthy (1895–1986), philosopher and writer who believed that each can solve his or her problems by a process of self-understanding that goes beyond intellectual speculation, adherence to a belief, or learning from a guru.

hair shorn like a half-moon in the front, thick long hair at the back. They would not talk while eating as they had recently been initiated into religious life with the sacred-thread ceremony. The one who served the food would try to tease them out of their vow of silence with, 'Would you like more curry? Would you like some buttermilk? Why, don't you like it?' And there was a boy of around five who had not yet had the sacred-thread ceremony. This child was so petrified that he would not even talk if his father was anywhere around. Jagannatha knew these children were growing up timid and self-conscious only because they were growing up in a wealthy landlord's house. But he could do nothing about it.

As he was going up to his room after his meal, Chikki came by. Jagannatha was upset to see her. Her face was so sad it seemed capable of breaking the strength of his resolve. To make her happy, he said, 'Gopala has written to say he'll be here for the festival,' and went up the stairs even as Rao came bustling in with the paper in his hand.

'Jagannatha, you've become news!' he cried, handing over a copy of the daily newspaper from Shimoga, *Jagruthi*. Jagannatha was amused to think how important the news must be if Rao, a politician by instinct, could be excited about it. *Jagruthi* had highlighted his wealth while praising his revolutionary concerns. 'The editor has already changed parties some three or four times,' said Rao. 'Tomorrow, there'll be letters to the editor in the Bangalore edition too,' he added enthusiastically and sat down to read the paper.

Jagannatha noticed how greatly Rao was concerned about him even though he did not think much of his plan of action. But, then, we love those whom we change, don't we? Rao loved this young man since he had been responsible for the change in him. That was the reason why Jagannatha loved Margaret even to this day, because he was responsible for the change in her. Only that which we change becomes truly ours.

He was not a politician by nature like Rao. Even Rao knew this. That was why he had asked him not to get involved in politics.

Rao sat quietly for a long time. Jagannatha kept writing. He was grateful he could sit with Rao without having to say anything to him; they were content to be together. This kind of a relationship was possible with only a few people. Sometimes, it was not possible with Margaret; they had to be teasing or petting each other.

Prabhu came after Rao left. He sat down and lit a Passing Show cigarette. 'You have to stand for elections the next time; you must not give up the seat to the Vokkaliga community,' he said. Jagannatha yawned to show there was no need for any talk. Prabhu asked Chikki, who had come up with some coffee for them, 'I hear you wanted some rope. How thick do you want it? I'll get it for you from Shimoga.' He waited until he felt Jagannatha would be more responsive and then he said, 'You and I could go and see the minister in Bangalore, Maharayare. We could submit a request to electrify the town.' He stood up to go saying, 'It's nice of you to fight for the welfare of the Holeyaru, but do you think they'll be grateful to you for it? Tomorrow, it's quite likely they'll vote only for the party in power.' And before leaving, 'It's good to be talking to scholars like you, Maharayare. The next time, I'll bring my son along. Tell me if he should become an engineer or prepare for the Civil Service exams.' He brought his palms together to bid goodbye. Jagannatha started writing again. He wanted to write down his thoughts. He took out a fresh notebook and began writing:

Right from the beginning, I've never thought about human limits; human possibilities have been my only concern. Ideas come in spurts. I'm dissatisfied with reality. That has been my problem: whether I was with Margaret or Peter, Tom or Reubens, sunbathing in Hyde Park or sipping beer at the Union Bar, I've played ball games with great ease with a lot of ideas. For a long time, I was under the illusion that I was totally free just because I could discuss anything with my friends. But slowly those days became a farce, those days when I could hold any idea I pleased, sway unfettered whichever way I wanted, my face flushed with excitement. Our ideas have to grapple with reality to be gauged for their worth. Now, my ideas will be useful only in as much as they can prepare these few Holeyaru to stand up for themselves, that's all. My very selfhood needs to take this test.

I could delude myself that the ideas I may be able to hold among the people of my class or with Margaret are real. But since the moment I felt the slavery of the Holeyaru diminished my humanity, I've begun to search for freedom in the truest sense.

Gandhi is more real than the free-thinker M.N. Roy though Gandhi is still kicking in the womb of God. It would be more worthwhile for me to wrestle with a rascal like Prabhu who manipulates the situation here for his benefit than to toss ideas back and forth in a discussion with Puranik.

Take, for instance, Dikshith of the Communist Party. Once when I was talking to him in Bangalore, I was quite irritated. Smoking a Charminar, he argued in English. He can't talk fluently in any Indian language, yet he thinks Gandhi's just a fraud. This man in a torn shirt and a baggy pair of trousers is so lost in his ideas, he's not even aware of himself. I said to him: You don't know these people at all; Gandhi knew this land. The rod we need to churn the environment with has to be tough. It will not do for an intellectual to be like an aerial catching sound waves; he has to be grounded in his environment, possessing its ruggedness. Only a man who is aware of the attraction Hinduism has for him can think any worthwhile thoughts here.

He laughed. You're right, he said, but first we'll have to change the economic situation.

Isn't there a connection between a devotee of Kali in Bengal and a militant Communist? I argued this way with him for a long time. But he merely shook my hand and said, as he walked away, right now my problem is the decision about wages.

There's no point in me trying to emancipate myself alone; hence this struggle. I could end up like Adiga, deluded that I'm detached from everything; I could convert my room upstairs into a bit of England like Puranik; I could become a realist trying to bloom as much as my petals will let me. But then, aren't there musicians who can always make any moment blossom amazingly? Why do we need to struggle for transformation? Change is an intrusive act that abrades to ignite. The way a flower rejoices in what dew may fall on it and glistens in what sunlight it gets is different. But how can I forget the way Nagamani put out her life?

And it's not as if I haven't known that sense of exhilaration while lying naked with Margaret on chilly nights; it was as leisurely as an alaapana, *the slow elaboration of the opening movement in music, it was the mystery of an exploding invitation of a whorl of clasping petals of a conch drawing me in, it was the lightness of a delicate red rose firm on a stalk, a rose that played hide and seek, weaving warmth with warmth as Margaret pressed further, her breath on my neck, a moment of slow release as I pushed away her hair from her face, not scared, not anxious. Neither covetous, nor hasty, it was like alaapana, now rising, now falling, now withholding, now releasing, it was the joy of stretching the moment for as long as we needed, a coitus in which we could prolong our pleasure by putting off the peaking moment. Such occasions were rare.*

But why did Margaret reject me even then? And why did I find her inadequate? Why do I want to feel real through these Holeyaru who neither sow nor grow anything on this soil, but are born here to wither away? Why was I dissatisfied with both Adiga's spirituality and my sexual intimacy with Margaret?

He read what he had written; he was not satisfied. Probably, he could have written the same thing some six months earlier. *I'm unable to draw out my innermost thoughts and see them. I'm still an idealist playing the same game; looking at myself in a mirror, one moment I'm euphoric and the next, depressed.*

Jagannatha felt he needed a walk before the Holeyaru arrived and so he went towards the farm. These days he could only fake an interest in the estate. Otherwise, he would become a farce in the environment. And so he went about pretending a concern, 'How're you, Sheenappa?' 'How're things, Shettare?' But their attitude to him had changed ever since they had heard the news. He had noticed that they were uncomfortable about their landlord mingling with the Holeyaru. They would have been quite happy to have him lording it over them so they could grovel under him. Then they could value his acts of kindness in as much as he was heartless. He could become a new person to them only through the change he wrought in them. Or else, they would be waiting for him to conform to the standard image of a turbaned landlord with a walrus moustache.

He stood under a mango tree. The trees were full of blossoms this season; Chikki must have planned to make enough mango pickle to last the next two years. Perhaps that was why she had asked Shastri the previous day to get her six large glass jars from Shimoga. Ants were crawling on the bark; big red ones that the Holeyaru fry and eat. They heat water in their backyards at night and have their bath; they have a hundred secret byways to happiness.

But my search is different. Tense and weary, he returned to the backyard.

He could see the Holeyaru coming in the distance, walking as if they were coming to work; they did not seem to be eager at all. Pilla may not know how good-looking he is. Jagannatha decided he would not talk about his project. 'Wait, I'm coming,' he said, and went up to his room and got the shirts and the dhothis. He also brought cakes of soap to wash the clothes. There were six that evening. He did not like to force them to come regularly; he gave each of them a shirt, a dhothi, and a cake of soap. The clothes were just like the ones he was wearing; shirts with a pocket, collar, and short sleeves, and dhothis with borders. In them, the Holeyaru had to look like men of his class.

'Come on, put on the clothes. Let's see how you look,' he said.

On some, the shirts were a bit too tight, on some others, they were baggy. They hesitated when he said, 'Okay now, tie the dhothi.' They tied it on only after much persuasion. In all their lives, they may never have worn a dhothi below the knees. Feeling awkward, they took them off. They folded their clothes and tucked them under the arm. Jagannatha said to Pilla, 'Come at the same time tomorrow. Have a bath after work, put on these clothes, and come. Don't feel shy. Ask the others to come. I've got clothes for them too.'

Pilla stood scratching his head. Then Jagannatha remembered. 'Is it okay if you get the money before the wedding? Anyway, there're two months to go. What's the hurry now?' he said. He gave them some tobacco to chew and sent them home.

The next day, Sripathi Rao brought the dailies published in Bangalore. He read aloud all the letters concerning Jagannatha printed in the readers' column. But Jagannatha was not interested in either the praise or the censure; he had not yet been successful in opening his mind to the Holeyaru. One of the letters condemning him said: 'This insistence on deliberately hurting the sentiments of the upper class through the entry of the Harijans into the temple is far from Gandhiji's philosophy ....' Another had argued in bombastic words about the difference between a devotee of God expressing his love for the Harijans by wanting to bring them into the temple and an atheist influenced by Western ideas wanting to destroy Hinduism. Dikshith of the Communist Party had said: 'It is certain that the proposed action will be futile as it has risen out of the idealism of a person belonging to the landed gentry; caste distinctions can be destroyed only through an economic revolution.' However, he had given a statement that he would support Jagannatha. Magadi Ananthakrishna, an organizer of the Sarvodaya Movement, had appealed to everyone to support Jagannatha in a venture dear to Gandhiji and Acharya Vinobhaji.[70] He had stressed

[70] A disciple of Gandhi, founder of *Sarvodaya* and *Bhoodan* (gift of land by landowners) movements.

the need for non-violence. He had persuasively argued that the entry of the Holeyaru into the temple would enhance the glory of Manjunatha.

'Do you know who this Ananthakrishna is, Jaganna?' asked Sripathi Rao, eager to narrate the story. He was one of Rao's companions during the freedom struggle, a great orator. He was disgusted with the caste prejudices of the Congress leaders of Chitradurga. He could not get a Congress ticket to stand for election to the Legislative Assembly. He had sacrificed his life in response to Jayaprakash Narayan's[71] call; an intelligent, friendly person; an idealist who had left home to join the struggle. Though he loved the good things of life, he was a decent man.

'He used to drink; perhaps he has given up now. Do you know how many tricks he tries, like me, to keep away from his wife?' Rao was beginning to open up. 'Very clever, he was very clever. I can still remember the speeches he had made during the Quit India Movement. He could've lived very comfortably. But he lost everything in the struggle. And then he got entangled in the internal politics of the Party and became corrupt. He lost his class. Disgusted, he joined the Sarvodaya movement. He's also a dreamer, do you know? I love these people, Jaganna, however bad they are.'

Rao's eyes were glistening with the warmth of his affection. Jagannatha felt a deep respect for Rao; the man could think so maturely about certain things. After he left, Jagannatha sat down to write in a fresh notebook. He was irritated with the sounds of the chanting and the rattle from downstairs; they signalled the midday worship to the household god, the saligrama, the black stone of Narasimha. Even as the worship was over, there was the gong from the temple announcing the final worship for the day to Manjunatha. Jagannatha felt he had become a ghost in his own town. He wrote: *God is worshipped even in my home. He is omnipresent; I can't grasp him with my fist. The crown of my childhood is on His head. How many days I've worshipped Him with Amma and come out of the temple and sat on the steps with her, feeling so serene! Monkeys would come and snatch away the prasada of bananas from my hands. Time moves drowsily here, worshipping God for various festivals*—Balipadya, Akshathadige,

[71] A Sarvodaya leader, a follower of Gandhi; one of the founders of the Congress Socialist Party in 1934.

Ganeshachowthi, Utthaanadwadashi, Mahalaya Amavasye—*ringing bells both big and small, and going through the endless cycle of life, mating, death. I trust the Holeyaru will shake it awake. But they creep like shadows. Since they have no personality, I remain a spectre.*

He came out in the evening and waited on the porch. Chikki was standing in the yard seeing the cattle into the shed. Jagannatha knew that she had been eating only one meal a day ever since he had talked about his plan. He found her cold war intolerable but there was no way he could get her on his side by talking to her about his plan. Silence was her weapon. He was angry with her. He felt her silence was the essence of the sterility of their lives.

Only when the Holeyaru came closer did Jagannatha realize that they had not lifted up the lower edge of the dhothi and tied it round the waist to leave their legs free; they had torn them lengthwise and worn half a strip each. The others who had not come the previous day had come wearing just a loincloth, eager to get their sets of new clothes. Jagannatha swallowed his anger. They looked ridiculous; feeling awkward about wearing something they were not used to, they had folded back the collars and mismatched the buttons with the button-holes. They stood like apparitions, in dread and embarrassment at wearing new clothes of this sort.

'What did you do with the dhothis?' asked Jagannatha, glaring at Pilla. He felt like laughing at their reply. They had to share the new clothes with father, uncle, elder brother, younger brother, even a visiting relative. So they had to tear the dhothis into strips to make enough loincloths to go around. They had no other choice as the elders had decided they could do with half a dhothi each.

'Give away even these half dhothis as loincloths. I'll get you new ones. You have to wear them whole. You'll have to walk in the market too, like me, without feeling awkward. You'll be coming to Manjunatha's temple with me. You're the new generation who'll have to awaken the rest of the Holeyaru from superstition.'

They stared at him perplexed; they had not understood many of the words he had used. Jagannatha felt embarrassed. Feeling useless and disgusted, he went into the house. He had to become more substantial, but how? He spent the night wondering. All he could do seemed to be to plough, sow, and wait for the rain. He woke up the next morning in a daze of disappointment and went for a stroll around the cashew grove. When he returned he felt he could hear Chikki's sighs all over the house.

Without realizing it, Chikki was hurting him, with the way she looked at him while giving him coffee, with her unkempt hair, with her face looking drawn with fasting, and more than all, with the silent suffering with which she searched his eyes during lunchtime in the empty dining room.

Sripathi came in with the afternoon post. Even though he did not support Jagannatha's plan wholeheartedly, he seemed to be quite excited with the response it was eliciting; sometimes, Jagannatha lost a little respect for him.

'Jaganna, did you notice? Gurappa Gowda hasn't issued any statement. Scoundrel! He can't say the Harijans shouldn't enter the temple. He's a Congressman, isn't he? And he can't say they can enter for then, he'll lose the votes of the upper castes. Whatever you say, Jaganna, the only people getting ready for a fundamental change in this country are the Brahmins, not the Shudras. That's because they're benefiting enough from the present arrangement; the Gowdas and the Lingayats[72] are getting most of the jobs in the government. It was the same in those days too, when the British were here; all these were in the Justice Party. And the funny part is that the Shudras are becoming neo-Brahmins.

'I believe, once the revenue minister, Bishte Gowda, had been to Gurappa Gowda's house for lunch. Gurappa served him biryani. Bishte Gowda ate the biryani. And then came the curd and rice. Now, isn't curd-rice a typical Brahmin dish? I believe the Shudra, Bishte Gowda, rinsed out the biryani from his mouth and then ate the Brahmin curd and rice. It didn't matter to him that both the courses would become one in his belly; he didn't want the Shudra dish and the Brahmin dish to become one in his mouth. That's the kind of people they are ...'

Rayaru had started to say something and had ended up saying something else. His awareness of the reality of the situation had made him a cynic; Jagannatha was upset. Instead of being upset that a Shudra was behaving in this way, Rayaru was gloating over his weakness.

[72] A community of Shiva worshippers, followers of Basavanna. They also call themselves Veerashaivas.

Jagannatha was sad about the snobbish mentality of the Brahmin that made him an outsider. To change the topic, he said, 'Rayare, what's in the paper?'

Rayaru opened the paper and read that Neelakantaswami of the Mysore Socialist Party would participate in the protest. 'Don't trust him, Jaganna,' he warned, 'This fellow protested against the Socialist Party because the secretary was a Brahmin and now he has set up his own party, the MSP or the Mysore Socialist Party. He's a Lingayat. You can't say when he'll join the Congress. There's another fellow with him, a man called Ranga Rao. The name sounds Brahmin but he's actually a Gowda. I hear he can't stand Brahmins. Our Sarvodaya Ananthakrishna knows all of them. By the way, he's written a letter too; he promises support. On the whole, you've provided a platform with an issue for these lazy politicians.' Rayaru laughed. But Jagannatha was worried that his serious intent would get watered down; his next struggle would be to find a way to preserve the sanctity of his action.

Feeling he should not get too upset about these things, he waited for the Holeyaru. The ten young men came in the evening, dour-faced, wearing their clothes like Jagannatha wore his, walking awkwardly. They would not sit on the mud floor in the yard for fear of dirtying their clothes; they did not have the courage to climb the few steps to sit on the cemented floor of the porch. They stood in the yard carrying their burden of guilt; it was impossible for Jagannatha to talk to them or to teach them. He paced about saying something to them; they stood staring at him without understanding a word of what he had said. He explained to them about an incident in a village in Mandya. 'Look, that Holeya made a mistake that anyone else could've made. But it seemed shocking to the upper-caste Hindus only because a Holeya had committed it. They tied him to a tree and chopped off his fingers. You're the majority in this country. If you stand up for yourselves, everything can change. So, you must come with me into the temple of Manjunatha, who's known throughout the country as a merciful god. We don't see you yet as human; to us, you're even worse than sheep and oxen. Therefore, if you can get angry, you'll begin to appear as human beings to us.'

It did not seem as if they had understood him, however simply he had put his ideas across. Looking at them as they stood there, as if they were not there, as if they did not deserve to be there, as if they were scared to be seen in such white clothes, Jagannatha could see clearly the harsh truths he and the Holeyaru would have to face. Suddenly he had an idea. His project would not materialize without a measure of cruelty; these men would not wake from their stupor without being assaulted. But could he, a humane liberal, mount such an assault against them?

After he had sent the Holeyaru away, Jagannatha went up to his room and stretched out on his bed. Looking out of the window at the fading trees on the hilltops, he felt disgusted with his own weakness. Why can't I peel away the scales and see the inside and outside more clearly? He felt like writing and so he took out a notebook and sat at the table and wrote:

I may wish to touch the Holeyaru with my lofty sense of idealism. But they may want to touch me out of envy. Then, I should not be afraid to arouse feelings of jealousy and greed in them. Doesn't Engels say that the reason for the march of history is the evil passions of men? If it is necessary for me to be cruel to abort our lives in the womb of Manjunatha, I should be prepared for it. Until the Holeyaru lose their innocence, this revolution cannot take off. And for them to lose their innocence, probably they need jealousy, greed, anger.

The Holeyaru should desire all that we desire. A Holeya youth should desire a Brahmin girl. A Brahmin girl should want to sleep with a Holeya. Without desire they will not become educated. From desire will rise pain and from pain, awareness. Right now, they are only spectres, shadows that are not expected to cross our path. Even Shankara, who said Man is a manifestation of the Divine, did not condemn untouchability. The reason? The Holeyaru did not stretch out their hands, they did not simmer with desire, did not boil over and become human beings.

They have no right to a good name, no right to wear such white clothes, no right to do any wrong. There's only one way they can get out of their wretched state in this country, and that's through bhakti. In this land of the lowly, they have the right only to be the lowliest. In this contest to be the lowliest, they have the right to become Alwars.

What a fraud this country has perpetuated by allowing only an ascetic the right to break social conventions! The Holeya has greater power than the Brahmin to humble himself before God. We're the crafty people who have made the Holeyaru believe that by carrying shit on their heads in this life, they'll earn the merit to be born as tulsi leaves at the feet of God in the next. Our society has lost the very significance of daily living by saying things like, 'only through sacrifice', 'only through humility', 'only by renouncing pride'.

Perhaps even the revolutionary who's fighting for some fruition in daily life may have to distance himself from it. This much is true: There has to be a birth of desire in the Holeyaru, a birth of jealousy. Perhaps only then will the foetus develop eyes, ears, nose, nails.

He had some buttermilk and rice, walked about in the yard for a while, and went back to his room. While reading Yeats' 'Easter 1916', his eyes grew heavy. He turned down the lamp and went to sleep, watching through the window, the glow-worms twinkling in the bamboo grove.

FOURTEEN

Saligrama

The next morning, Jagannatha woke up in high spirits. He washed his face, had his coffee, and went for a stroll in the cashew grove. The tender sunlight looked lovely, glistening on the damp cobwebs and the dew on the green grass. The gopura of the temple glinted like a jewel. He remembered every detail from Margaret's letter. He realized how necessary celebration was to his very nature but was not upset about it. It can't be helped; that's the way I am, he thought, and looked around for kakay trees. As a child, he used to be very fond of the kakay and hibiscus berries of this hill.

He felt he had intuitively come to some decision but he was not quite clear what it was. He sat writing for a while after breakfast and then took a walk towards the market. He was not uncomfortable that the people on the street were looking at him with hate or fear. He stopped to speak warmly to Venkatakrishnaraya. As usual, his hair was unkempt and his forehead, smeared with sacred ash. This man was known to get up at four every morning, have a bath in cold water, pray for two hours, then wash his cattle, smear their forehead with kumkuma, worship them, give them their morning feed, milk them, and then go to the Manjunatha temple to chant till noon with his eyes closed. At least twice a week, he would stand under a peepul tree and look out for an eagle, the Garuda; he would not have his lunch until he saw one. If anyone asked him why he followed the rituals so diligently, he would reply in all seriousness, 'I hope I'll be born in America at least in my next birth.'

Jagannatha said to him, 'How is it you're home today?'

'My wife is having her periods,[73]' he said, 'and so I'm cooking.'

Perhaps he hated Jagannatha but he would not show it.

Jagannatha met Vasu in the town square. Deeply concerned, Vasu began to advise him. 'Why do you want to mingle with the Holeyaru and incur the wrath of the town?' but, suddenly, he became deferential, using the plural, *neevu*, for *you*, 'You people are educated. You are also rich. You can somehow survive. As for me, my plan to open a store is floundering; I may have to come to you for a loan,' he said and walked away. Jagannatha did not have the courage to drop in at Nagaraja Jois' place. The home of the bereaved looked desolate.

And then he saw Sripathi Rao writing out an application for someone. Poor man, it was his plight to render free service.

Jagannatha thought he should give the Chivas Regal whisky he had brought from England to Puranik. It would have been nice if he had known Puranik's birthday.

He met Ganesha, the son of the chief priest, carrying a bottle of medicine. He felt the boy's face looked strange. His body was that of a stripling but his face with its sunken eyes looked old. His mouth looked as if it were sealed. He was staring at him and so Jagannatha smiled. He was surprised to see Ganesha stopping as if he wished to talk to him. He stopped too. It was painful to see Ganesha stammering desperately, trying to say something, but Jagannatha did not show his distress. He waited for him to say whatever it was as if that was the most natural thing to do. Contorting his face, Ganesha struggled to say,

[73] A woman is considered unclean during this time; she cannot do her household duties and has to stay apart from the family.

'Do you have any of Sharatchandra's[74] novels?' Jagannatha was amazed to find him so outgoing. 'I do. Come home any time,' he said warmly and walked on so as not to embarrass him any further.

Lunch at home was as usual, with the family priest and the cook's sons. He tried to talk to Chikki but failed. He rinsed his hands clean and was going upstairs when he stopped for a moment in front of the prayer room; it was fragrant after the puja with fresh flowers and tulsi leaves. His decision grew firmer but he did not want to think it through right then; he thought it better to sleep for about half an hour. He stretched out and closed his eyes. He tried to still his turbulent mind; he needed to conserve his intensity and his energy for the evening. He let his mind wander and laughed to himself. Once, during a dance session arranged by some West Indians, Margaret had dragged him to the dance floor as soon as the music had started just to loosen him up. But he could not move his feet to the rhythm and he was perspiring. How stupid he had felt! How Margaret had laughed at him! 'Jagan, relax,' she had said, as she tried her best to ease his tense body to sway to the beats and failed. Among the blacks dancing in total abandon, he had stood like an idiot with his arm round her waist. Margaret had been angry. 'You don't know the joy of life in dance and music, you fool!' she had said. He had not been able to relax completely even after a few pegs.

Jagannatha sat up suddenly. He took out the bottle of Chivas Regal from the trunk, wrapped it in some paper, and combed his hair. He took the car out of the garage and drove towards Puranik's house. It was a long, circuitous route by car and the road was bad, full of potholes. At last he reached Puranik's place, which was like an island, parked the car, took the bottle of whisky, and rang the bell. The Gurkha arrived after he had rung twice, saluted him, and, seating him in the foyer, handed him a slip of paper on which to write his name, put it on a tray, and took it upstairs. Puranik came down in an old but smart, silk dressing gown and a pair of slippers. He shook hands with Jagannatha and said, 'Sorry, I'm not dressed.'

[74] Sharatchandra Chattopadhyay (1876–1938), most popular Bengali novelist. He represented rural Bengali society and wrote against superstition and social oppression.

'That's all right. I should apologize for visiting you unexpectedly,' said Jagannatha.

'Not at all. You must feel free to drop in at any time,' said Puranik, taking him upstairs.

Jagannatha noticed Puranik's graciousness in welcoming him without asking him why he had come.

'I'm busy, I should be going. I thought I'd see you for five minutes,' said Jagannatha shyly as he handed over the whisky.

'No, you mustn't give this to me. This is liquid velvet,' said Puranik, while taking the bottle with great excitement and thanking him. 'Come, let's celebrate. I'll fix you a drink,' he added.

'Sorry, but I've just had my lunch.'

'Then, some liqueur is the right thing for you,' said Puranik persuasively, while pouring out some into a long-stemmed glass and handing it to him. He poured out some for himself too and said, 'Cheers!'

Puranik started talking, 'The Labour Party appears to be winning the election this time too. The prediction of *The Daily Herald* failed.' A faded photograph on the radio caught Jagannatha's eye. He had not noticed it the previous time. He went up to it and, staring at it with interest, said, 'If Labour comes to power, they'll act like the Conservative Party. But if the Conservatives come to power, they follow the Leftist policy in many areas. British politics is strange.' Puranik noticed Jagannatha staring at the photo and said, 'That was taken many decades ago, when I got married.'

It was a curious photo. Puranik's wife was standing beside him. He was in a turban, coat, and kachche panche. His wife had wrapped the sari round her shoulders and parted her hair in the middle, knotting it up at the back. She was leaning against him and smiling at him, with face upturned. Jagannatha was attracted to the large lapels on his three-button coat, which he had buttoned down fully. Above all, the one detail that seemed to distil the essence of this revolutionary wedding was the absence of the garlands and crowns that usually adorned bridal couples in photographs; both groom and bride were holding books and prominently, against the chest, as in pictures taken on graduation day. The expression in their eyes seemed to say they felt different and distinct in posing this way with books. Below the picture were their names and a legend to say this was taken on the occasion of the remarriage of a virgin child-widow. While Jagannatha stood mesmerized, taking in every detail in the picture, Puranik said, 'Have you succeeded in shocking the medieval citizens of our town?'

Jagannatha smiled. 'Well, at least an attempt is being made,' he said. He put down his glass and, shaking Puranik's hand, said, 'I'll come again. I should be going now. Sorry.'

'Thanks for the wonderful whisky. Nothing could've pleased me more,' said Puranik, picking up his pipe. He walked Jagannatha to the gate and saw him off saying, 'Come again.'

Jagannatha felt elated as he returned home. But, by the evening, he began to feel a little nervous. He wondered why he had suddenly gone to see Puranik; he was a little surprised at his own behaviour.

Jagannatha saw the Holeyaru standing a little beyond the yard; he had been waiting for them eagerly, but also with some anxiety. He felt a little weak in the legs as he came down the stairs. His palms were damp. They're standing beyond the yard; they're standing there hoping for nothing, he said to himself as he came out to the veranda. 'Wait, I'll be back,' he said to them and went in again. They listen to everything like morons; now they stand in their dhothis looking like criminals. Jagannatha was troubled. Perhaps they should feel they have been whipped. Then they might wake up. They might fall into this world of deceit, fraud, greed, and may stretch out their hands. They might yearn, they may learn.

His resolve hardened. Jagannatha stood at the door of the puja room.

Brass lamps were shining in the dark room, a casket held the saligrama of the household deity, Narasimha. People believed that if it was polluted in any way, a black cobra would enter the house, a fire would burn down the farm. It was supposed to be a thousand years old. For generations now, the members of the family had eaten their meals only after drinking holy water sanctified by being poured over the stone.

After another ritual bath, the family priest came and topped up the oil in the lamp in the puja room. Jagannatha felt this lamp that burned day and night also had a smell of its own. There was also the aroma of sandal paste, the stale yet sweet fragrance of wilted tulsi leaves, conch flowers, roses, red sampige mingling with the smell of scented sticks.

He saw the tongue of flame that had burnt continuously, from wick to wick; the caste-thread ceremony was done before this wick and the wedding ceremony was conducted in front of the fire lit from this flame. Chikki says this fire could have been burning for a thousand years, like an eternal light.

Sometimes, Jagannatha was amused by this idea of eternity. A little of today's curd is added to a bowl of milk to make the curd for tomorrow and that is how curd is set day after day for a whole year; Chikki makes fresh curd once a year by adding Swathi rainwater to milk. But this lamp has been burning for some hundreds of years, providing fire for the home. After all, this lamp was being maintained by a salaried priest of the family. Was it not possible that the lamp had run out of oil because the priest had forgotten to top it up? Could he not have struck a match quickly and re-lit the lamp? Anyway, that was the belief; it was the family lamp lit by the forefathers and burning for a thousand years.

Should he go into the room and bring out the saligrama right then, in the presence of the priest? Could he go in with his shirt on, thus polluting the prayer room? Should he bring it out together with the casket? Jagannatha's heart began to pound. His feet were perspiring. He felt there was no turning back now, and so he went in. The priest was horrified to see the master polluting the room with the way he had entered it.

Jagannatha had to pretend that he was not doing anything unusual. And yet, the shock on the priest's face made him put out his hand as if to protect himself. Though no one was holding him, Jagannatha held his breath and pushed forward as if his whole family was pulling him back as he lifted the saligrama together with the casket. Though he knew that the pressure he was feeling was ridiculous, his eyes were burning, his face was warm. The priest who was standing behind the burning lamp had become a long shadow. Jagannatha tried to smile but his face merely contorted as he looked at the priest who did not know what to do.

Pretending to adjust the wick and trying to smile, he asked, 'Did you want something?'

'Nothing,' Jagannatha said softly, and then added apologetically, 'Just for five minutes. I'll bring it back.'

Controlling a desire to run out, he walked out of the puja room, stooping a little at the door. He walked slowly towards the veranda. Though he knew there was no need to do so, his fist was clutching the casket in a painful grip.

He came down from the porch to the yard. He controlled his desire to look back. And yet he felt that Chikki, the priest, the cook, and their children were at the door, staring at him. He could feel Chikki's eyes boring a hole in his back. He could have freed himself from his anguish by turning around and staring at her, eye to eye, to reject her plea. But he was too terrified to look back. Perhaps he felt it would be too cruel to stare at her in the face and reject her. The hand holding the casket was damp. This saligrama of Narasimha had probably never crossed the threshold. Chikki may be standing there too shocked to speak. She might be drawing him back with her prayer, with all her spiritual strength gathered in her eyes. He wondered why he was still standing there and looked ahead. The Holeyaru who stood beyond the yard, dressed in white, looked like orphans. Their eyes did not look as if they hoped for anything. They were just looking at Chikki standing at the door, and at him. They did not know what would happen next. They were not concerned.

Jagannatha walked slowly. The sun was a red ball of fire on the shoulder of a distant hill. The soft light of the evening lay on the grassy slopes. From the base of the hill, the last bus from Shimoga was slowly climbing up the snaky road, raking dust in its wake. The cattle were meandering their way towards the shed with their cowbells tinkling. Chikki should have been there by the shed watching them. Kaveri came by with a load of firewood, her sari tucked high, and walking quickly because of the weight on her head. She had found these Holeyaru dressed like their master in white shirts and white dhothis ludicrous and she giggled.

Jagannatha suddenly felt the whole situation was absurd: 'To me, this saligrama is merely a ball of stone. And yet, what an intense drama around it! Why do I think it's a momentous experience for the Holeyaru to be able to touch this ball of stone? Is there any connection between the way I'm converting this yard into a magnetic centre with the Holeyaru before me and Chikki behind me, and the person I am, who, after a clear and logical deliberation, has arrived at the scientific conclusion that God does not exist? Jagannatha wondered.

In a flash, Jagannatha saw that he himself was making a ball of stone into the saligrama by wanting to make the Holeyaru touch it. And yet, he stood as if he could not move. Making a great effort, he looked back. The entire household had gathered there with Chikki. In a corner of the veranda, even the farmhands were huddled together. Chikki's mouth might have gone dry or else she would have surely called out to him. She was standing like a mother looking at the body of her son being taken to the cremation ground. He was fully aware of all that she could be thinking about the thousand-year-old saligrama of Narasimha that had never crossed the threshold of the family home. He felt as if her eyes too had bored into him; the ball of stone his fist was gripping burnt like live coal.

Was he doing it for the Holeyaru or for his own self, to reject his Brahminism? Was he becoming an ascetic like Adiga through such a renunciation? He felt confused; Marx and Russell, from whom he had learnt so much, seemed to be evaporating from him.

He tried to clarify his argument to himself once again: 'These Holeyaru who do not hope for anything are standing here like formless ghosts. I can't continue to stand here vacillating. The moment my decision weakens, Chikki's eyes will invade me and conquer me. The person I am at this very moment, holding the saligrama aloft, and the person I could be, retracting my decision in a weak moment, are not two different personalities. Why did the plan to do this enter my head? It's because I want the Holeyaru to touch the deity of my home before they enter Manjunatha's temple in the town. Otherwise, my resolve will not be real, it cannot be firm; the Holeyaru will not forsake the old to receive the new. If I can brace myself for the anguish that is inevitable with this act, I would've learnt the first step towards coping with what I'll have to suffer later to bring about the transformation. This is how I had thought my plan through and my thinking is right. Now, I must take the first step or else Chikki who's standing behind me will win. He turned once again and looked at her reproachfully. The whole house looked ghostly; it had rejected him, casting him off like some shrivelled scrap lying in the yard.

This situation of fear and anxiety might have already instilled panic in the Holeyaru, who stood there like criminals in their white shirts and dhothis. They might turn and leave if he did not step forward to cross the yard and thrust the stone at them. As soon as Jagannatha realized that the situation demanded immediate action, he started walking quickly towards them.

While walking, he thought: 'The most important question is this, why has God possessed me this way? Why has the ball in my hand that I want to establish as a mere stone become the saligrama? Why do I hear bells ringing inside me? I'm walking like a priest performing a strange ritual; I'm making this stone the saligrama with every step I'm taking, while asserting all the while that it's just a stone and not the saligrama. The eyes of the Holeyaru look at me like those of cattle that look up while grazing, expecting nothing. Even they expect nothing. They have no past, no future. The eyes at my back have compassion; they're drawing me to them. Will I turn back now? Or will I change sides and bear fruit in the minds of the Holeyaru? I must see.

He went close to the Holeyaru and stood before them. They moved backwards; their master had come too close to them. As he lifted the lid of the casket, he felt his action was so absurd that if the conch and the temple-gongs were sounded at the moment, it would be a fitting comment on what he was doing. But the grave moment, in which he held the bare black ball of stone in the palm of his hand, stretching it towards the Holeyaru, enveloped him slowly; he was hardly aware of it. The nerves on his neck stood out. He spoke in a deep, trembling whisper.

'Touch it,' he said.

He looked around. The sun was setting. At the door were Chikki and the priest, staring astounded. Janardhana Shetty was also there, in a corner of the yard. Watching from another corner were some farmhands of the Vokkaliga caste, with their knives tucked at the waist. Kaveri stood wiping her face, leaning against the veranda. In front of him stood the Holeyaru, looking like idiots. He trembled. His hair stood on end. Jagannatha spoke to them in a cajoling voice.

'Touch it,' he pleaded.

All that he wanted to say was stuck in his throat: 'This is primary matter, touch it; I hold my life in my hand as I offer this to you, touch it; touch the deepest part of my innermost being; this is the propitious moment of evening worship, touch it. In vain is the eternal flame burning there in the puja room. The people standing behind me are pulling me towards them, reminding me of countless obligations. What are you waiting for? What am I offering you? This is the way it is: only because I offer this to you as a mere stone, it's become the saligrama. If you touch what I offer you, it'll become a mere stone to all of them. My anguish is becoming the saligrama; because I offer it to you and because you touch it and because they see you touching it, let the stone become the saligrama and let the saligrama become a stone, even as the evening deepens. Pilla, you're not scared of the wild hog or even the tiger. Come on, touch it. After this, you'll have just one more step to take, enter the temple. Then, centuries of belief will be turned upside-down. Now, come on, touch this. Touch it now. See how easy it is. Touch it.'

His hand was perspiring. The Holeyaru drew back, stunned. They and those people watching him and the evening had all rejected his anguish. Jagannatha tried to understand the situation with whatever wisdom he could muster. He knew; these men would have seen the practice of suspected thieves being asked to touch a blessed coconut. A plate of reddened rice and, on it, a coconut smeared with kumkuma and with its tuft sticking out, looking like a face. They would have seen people touching it one by one until one man, when his turn came, fainting with his nerves standing out, being unable to breathe. And then Bhootharaya with the singara in his hand, smeared red with kumkuma and trembling in a frenzy coming to punish the guilty one. The same Bhootharaya must have manifested himself to them in that auspicious moment when he offered them the ball of stone.

'This is just a stone. Touch it and see, you'll know. If you behave like this, you'll remain idiots forever.'

He spoke to them gently, the way he did every evening while teaching them to read and write. But who knows what happened to them—all of them stepped back together. Their faces contorted with fear, they struggled, not being able to stand there, not being able to run away. Jagannatha, who had desired this auspicious moment when the Holeyaru would touch the saligrama, suddenly felt a fury rising from within him.

'Come on, touch it,' he said. Seeing their master coming at them, the men retreated stupefied. Jagannatha had become cruel now. The Holeyaru in front of him seemed like worms crawling on their bellies—disgusting.

Gnashing his teeth, he hissed at Pilla, 'Hey, Pilla, touch it! Come on, touch it!'

Pilla stood blinking. Jagannatha felt that all he had told them all these days had been a waste. In a terrible voice, he shouted, 'Touch it! You here, touch it!'

His voice sounded like that of an animal provoked. He was startled to hear his own voice coming out like that. Except for cruelty, all other feelings had left him. He looked more frightening than Bhootharaya.

'Touch it! Touch it! Touch it!' he screamed. Stunned by the pressing, piercing yell, the Holeyaru stepped forward mechanically, made a ritual of touching whatever Jagannatha was holding out to them, and stepped back quickly.

Jagannatha, weakened by cruelty and grief, threw away the saligrama. His anguish that had been firm and upright until now had ended, crushed and contorted. For a moment, he had lost even the basic human concern Chikki had for these people whom she considered untouchable. The Holeyaru had appeared as meaningless things to him. He stood there, head drooping. He did not know that the Holeyaru had left; it was too dark to know that there was no one else around him, anyway. He wandered about feeling disgusted with himself. How we died losing what little humanity we had, the Holeyaru and I, when they touched the stone! Does the fault lie in me? Or, is it outside, in the society we live in? He did not know. He walked for a long time in a daze and went home. Chikki had shut the door of her room. The family priest and the cook had bundled up their belongings, preparing to leave. Shanbogh Shastri, who had been watching everything through the window until now, came forward.

'Shastri,' said Jagannatha calmly, 'these people seem ready to leave. Calculate their dues and pay them. Give them a bonus of a month's salary. They may not be able to get another job in a hurry.' The priest and the cook were looking at him as if he were a lunatic.

'We're going,' they said, pressing their palms together. He realized that now he and Chikki were the only two left in the house, and he felt sad.

As he was leaving, the cook said, 'I've left your breakfast on a plate. It's in your room.' He had done his last duty.

'Okay, you may go,' said Jagannatha and went inside.

FIFTEEN

The International School

'Politics is not enough.'

It looked as if Desai's argument was rising to another level. Jagannatha was waiting for a pause when he could go out and ask Budan to leave the car at a garage to be serviced while he had his lunch; he would be tired after driving all the way from Bharathipura to Bangalore.

'Excuse me,' he said after a while and went out. He gave Budan some money and sent him off. When he returned, Desai seemed to have forgotten him. His intense expression of a moment ago seemed to have waned now. He appeared relaxed, reading something, one leg slung over the other and swinging. The glass windows on every wall let the sunlight into his chambers that looked spacious and welcoming with comfortable sofas, but his mind did not seem to be aware of his surroundings.

His face was not one of those familiar, colourful, well-rounded ones Jagannatha had seen on calendars. It was long with sharp features—clean-shaven with sunken cheeks and a broad brow. Not the wide eyes in the pictures, but small ones with a piercing look. But they were gentle and mild. When he stood up, the man looked stocky and trim, like the owner of a candy-store. Looking at him Jagannatha felt a new awareness of the situation at Bharathipura wash over him; the critical was leaning towards the ludicrous. In 1942 Desai had been a hero of the Quit India Movement. The British government of those days had announced a reward of ten thousand rupees to anyone who would capture him; he had escaped from prison. He had been one of the leaders among the young men in Bombay who had shouted, '*Inquilab Zindabad*'.[75] Now he was the head of an International School.

As soon as Jagannatha entered his room, Desai had shaken his hand warmly. He had spoken as if to an old friend, telling him he had not been keeping well lately. Jagannatha had been able to complete his business with him in five minutes. 'Margaret had written to me too. She can start working here from next June. I knew her father,' Desai had said and had also asked, 'Did you have to come all this way for this?'

Desai's personality exuded a gentle refinement and Jagannatha began to feel comfortable in his presence. He was able to enjoy the flow of conversation without the burden of the situation at Bharathipura weighing him down. Desai sent the peon to get them some tea and said, 'You've been making news, haven't you?'

Jagannatha felt he could tell Desai about his innermost struggles. 'Neither we nor the Holeyaru are really ready for this, Mr Desai. That's why I feel it would be stupid of me to take them into the temple as if to boost my ego. And so I'm wondering if I should drop the whole plan. Perhaps it would be better to wait a bit. Of course, it needs courage to shelve it. I've come away for a day to think about it calmly. What do you think?' But Jagannatha did not say anything. He sat there turning over these thoughts in his mind while listening to Desai. He felt Desai's new dentures could be hurting him, or perhaps he was someone who could be mesmerized by his own words.

Desai stressed each word as if he was pouring his very soul into it. He explained why politics was not enough, narrowing his eyes and looking fixedly at Jagannatha. He spoke English in a typically Victorian

[75] 'Long Live the Revolution!'—a slogan from the days of the Indian freedom struggle.

style, in long tortuous sentences and with a Maharashtrian accent. The truths so close to his heart should have come out in a gentle whisper, not in such rhetoric; Jagannatha felt irritated. He could not pay much attention to what Desai was saying because his choice of language made an intensely personal sharing of experience sound like an oration.

'I had a traumatic experience when India became Independent,' he said and stared at Jagannatha silently. Perhaps he was waiting for the profundity of his statement to sink in. Perhaps he expected Jagannatha to react. But Jagannatha remained aloof, refusing to be drawn to its intensity.

'I was in Paris when India gained Independence,' Desai said, 'I had a strange feeling as I read about the news in the papers, an awareness that this would have happened even if I had not fought in the freedom struggle of 1942, offering my very life for the cause. The awareness that Independence would have come to us anyway made me feel as if a deep trench had opened up in my life; as if I had been living in an illusion. History rolls on even if we're not here. The logic behind its needs and constraints is different. After all, we have just one life to live and it's wrong to peg it down to a single purpose when it is hankering after love and fulfilment. History is impersonal and so ...'

As Desai continued talking, Jagannatha's attention was drawn to his hands that he flourished as if he were making a speech. 'And then I read Aurobindo, and met JK and spent some time with him. The only revolution, the only meaningful revolution ...' When Desai said, *the only revolution*, he stressed each word, as if he was sending it out with the strength of his conviction. 'Look!' he continued, 'You know how it happens? How it takes shape in the stillness of your being? When the breakthrough comes ...' Now he stood up. Even as he was staring at Jagannatha, his eyes filled with tears and his face softened. Jagannatha wondered if Desai needed someone to listen to his story every time he wanted his breakthrough to come alive to him. Perhaps he would live in this room as a ghost if he could not enter this other world of awareness and subdue it again and again by narrating it to someone. Jagannatha wanted to say, 'A politician who always lives in the public eye tries to survive in his shell barely breathing, and yet he imagines even that minimal life to be like basking in a blaze of light; tell me why.'

He wanted to shock him.

Desai might have felt Jagannatha's interest in his fervour slipping; he suddenly looked downcast. Jagannatha thought of his mother. Probably, the breakthrough Desai is talking about is possible only within the warm intimacy of family life, as in a nest. The sense of well-being, selfishness, bestiality, piety, tenderness, and the unexpected joys—everything in it kneads one's life to a fine consistency. A bachelor like Desai could only imagine it, but my mother has withered away like a fragrant flower that surrenders itself to the breeze. Hers was not the sense of achievement that comes with being kindled, burning, and going out.

The peon came in with the tea. With great relish Jagannatha ate the cream-cake baked in the kitchen of the International School. He saw Desai sipping his tea absent-mindedly and tried to change the topic. But somehow he got the feeling that Desai would continue to be this way until he could find another occasion to trigger his enthusiasm.

'One needs to reach a boundless state for such a struggle,' Desai started talking again, 'And you can experience that state of freedom only in the stillness of your being,' he explained. But why is he bellowing out the words? Couldn't Amma have possibly achieved such a state? Appa had managed the estate. Not a playful person, he had been preoccupied with wealth. It was impossible to say if Amma had really loved him. Then, did she ripen and die by merely tending the guests, the home, the cattle, and the garden, her aches and pains, and her singing? Surely, Amma couldn't have been aware of the philosophy Desai is expounding. How difficult it is to say that something so inexplicable is real! Not just to me but to Desai as well, as much as he's trying to explain it to me. Or perhaps he knows, but he's a lost man because he doesn't have the right words to express it.

'Come and see the school,' said Desai, leading him out. There were children from America, England, and Germany. 'We try to bring them up without any kind of conditioning,' he said. The school was set in spacious and pleasant surroundings. Jagannatha saw some Indian and European children playing under a tree.

'What are the fees like?' he asked softly.

Desai looked embarrassed, 'It works out to at least four thousand rupees a year per child. I feel sad we can't provide such education for poor children.' Jagannatha felt Desai's discomfort was genuine. He felt bad that he might have hurt him. He walked eagerly towards the gazebo where an art class was going on. A red-haired American teacher in a sari had raised her hand to slap an Indian child who had accidentally spilt some paint. Seeing someone walking towards her, she said, 'Don't be clumsy, child,' and slid the raised hand quickly to her hip. Desai deliberately ignored it and introduced Jagannatha to her. Jagannatha looked enthusiastically at the pictures the children had painted and walked out.

Desai said he would see him to the gate. They were walking down a tree-lined avenue when Desai started talking again. 'See what we think of sex. When my nephew was going abroad to study I said to him, "You're a young man. What do you think of sex? America is not like India; there's greater sexual freedom there. Not that I'm saying sex is wrong, nor am I saying it's right. There's a problem here, that's all. When you sleep with a woman, both body and mind become tumescent. In the sexual act the body becomes detumescent but not the mind. Man isn't really soothed by sex; that's the problem. That's why you need tenderness. Together with wanting to enjoy sex, you must want the woman also to enjoy it. Look, the problem is to bring the mind to detumescence." This basic problem bothers us more than our political and economic struggles.'

As they had reached the gate, Desai did not know how to end the conversation. He put out his hand.

'Bye,' said Jagannatha.

'Come again,' said Desai. 'Don't ruin your peace of mind over politics. Keep coming here as often as you can. We have a guest-house here. You can spend time with the children,' he added, coming to the point at last. Desai could rise beyond the irony of his situation at least for a few moments. Jagannatha felt a regard for him.

'Could you please give me a lift till Bangalore city?' asked the manager of the school as Jagannatha got into the car. On the way Jagannatha asked him, 'Don't you prepare the children for the Board exams?'

'After spending so much, do you think the parents will keep quiet if we don't?' 'Mr Desai tries very hard to train the children without conditioning them. We can't help but compromise,' replied the manager.

A little beyond ten miles they reached Bangalore. The manager got down saying, 'You must come again. I'll send another letter to Margaret tomorrow.' Jagannatha felt he was just the down-to-earth manager the dreamy Desai needed.

Jagannatha stopped for lunch at a restaurant. He had come to Bangalore thinking the trip might clear his mind. He had not slept the night he had offered the saligrama to the Holeyaru. In the middle of the night he had gone towards their huts to wake them, but had returned, unable to gather enough courage. Was his decision to take the Holeyaru to the temple premature? He had come away to Bangalore to sort it out in his mind. He was ready to drop the plan without a touch of egoism. But he also wondered if that was the right thing to do.

He was a little confused after what Desai had said. He felt his plan could be unrealistic. In all the time he had spent with the Holeyaru all these days, not a moment had been a real experience, either to him or to them. He feared his life would become desiccated with such artificiality.

As soon as he finished lunch, Jagannatha got into the car and said to the driver, 'Budan, let's carry on to Bharathipura. If you get tired, let me know; I can take over for a while.'

Over and over again, Jagannatha had felt he would not be able to come to any decision being in Bangalore. 'I must go home again; I must walk about inside the house where not another soul is stirring. I must see Chikki; she must be weighed down with sorrow. I must face up to the reality of the situation and assess how badly the Holeyaru need my plan of action. Also, I have to be patient. If I feel at any point that whatever I'm doing for them is a cover to satisfy my ego, I should have the courage to withdraw it at that very moment.

'I had a strange feeling while talking to Desai, didn't I? I watched him with amusement but I listened to him with respect. Everything seemed a sham and yet his intensity seemed to disturb me. Was he trying to tell me why it was unnecessary to take the Holeyaru into the temple? I could see holes in his argument as he was struggling to explain the truth behind the recurrence of events in cyclic time.

'Anyway, all this speculation won't help; I'll never know whether I'm right or wrong in what I'm setting out to do. The Holeyaru of

Bharathipura will decide that. As for me, I have to push my plan as far as it can be moved forward; try and be the driving force behind it; wait and see how it works; and if, at any time, I feel it's pretentious, I should withdraw—this is all that I can do.

'If I don't lend myself to a great cause, I'll stay soulless.'

SIXTEEN

The Police Station

By the time Jagannatha reached Bharathipura that night, it was nine o'clock.

There was no one in the house, except Chikki and a farmhand. Seeing Chikki's drawn face, Jagannatha wanted to say, 'I'm not an idiot, Chikki. If I feel my decision to act is premature, I'm willing to scrap the whole project.' He tried to tell her that but couldn't. 'I'm tired. I'll have a bath and come for dinner,' was all he said as he went towards the bathroom. The copper pot over the wood stove was ever ready with hot water and he bathed until sweat poured out of his body.

Chikki served him dinner. He had some rasam and rice and went up to his room. There was the December chill in the air. He sat reading for a while, then turned off the light and lay down. He had no zest for doing something that brought him no joy; the ambience seemed to leave him in a stupor. He relaxed as soon as he had covered himself with his shawl and stretched his legs. He loved the time he spent alone in bed before dozing off because he was too involved with people during the day to make time to be with himself.

He remembered the letters to the editor in the day's paper. He had not found any of them worthwhile, neither the ones that had criticized him nor the ones that had supported him. His mind meandered. Will Margaret like the school? Won't she be very disappointed to see the difference between Desai's vision for the school and the way it is really run? He decided he would write to Margaret about Desai. He remembered his mother, and then the play *Coriolanus* that he had watched at Stratford, and the way he would sit up all night as a young boy watching *yakshagana*[76] performances at his family's expense every year during the Chariot Festival. But this year no one had come to ask him to host the performance; he felt hurt.

He was just about to drift off when he heard someone shouting, '*Ayya! Master!*' There was terror in that voice. Jagannatha got up, got the torch, and came down. The night was pitch-dark as the moon was waning. Some people were standing beyond the yard, wailing.

In the light of the torch, Jagannatha could see Pilla's parents. Pilla's father stood shivering with nothing on but a loincloth. His hair was dishevelled and his eyes were red. His breath smelt of toddy. 'What happened?' asked Jagannatha, gently.

Pilla's father was in a panic. Jagannatha asked him many questions but all he could tell him was that the police had come that night and dragged Pilla away. He did not know where, he did not know why.

'Go back to your hut, I'll go and get him,' said Jagannatha to pacify them. But they still stood there crying and Jagannatha had to scold them. He drove straight to the Bharathipura Police Station in the clothes he was wearing.

As soon as he saw Jagannatha, a *daffedar* with a handle-bar moustache stood up and saluted him. 'Who's on duty here?' asked Jagannatha, authoritatively.

'I, Sir. Why?'

'Please call the inspector.' Jagannatha sat on a chair across the table. The daffedar remained standing.

'The boss is sleeping, Sir.'

'You've brought one of the labourers on my farm, Pilla, to the police station. I've come to find out why,' Jagannatha said angrily.

[76] A popular dance-drama form of Karnataka based on classical themes.

'There's a case against him, Sir. A criminal case.'

'What's the case? Tell me. I'll bail him out if necessary. Release him from the lock-up first.'

The daffedar looked flustered. Still standing, he said courteously, 'Those Holeya sons of whores, think too much of themselves, Sir. That Pilla has tried to molest a Shetty girl. We got a complaint and so ...'

'Where's the statement? Let me see it.'

'The girl's family said, "We don't want to lodge a complaint; it'll become a scandal. Just thrash him, teach him a lesson, and let him go," Sir,' said the daffedar, looking scared now.

Jagannatha was furious.

'Such a procedure's against the law, daffedar. Do you realize what can happen if I complain to the DSP about you? Where's Pilla? Where's the girl's family?'

'They also work for you, Sir. Don't you know one of the Shettys, Sheenappa? He's the one. He said, "Master's not in town; he'd have come and complained personally had he been here."'

'Where's Pilla? Show him to me first.'

'Then we'll file the complaint, Sir.'

Jagannatha felt the daffedar was not willing to release Pilla so easily; he threatened him, raising his voice, 'Look, I'll have to create trouble by complaining that you've not acted according to the law. First show me where Pilla is.'

'I don't want to sound disrespectful, Sir, but these Holeya sons of bitches ...'

'Hey, daffedar! Where's Pilla, tell me?'

Jagannatha stood up trembling with fury. The daffedar picked up a bunch of keys and went in. He unlocked the cell and stood by, silently. Jagannatha flashed his torch and looked in. Pilla was crouched in a corner. He did not seem to be aware of himself. When Jagannatha said, 'Pilla,' he lifted his head painfully; his face was battered. His eyes were swollen and blood had streamed from his nose and mouth. It didn't look as if his eyes could see well enough to recognize him. Jagannatha went closer and saw him in the light of the torch. The white clothes he had given him had bloodstains all over. The collar and sleeves had been ripped away.

'Are you men or animals?'

'Sheenappa's men had hit him on the face, Sir. I did give him a few thrashes to get him to talk. Otherwise these fellows don't open their mouths, Sir.'

Jagannatha felt very tired. The daffedar did not think of Pilla as a person at all. His indescribable cruelty was backed by centuries of ignorance. A Holeya had desired a caste-girl. No doubt it is wrong for any man to abuse a woman, but it was considered a grievous crime because he happened to be a Holeya. Jagannatha knew how natural it was for anyone to see it this way; there was no point in getting angry with the daffedar. Swallowing all his anguish, Jagannatha said, 'Pilla, get up. Come.'

The strong and well-built Pilla was huddled in a corner like an animal cowering in fear.

Jagannatha's guts wrenched at the bloodstains on the white shirt.

'Get up!' said the daffedar roughly and Pilla cringed even more, like a frightened worm.

'Leave him alone, daffedar,' said Jagannatha and put out his hand to help him up.

'Why are *you* touching him, Sir? He hasn't lost consciousness. He'll stand up on his own,' said the daffedar, trying to throw his weight about.

Ignoring him, Jagannatha held Pilla gently by the arm. Pilla seemed to shrink in a panic as Jagannatha touched him. 'Don't be scared, Pilla. Come with me,' said Jagannatha, oblivious to his fear. He walked him slowly out of the lock-up and helped him to sit in the car. And then, noticing the daffedar staring at him as if he could not believe his eyes, Jagannatha said, 'I'll talk to the inspector tomorrow, if necessary,' and drove away.

Pilla would not climb the patio. After Jagannatha had helped him, he refused to enter the hall. Jagannatha woke up the farmhand to light the gaslight and went in, got some tincture of iodine, cotton swabs, and Dettol, and took off Pilla's shirt. Pilla squirmed under his master's gentle nursing care. His dark skin was covered with welts all over. Jagannatha washed his wounds, swabbed them with a few drops of tincture, and made him lie on a mat. And after he had helped him to drink some brandy, Pilla seemed to recover a bit.

Pilla started shivering as he had no clothes on. Jagannatha fetched one of his own shirts, a dhothi, and a blanket. He helped him to wear the clothes and gave him the blanket to cover himself. Pilla's face was disfigured by fear. Jagannatha asked him gently, 'Had you drunk too much last evening?'

Pilla nodded. He struggled to sit up.

'Is it true that you did it, Pilla?'

Pilla fell at Jagannatha's feet from where he was sitting.

'Che, get up,' said Jagannatha.

'Who is it? Kaveri?'

Pilla's silence said that it was.

'It's not wrong to desire a girl, Pilla. But it seems like a sin to others because you're a Holeya. It's wrong to force someone who's not willing, that's all. Now tell me everything that happened.'

Jagannatha was amazed to see that, for the first time, the atmosphere between them had cleared. Pilla spoke with difficulty; for the first time, the words were man to man. This scene of the two of them squatting opposite each other on the patio in the gaslight remained etched in Jagannatha's memory.

Pilla had not forced himself on Kaveri. He had been drunk. He was singing to himself and staggering down the road. The people at the toddy shop had laughed at his white clothes. He had been angry, and he was flattered too. As he was coming down the road in the gathering darkness, he thought he had seen something in the bushes. Going closer, he saw Janardhana Shetty taking off Kaveri's clothes. They had not seen him standing there. He did not know what had come over him while watching them. He only knew he had gone straight towards Kaveri who was naked by now. Shetty had seen Pilla approaching with a raised hand and had fled. Kaveri had covered herself. Pilla had stood mesmerized. Suddenly, Janardhana Shetty had sneaked in from behind and hit him on the head. Pilla had lost consciousness. When he came to, he was alone. He had got up and walked home. He had not told anyone at home what had happened. His parents might have thought he had hurt himself in a drunken brawl. After some time, during the night, a daffedar had come and dragged him to the police station, given him a sound thrashing, and put him in the lock-up.

Jagannatha felt strange to realize that Pilla had desired the same girl that he had. The dark, sturdy body that sat in the gaslight was like his own, carnal and alive. Now he felt he could really touch him.

'Pilla, you must all come into the temple with me without fear, okay?' Jagannatha's voice shook as he asked. He thought he saw a friendly look on Pilla's face and was happy. He felt he could start talking about something serious at last.

'Would you like to sleep here or would you rather go home?'

'I'll go home, Odeya,' said Pilla as he struggled to his feet.

'I'll walk some distance with you,' said Jagannatha and took the torch. He held Pilla as he was limping.

'Don't touch me, Odeya.'

Jagannatha was happy Pilla could talk about it so openly.

'You ass! What'll happen if I touch you?' he said to tease him.

Jagannatha walked up to the huts where the Holeyaru lived. He would have liked to go in. But he knew the Holeyaru believed that misfortune would befall them if a Brahmin entered their homes. And so he felt it was improper to go in uninvited. He stood at a distance and said, 'Don't be frightened, Pilla. All of you come and see me tomorrow.'

He went home and lay down. Chikki was still awake but she did not ask him any questions.

He had held out the saligrama to Pilla and Pilla had reached for Kaveri's body that had aroused him too. Even as Jagannatha was trying to understand what could have aroused Pilla, his mind went back to the day he had stolen Adiga's five-rupee note and to the way he had watched, mesmerized, Sheenappa stealing coconuts from his grove—he could not figure out what kind of a person he really was.

He went to sleep, exhausted.

SEVENTEEN

The District Commissioner

Kaveri did not turn up for work the next day, nor did Janardhana Shetty. Pretending as if he did not know anything about the previous night, Shanbogh Shastri asked, fawning disgustingly, 'Shetty's farmhands are saying they will not be coming to work from now on. What shall we do?'

'We can always go to some district in Kanara and hire labour,' Jagannatha replied and turning to Rao's son, Ranganatha, asked, 'Is your father at home?'

'He said he'd be going to get the mail,' answered Ranganatha and turned his attention to making entries in a ledger.

Jagannatha came out of his office and walked about. He saw Rao coming towards him and his spirits lifted. He waited for him in the yard. Rao was walking briskly; he looked perturbed. The family priest and the cook had spread the news all over the town of Jagannatha offering the saligrama to the Holeyaru. Rao had heard the people's comments and had come to see him the previous day. And when he learnt that Jagannatha had left for Bangalore unexpectedly, he had been worried.

Jagannatha took him upstairs and told him in private about the police beating up Pilla.

Rao had heard about that too; he feared it might lead to public violence.

'The moment I feel my plan of action is premature, I'm willing to withdraw it, Rayare.'

'After all that's happened, you may not be able to retract now, Jaganna.' Rao sighed.

Jagannatha wanted to tell him he was really happy Pilla had desired Kaveri but he kept quiet; he did not think Rao would understand.

'What's in today's paper?'

'Nothing much. As usual, there're a few letters to the editor. And there's news of Neelakantaswami and Ranga Rao heading towards Bharathipura to participate in a campaign here. They're members of the Mysore Socialist Party. Magadi Ananthakrishna has written to me that even he'll be coming to represent the office bearers of the Sarvodaya Movement. That's about it.'

'Rayare, Chikki hasn't been talking to me at all. I feel she's very upset. Also, we don't have anyone to cook for us. Could you reassure her, please?'

'I'll do that, Jaganna. Do you know why I came here so quickly? You'll have to do something immediately. The district commissioner at Shimoga, Satyaprakash, is a Harijan. You'll have to go and talk to him. Ask him to send us police protection during the Chariot Festival to prevent any violence. You might've read about the torching of Holeyaru in Andhra Pradesh. We can never be sure such things won't happen here.'

Jagannatha felt Rao was right.

'Then I'll leave for Shimoga right away. I'll be back by the evening. You stay with Chikki and cheer her up.' said Jagannatha. He changed into a fresh shirt and dhothi and left.

On the way, Vasu signalled for him to stop the car. Prabhu and Nagaraja Jois were with him. Jagannatha needed to be alone. But Vasu said, 'Are you going to Shimoga? Then, we'll come too.' And it was only proper to give them a lift.

Vasu began chatting about some north Indian maker of Indian sweets in Shimoga; they were going to bring him down to Bharathipura to set up his stall in time for the festival.

'Why have you taken on so much, Jaganna? What for?' he asked.

Jagannatha drove on without answering. Jois said to Vasu, 'Whether Jagannatha Rao's doing the right thing or not is not so relevant now; there's another issue that's more important. It is said in the Upanishads, if one seer could see everything, he'd know the absolute truth and there'd be no need for other seers. Jagannatha Rao's only trying to shake up what has been hidden. Beyond that ...'

'Why are you going to Shimoga, Joisare?' asked Prabhu.

'You see, my son is barely thirty years. And you know about Nagamani. What else can I do? There's a family that's willing to give their daughter in marriage; they don't mind that he's a widower. But he's an educated man. So I must consult him before setting the date for the wedding some time next year,' said Jois, sighing.

Prabhu asked Jagannatha, 'Why didn't you get a new car from England?'

'No particular reason,' he replied, listlessly.

'Anyway, good cars can't last long on these roads; they're so bad. And after Independence nothing gets done without greasing palms.'

Jagannatha adjusted the rear-view mirror, implying that he did not like to talk while driving. Prabhu said to Vasu, 'Have you heard about the new DC, Satyaprakash, Vasu? He doesn't do any work unless he's bribed. He's a Harijan, after all. Who's to stop him, tell me? I hear he's also related to some minister.'

To irritate Jagannatha, Vasu began to describe the disasters that might happen if Holeyaru were to rise socially. From a tirade against a Holeya Member of the Parliament who was supposed to have tried to make advances to a lady in the room next to his when he was in Delhi and was ticked off by Nehru, Vasu moved on to jokes about a Holeya minister and his wife, 'The very day he was made a minister, this man and his wife went to Bangalore and checked into a posh hotel. They took a room with bath, and the wife went to the bathroom as soon as they had settled in. She didn't come out for a long time and the husband got worried, so he peeked in. And what did he see? His wife seated on the floor, stupefied by the tiling. "Look at the floor!" she says, "We can eat and sleep right here, can't we?"'

Jagannatha slowed the car and stared angrily at Vasu who was sitting beside him.

'Shut up. You've become disgusting,' he said.

Vasu was taken aback to see him trembling with rage. Prabhu changed the topic.

'Jagannatha Rao hasn't got my point at all,' he said, 'If we rely on Gurappa Gowda to improve our town, that'll never happen. He'll only see to whatever will benefit the Gowdas—scaring the shanboghs, paving the roads where the wealthy Gowdas live, and getting the amaldhars transferred. Beyond this, he's of no use to anyone. Only you can do something if you put your mind to it.'

Jagannatha nodded but said nothing.

Vasu had tried to treat Jagannatha's fury as a joke but it had not worked, so while getting down he said, 'Sorry.' Jagannatha dropped them off at National Lodge and went on to the district commissioner's office.

SATYAPRAKASH, BA, BL, IN

Jagannatha saw the board, wrote his name on a slip of paper, and sent it in through a skinny man seated on a high stool. The man had the marks of a Madhva Brahmin: a black line drawn vertically in the middle of his forehead, and tiny imprints of the conch, and the chakra on his temples. On his tufted head was a dirty white cap. Though he was not wearing any slippers, this poor Brahmin, as emaciated as Balarama's[77] cow, had the other trappings of a peon's uniform: a white coat and loose trousers. As soon as he heard his boss press the bell, he would dart in like an arrow and then rush out. He reminded Jagannatha of a magician at the fair who would move a camphor ball in and out of a box by a sleight of hand while chanting, '*ullai, pidhai, ullai, pidhai* ...' For touching the Holeya commissioner's hand every time he gave him the visitor's slip, the peon would probably be doing his ritual cleansing every evening: having a bath, changing his sacred thread, having some panchagavya to purify himself to be a proper Brahmin householder. Jagannatha looked at his drawn face with compassion.

[77] Krishna's older brother, who was as poor as any other cowherd though his brother was God.

The peon was not impressed by his clothes. '*Sahebru* is busy, you'll have to wait.'

'Please give the slip to him,' said Jagannatha politely. The peon grimaced and went in. Perhaps, Satyaprakash was venting all his resentment against the upper class on this poor creature. It struck Jagannatha how difficult it is to understand a country where a Pilla, a Satyaprakash, and even a man like this poor Brahmin could coexist.

When he emerged, the peon's expression had changed to one of respect because his boss had asked to see Jagannatha immediately. He opened the door and bowed deferentially. Satyaprakash stood up to shake hands. He was short, dark-skinned, and pock-marked. His crude broad ears looked conspicuous. His desire to please was obvious in his manner. His broad, servile smile seemed to say to everyone he met, 'You are everything to me.' It was easy to guess how this man might have climbed so high so quickly.

'Please come in. Do sit down. You've honoured me with your presence.'

Satyaprakash's Kannada sounded artificial. 'When an untouchable young man becomes an officer like this, he also loses his authenticity, doesn't he?' Jagannatha thought.

'Which town do you come from?' Jagannatha asked a few such openers and looked around the room with curiosity. On one wall were pictures of Gandhi, Nehru in a rose garden, and the chief minister of Mysore. On the wall behind Jagannatha was a large picture of Manjunathaswami. It looked as if it had been there for a long time; there were faded stains of scented sticks, turmeric, and kumkuma. The fresh ash of that day's incense sticks lay on the photo frame. Running his hands over the khadi tablecloth and fiddling with the bell, Satyaprakash spoke as if he were reading from a book.

'I am from Tumkur, Swami. If our society has to improve, young men like you will have to commit themselves to serve the country. As Karanth has said, you have returned to the soil. The other day, when I had been to Bangalore to attend the Deputy Commissioners' Conference, I told Narayan about you. You know Narayan, do you not? He is related to me, his wife and my wife are sisters. He is the health minister. He was very happy.'

Jagannatha sat quietly. The phony ambience sickened him; paper flowers on the table, coffee stains on the tablecloth, and Satyaprakash's fingers restless to press the bell.

'I heard you had lived in England? Even I had gone on a tour. To Japan. You know the cooperative movement? In connection with it. What a country! I was astonished to see it. Our people are disgustingly lazy. Take my people, for instance. See how many facilities the government has provided for us! But they misuse everything. Students in hostels eat free food and waste their time drinking. That is why I tell them, "Look at Brahmin boys, the way they study hard even if they have to study under street lamps." Take my peon, Govindacharya, for instance. His son and mine will be appearing for the Board exam together. His son has passed in the first division throughout, but my son has not been able to get through a single class without grace marks. And what does my son lack?'

Satyaprakash's fingers pressed the bell at last. The peon hurried in and stood with his head slightly bowed. 'Acharya, go over to my house and get some good coffee in a flask,' said Satyaprakash to him, and turning towards Jagannatha, he said, 'The coffee in the canteen is not good, Mr Jagannath.' He had addressed the peon in the respectful plural because he was a Brahmin. Jagannatha was curious about this man. 'Perhaps he's arranging for coffee from his home to see if I'll drink it. He might have deliberately managed to get a Brahmin for a peon but uses the plural while talking to him. He speaks a stylized formal Kannada very courteously, but probably he's seething inside. He's doing all he can to impress me because I'm an educated Brahmin. Why, Pilla may become like him some day. Since I've put my hand to the wheel to turn it, I suppose I must be prepared for such things too.'

'Perhaps you know why I've come to you.'

'I guessed, Mr Jagannath. It is a great job you are doing. Take me, for instance, I have been to almost every temple in the country—Tirupathi, Rameshwara, Madurai. No one has stopped me anywhere. First, my people have to become educated; they still live in their superstitions. And also, there is so much of infighting among us; the right-hand people cannot tolerate the left-hand people. I have no sympathy for some of my people. People like you will have to reach out to them and help them. You know who encouraged me? A Brahmin teacher at Gubbi High School.'

The coffee arrived. Jagannatha was troubled by the irony that he could not have a normal relationship with people like Pilla and Satyaprakash. Some kind of artificiality crept in. The peon poured out two cups of coffee and brought it to them. It was much too sweet and had some blobs of cream floating in it. Jagannatha swallowed it with great difficulty.

'Mr Satyaprakash, I came to tell you that there might be some trouble during the Chariot Festival. There may be violence against the Harijans. So I've come to ask you to arrange for police protection.'

Jagannatha waited for his reaction.

Satyaprakash put on a wise expression and said, 'That was what I was about to say, Mr Jagannath. I have already received many representations. Do not have your entry to the temple programme during the festival. Do it quietly on another day. I will come and be with you. Our country is known for peace. The day I reported here as DC, the members of your temple committee had a special puja and sent me the prasada. People will change in due course anyway. Is it not said, "What the Saivas worship as Siva[78] is worshipped by others by a different name?" This is what Nehru called religious tolerance. Slow and steady … that is my policy. I consider you as a Harijan and request you …'

Satyaprakash rose to his feet and brought his palms together in respect. Jagannatha still had the bad taste of the sweet coffee in his mouth. Sick with disgust, he too stood up.

'We can't go back on our decision. If the Harijans aren't ready, that's a different issue. I've just come to inform you that the law and order situation is your responsibility.'

Jagannatha spoke courteously but sternly; Satyaprakash looked shaken. He walked with him, muttering something about peace and non-violence and about how the Harijans cannot continue to live in resentment; they had to be educated first.

And, bringing his palms together, deferentially led Jagannatha to his car.

[78] Satyaprakash, a Holeya, fumbles with /*sh*/ and /*s*/ sounds.

EIGHTEEN

Preparations

Neelakantaswami and Ranga Rao, members of the Mysore Socialist Party (MSP), came directly to Jagannatha's house carrying a bag and flag. Sripathi Rao welcomed them, got Chikki to serve them some coffee and eats, and settled them in a spacious room next to the office. As soon as Jagannatha arrived, Neelakantaswami introduced himself: he was an MA in political science doing his final year of law; president of the Law College Association and secretary of the MSP. Ranga Rao added that no public function in Mysore was complete without a speech by him. After being complimented in this way, Neelakantaswami introduced Ranga Rao, 'He's done his Master's in political science and is engaged in research right now. He's building up the party.'

He then explained why he had to leave the Socialist Party and form another: the president of the party had misused his position for personal gain; he had appointed a man of his own caste as secretary, etc. While he talked Neelakantaswami tugged at a strand of curly hair from his head until he pulled it out, stared at the root, dropped it down, and then fingered another strand in the same place. Jagannatha found it disgustingly painful.

'Rest for a while. I'll see you later,' he said and went up to his room.

Sripathi Rao followed him. He shut the door behind him and said softly with great concern, 'You'll have to deal with them carefully, Jaganna. Do you know what they were saying to each other? I don't think they knew I was standing outside. Neelakantaswami said, "What about making Jagannatha Rao the president of our party?" To which Ranga Rao replied, "A Brahmin is a Brahmin." Ranga Rao is a Vokkaliga and Neelakantaswami's a Lingayat. Of course, there's no love lost between them. But Neelakantaswami said, "It's a strategy, Ranga Rao. He'll be a good candidate to field from here during the next elections." I was very upset to hear them. And do you know what Ranga Rao did as soon as he came here? He changed his clothes, went to the temple, and brought some prasada. When I said, "That wasn't the proper thing to do," he said, "Anyway no one knows me here, so it's okay. My mother was a great devotee of Manjunathaswami." Neelakantaswami too scolded him but for a different reason; as a Lingayat he doesn't care much for the prasada from a Brahmin temple. Why am I here telling you all this? Because you're new to politics. Be careful!'

Rao had been quite dramatic and Jagannatha listened to him quietly.

'We may have to make such people serve our purpose,' he said.

Rao laughed, saying, 'You're an idiot. They're planning to exploit *you*. You wait and see.'

Jagannatha told him about his meeting with the DC.

'I knew this would happen. He's thoroughly corrupt,' said Rao as he stood up. Jagannatha stretched out on his bed.

'There may be many others coming to see you and staying on to eat. Chikki can't cope alone. I'll send my wife over.'

'Did you comfort Chikki, Rayare?'

'Yes, I did. She said she's sent for Adiga to purify the saligrama and install it again. She weeps saying, "How can I eat without drinking its *teertha*?" I feel sorry for her. Anyway, she's looking forward to Gopala and he'll be here tomorrow.'

Jagannatha had always been amazed by the love his mother and Chikki had for Gopala, clerk Krishnaiah's son. He was happy to know he was coming the next day. More than anything else, he wanted Chikki to be cheerful.

As he was leaving, Rao said, 'Tell those Holeya young men not to go about the town in white clothes, Jaganna. There may be trouble if they're too visible.'

That evening, the Holeyaru came to him. Pilla was with them, despite his aches and pains; Jagannatha was happy to see him: *There's a friendly look on his face, isn't there? Something I've never seen before.* He told them he had been to see the DC. 'He belongs to your caste,' he added, to encourage them. 'And these two men have come from Mysore to help you enter the temple,' he said, introducing Neelakantaswami and Ranga Rao. He asked Neelakantaswami to talk to them about socialism and went into the house, thinking he might feel inhibited in his presence.

Rao's wife, Bhagyamma, and their daughter, Savithri, who had come home for the holidays, had come to help Chikki. Jagannatha went out for a stroll down the hill.

Rao also stayed on for dinner. Jagannatha was happy; for the first time there was a Lingayat and a Vokkaliga eating in his house.

Chikki served them silently.

'There'll be a few more members of our party arriving tomorrow,' said Neelakantaswami.

'We intend to start a Farmers' Association here,' hinted Ranga Rao.

The next day there was a letter to the editor in the newspaper from the Brahmin Youth Association of Bharathipura condemning the entry of Harijans into the temple. Two letters came in the mail bus for Jagannatha. One was from Ramesh Chandra, Reader in sociology, University of Mysore. Jagannatha had known him for quite some time. He was from Nanjanagudu, from a famous Hoysala Karnataka Brahmin[79] family. Though he used to wear earrings until he graduated, he had learnt to wear a three-piece suit in England. And he would wear it without spoiling the creases. He would sit slightly bent, wiping

[79] A sub-sect of Brahmins who worship Shiva.

his glasses with his handkerchief, and all set to launch into a serious discussion, giving everyone the impression that he was an intellectual. He would support the Indian caste system in a very subtle way. 'Do you know how wealthy the kumbaras[80] are?' he would say but, at the same time, he would condemn racism in England.

When Jagannatha said, 'You're a hypocrite,' he would say, 'May I have a cigarette, please?' And after lighting it, he would continue, 'I do understand your concern. But, Jagan, see what's happening to the educated Shudras. Look at the state of the Mysore University. There's always some conflict or the other between Vokkaligas and Lingayats. The university that had men like Radhakrishna and Hiriyanna, now has some Kalappa or Siddappa misusing his clout. *This* is what we should condemn. What's the point in condemning the caste system, tell me?'

Ramesh Chandra represented Indian hypocrisy in all its innocence. He would earnestly argue that it was acceptable for Shudra women to commit adultery but not for Brahmin women; that there were no neurotics in India; that Indian culture was better than European culture; that we would not have had electricity and railways if the British had not come to India and taught us English; that we should have got our Independence a little later; that it was wrong to have given voting rights to illiterate people; and he would say, 'The English are obsessed with cleanliness but they don't wash their bottoms, do they?' Jagannatha would watch his well-trimmed moustache and the way he would earnestly hold his hands to his chest, and stifle a yawn.

Ramesh Chandra's future had unfolded exactly as Jagannatha had expected. This man who believed in the fidelity of the Indian wife fell in love with a girl in England. Jagannatha knew that Ramesh knew he would never marry the girl. While returning to India he pined for his lost love the way he had appreciated the tragic sentiment in Western literature. On his return, he praised Western cleanliness, honesty, and political maturity, impressing a Hoysala Karnataka Brahmin executive engineer. After 'seeing' a few other prospective brides, he ended up marrying the engineer's plain-looking daughter. In the wedding invitation, he had carried 'MA (London)' after his name.

[80] The potter caste.

Ramesh Chandra had written in his fine hand: *I appreciate your struggle to bring Existential Socialism to Bharathipura. But as a sociologist I don't think your efforts will be worthwhile. The problem of the Harijans will have to be settled eventually through the process of urbanization only and not through the programme you have planned. Right now, intellectuals like you will have to confront neo-Brahmins like the Vokkaligas and the Lingayats who are in power. You may not be aware of the way these two groups are fighting for the position of vice-chancellor at the Bangalore University; they are desecrating the sanctity of academia. It is the same in Mysore too. If merit were a priority, I would have been a professor but ...*

The other letter was from England, from Chandrashekar. He read it over and over again as it had upset him very much.

Dear Jagan,

Margaret has told me everything. My brother had also written from Bangalore. But I think I know you better than anyone else. Your idealism has grown a paunch with your daydreaming and now you want to trim it down to an athletic figure through this struggle. You like to suffer. Your tragedy is that you'll become a hero of another sort, that's all. Do you know why? Because you'll never be able to love the Holeyaru. Your personality is too absorbed in itself; it's incapable of loving anyone else. Squirming with jealousy as I am, I know more profound truths through human frailty than you ever can, living in your idealism. You're only moving from one kind of pomposity to another. I'm surprised that I'm filled with jealousy, love, and hate for you even though I know how hollow you are. I guess it's my misfortune to live my life deriding lucky people like you. I'm writing to you frankly, condemning your phony liberalism because only I can tell you the truth as it is. Margaret does not accept what I say but I know, deep in her heart, she knows I'm right.

Yours affectionately,
Chandrashekar

Jagannatha went looking for Neelakantaswami to forget Chandrashekar's letter. He was busy preparing a report for the press about a meeting the secretary of the Mysore Socialist Party had had with the Holeyaru of Bharathipura. As soon as he saw Jagannatha, he said, 'You'll have to issue a statement condemning the local MLA.'

'We'll do that. But don't you think it'll be good to talk to him first?'

'Gurappa Gowda is a crook. I hear he's gone to Bangalore not to get involved.'

Jagannatha did not feel like talking. Every word from Chandrashekar's letter had stabbed him like a dagger even though there were many lies in it. He took Neelakantaswami and Ranga Rao into the house, had some coffee with them, and said, 'I've got something to do. I'll be back.'

He went looking for Sripathi Rao. He had not turned up yet, though his wife and daughter had been helping Chikki in the kitchen since the morning.

Even as he entered the main street in the town, Jagannatha saw a few people carrying flags and coming towards him. Looking at the flags, he guessed they must be from Neelakantaswami's party. He stopped and pointing towards his house, said to them, 'Go home and rest awhile. I'll be back in an hour.' The young men looked happy as if they were there for a fair or a picnic. One of them said familiarly, 'Yes, Comrade.' Jagannatha was embarrassed but he did not show it; he walked away towards Rao's Khadi store.

The shops down the main street were decorated for the Chariot Festival. No one spoke to him. Jagannatha was upset that he had been rejected by the streets of the town of his birth. Rao had closed his shop and was on his way to Jagannatha's house. He was happy because he had heard that Magadi Ananthakrishna of the Sarvodaya Movement was arriving that evening. He was eager to see his close friend who had been with him in jail during satyagraha. As they walked homeward, he talked animatedly to Jagannatha about his friend. Jagannatha was wondering why he had sought out Rao because Chandrashekar's letter had upset him. And, so, he was listening to Rao's story only half-heartedly, but was stunned to hear what Rao had to say during the course of his narration.

NINETEEN

Magadi Ananthakrishna

'Ananthakrishna is younger than me. Not much, just about four or five years,' said Sripathi Rao to Jagannatha, 'He never keeps a secret from me. Listen, I'll tell you the tragic story of his life. There's a lesson in it for idealists like us …

'Ananthakrishna joined the freedom struggle when he was very young and went to prison when he was doing the Intermediate course. He thought, like thousands of other young men, that this kind of education prepared us for servitude, that it wasn't possible to be truly educated in a college. He was a good student of literature. Do you know how well he writes and talks even now? Some of his family had served in the police department and his father was a clerk at the collector's office. His father remarried after his mother's death and his stepmother enjoyed being cruel.

'His father didn't want Ananthakrishna living in the house; he was embarrassed by a son who condemned the government he was working for. The stepmother didn't want him at home either. There were young daughters to be married and she felt she could do without people's comments that the son ate with people who belonged to unacceptable castes. Anyway, the home was a burning ghat, bereft of love and compassion. Of course, the freedom struggle could have also been a reason, as it was for many young men like Ananthakrishna. He left home.

'In those days of the struggle it wasn't difficult for freedom fighters to get a bite to eat somewhere. They'd travel from town to town, eat wherever they set up camp, and make speeches. And what speeches he delivered! In this way, Ananthakrishna became a favourite with Congress leaders. Even if you woke him from sleep and asked him to speak, he would do just that. Ananthakrishna was heady with success; he travelled all over the country. He lost all contact with his family. He always lived as if he had no private life. He knew people came to him for his eloquence, they followed him, and they praised him. He went wherever he was invited, becoming a speech-making machine. Sometimes I used to wonder if there was anything in him beyond his exquisite eloquence.

'Ananthakrishna was an attractive person too; he believed every word he spoke. Caught up in his idealism, he had gone to Gandhiji's ashram once. There he became Gandhiji's favourite disciple. He would fan him while he slept, go for walks with him, and would translate into Kannada whatever Gandhiji wrote in his paper, *Harijan*. Whatever Ananthakrishna did, he did with style. It was when he was in Gandhiji's ashram that he virtually jumped into a well.

'In the ashram, there was a Naidu girl, an orphan. She had been brought up very strictly. Ananthakrishna met her while on duty as volunteers and became friends. As a volunteer, she had been hoping to meet a fellow-volunteer and settle down. And Ananthakrishna had been waiting for a chance to prove his idealism to the world; he had decided on an inter-caste marriage. So he asked her if she'd marry him. "Let's ask the Mahatma," she said. You know Gandhiji. He preached to them that they shouldn't marry for lust; they should have sex only to have children and should otherwise practise celibacy together. And he also decided they would be married during the next mass-wedding.

'The day of the wedding arrived. Ananthakrishna and the girl were standing under a tree. She was leaning against the tree, explaining to him how the two of them could serve the country together. She hadn't touched him until that moment and he hadn't touched her either. They hadn't even felt the need to. They hadn't had any kind of intimacy beyond talking to each other this way.

'The auspicious moment for the wedding was approaching. Both of them stood there under the tree looking like convicts in their new, coarse Khadi clothes. She had made her flat chest flatter with the blouse stretched tightly across it. Ananthakrishna stood listening to her, trying to look interested. She wasn't saying anything new; she was only spouting what he had been saying all along.

'Now, Ananthakrishna had a great taste for literature. He had memorized *Muddanna-Manorama Dialogues* and Kalidasa's *Shakuntala*. As he stood listening to her profundities, his attention wandered to her slightly protruding teeth, long nose, flat chest, small elephant-eyes, and her narrow forehead. Her well-worn words began to buzz around him like bees. And Ananthakrishna panicked. Won't the same forehead, the same teeth, the same nose, and the same mouth, the same words said in this same stance go on forever? His mind was screaming, "She's ugly, I can't possibly marry her." His body revolted against having to sleep with her. He thought he had to run away from that spot to save himself. But his legs wouldn't move and his eyes couldn't stop staring at her forehead, nose, and teeth. As strong as his urge to break free, was his rising sense of helplessness that he could do nothing about it.

'"Why are you staring at me like an idiot?" she said.

'Ananthakrishna moved his pale face from side to side very slightly, swallowed, and tried to talk.

'"We must set up an ashram in Srirangapatna. We have to look after orphans ..." she continued her monologue.

'They got married, they had a child. He's worn out. Even now he says to me, "You know Sripathi? In all my life, I've had but one genuine feeling—that she's ugly. But I was holding on to an ideal I couldn't let go."

'Eventually, even his thinking became phony. He used to love spicy rice dishes like puliyogare and bisibelebath. But she didn't use any spices in her cooking; she served boiled vegetables. And she didn't make coffee or tea at home. For a year Ananthakrishna somehow endured being obedient to his wife. And then he started eating spicy food on the sly. He even started drinking. His wife threw him out of the house and complained about him at the Congress office.

'The Congress party cast him out, like crushed sugarcane, when they had no more use for him. They didn't give him a party seat because he's a Brahmin. Ananthakrishna had sacrificed the best years of his life. He decided it was better to do padhayatre with Vinobha Bhave than to live with his wife. He gifted his life to the Bhoodan Movement.

'I still feel Ananthakrishna is a very great man, Jaganna. He may be a dejected man but he has matured. True, he drinks, but he talks with real concern about Sarvodaya. You can't really tell how a man turns out. There are kinks in his life, no doubt, but Ananthakrishna's living for an ideal even today. He isn't a loser like me. He's disillusioned but is still trying, struggling for an ideal.'

TWENTY

Approval

Jagannatha was bewildered. Chandrashekar's letter; the story of Ananthakrishna; the Holeyaru who were not any closer to him than they had been when he began his work with them; Bharathipura that lived for itself; and Sripathi Rao's insight that no real change is possible—all these were too much for him to take in.

As they walked up the hillock, Jagannatha said to Sripathi Rao, 'Rayare, our being is not like our awareness. You can call this hypocrisy if you like. I can't yet love the Holeyaru. Though I do know that history makes possible many things that seem impossible, my being is repelled by Satyaprakash, it behaves artificially with the Holeya youth. True. This is what I call anguish. The split between awareness and being is inevitable in us. Animals don't have this problem at all. History that has created me this way is even now plotting to create another reality, even through me. But its field of action is as much in Bharathipura as it is in my awareness. So many things are needed for the seeds of history to sprout, even those that we can see with our myopic vision. Look, Rayare, a conservative can't understand this angst; he sees only the present reality in human nature. But people like me, who can see the viewpoints of both reality and possibility, can't escape suffering.'

Jagannatha could no longer feel the enthusiasm he had felt when he had begun speaking to Rao, who in turn did not seem to think what he had said was true though he had understood the whole argument; such things had been discussed many times over. Unless the reality in Bharathipura changed; unless the Holeyaru were ready for the change; unless what seemed to be sprouting in Pilla took firm root—my ideas will remain mere shadows.

Jagannatha was moody at lunch. 'I can't love anyone who's seated here with me; I've exposed Chikki, who loves me, to a deep sadness. No one I can relate to will ever eat here again.'

Next to him, Ranga Rao was mixing just enough curry with the rice to make it into balls that he tossed into his mouth. The way he made a hole in the mound of rice on his leaf and asked for just a spoonful of curry to be poured into it, and the way he rolled the balls of rice as if he were offering *pinda* to the ancestors, disgusted Chikki. This was not new to her; she had seen Shudras eat this way elsewhere. She was repelled by a Shudra sitting in her dining room and eating this way, and her repugnance affected Jagannatha too. 'I must become insensitive,' he thought, 'I don't know how to destroy the caste system that is destroying my humanity. It has created different worlds for everything we do; from the way we eat to the way we clean ourselves in the toilet. I've no other way but to condemn myself with impotent rage, no other way but to be a homeless spirit in such a society. However phony it might seem, I've probably no choice but to go against my feelings; it's a necessity. I have to learn to love this Ranga Rao, this Satyaprakash—or at least to understand them.'

'Mr Jagannath, I've written a book on public administration,' said Neelakantaswami.

'Oh, really?'

'I'm getting it published. I'm trying to get the Maharaja to write a preface.'

'But, you being a socialist ...' asked Jagannatha, casually.

Neelakantaswami said, smiling, 'That's just a strategy. Or else, who'll publish my book, tell me? There's a lot of casteism in the Kannada publishing world.'

'Really?'

'Of course. Now my book is getting published in both English and Kannada. It may be used as a textbook. Then, what I say will have some value. Even the party will benefit from it.'

Neelakantaswami spoke without any embarrassment. Jagannatha was amazed at his optimism and his energy. 'The rascal! But, probably, it'll be he who shapes the future ... until people like Pilla stand up to rise above him. The Brahmin is cultured and refined; he is too timid to act out his convictions and hypocritical enough to look calm when he's seething inside. But these Gowdas and Lingayats have a shameless courage, energy, and youth. In this changing society, these people will become self-centered demons, eager to grab everything. And another day, Pilla will kick these neo-Brahmins. Then, perhaps, even he'll become ingratiating like Satyaprakash. Among the seeds of history, some may be mouldy, some may rot, some may germinate, and some like me may become manure.

Though he felt his words might hurt, Jagannatha said, 'Listen, I think it's dangerous, the way you're trying to get the Maharaja to write the preface and justifying it as strategy. It's vulgar too. I heard Ranga Rao went to the temple and brought prasada as soon as he came here. I'd like you to be pure in your behaviour if you want to join me in what I've set out to do.'

Neither Neelakantaswami nor Ranga Rao seemed upset.

'I see what you mean,' replied Neelakantaswami and continued eating. In a society where success alone matters, it's difficult to make out the value of what's passing and what's lasting; to Neelakantaswami, success is everything. In those days, the Brahmins grabbed what they could; today he's grabbing. No one has lost sleep over the plight of Holeyaru, though this land has had the concept of dharma for thousands of years.

Rao had eaten his lunch without saying a word. He was happy with the way Jagannatha had spoken frankly to them. But Jagannatha was furious that he could not shake Rao's belief that all non-Brahmins were like Neelakantaswami and Ranga Rao. As he rinsed his hands he searched for words to hurt him. Neelakantaswami's men had rinsed their hands and were plucking some guavas in the backyard without asking Jagannatha or Chikki if they could. Jagannatha went upstairs saying he would rest awhile. The socialists went with Neelakantaswami to look around. Rao also went with them.

Jagannatha was astonished. Ganesha, the temple priest's son, had come right into his room. He sat up and pointing to a chair said, 'Please sit down.' Ganesha closed the door and sat down, his eyes bright with enthusiasm as he stared at Jagannatha. Dirty shirt, dirty dhothi, the body like an unripe fruit with a face that was prematurely old. A sad figure of a man neither young nor old. His head had not been shaved for months; his tuft was longer than his hair. A scraggly beard on his chin and pearl studs in his ear lobes.

In his eagerness to say something, Ganesha started stammering.

'Do you want books?' asked Jagannatha to help him out and brought him a few of Sharatchandra's novels; they had been his mother's favourites.

'Don't tell anyone that I'm here,' he stuttered while his eyes spoke volumes. His stammer was like the birth pangs of truth being born.

Not knowing what else to talk about, Jagannatha asked, 'Are you the eldest?'

Ganesha nodded, still staring at Jagannatha.

'Are you married?'

And then he felt he should not have asked because Ganesha looked sad when he nodded again. He seemed to have something to say and Jagannatha had to create the right ambience of ease in which he could say it. He sat looking at Ganesha with empathy. There was a restlessness in the way Ganesha was sitting. It looked as if this person, who could be anything between a youth and an old man, had a lot of pent-up feelings. He reminded Jagannatha of the Holeyaru with their vacant expressions. It was not just that he looked odd; his wan face told the story of hundreds of years of inbreeding.

'What you're doing is right,' Ganesha said to Jagannatha, perspiring. At last he was able to express what he had come to say.

'I'm going,' he said and walked out of the room with long strides. Jagannatha came down and stood staring at Ganesha loping down the hillock. He was amazed that the short, unhealthy body could walk so briskly.

TWENTY ONE

Margaret's Letter

Jagannatha shut the door of his room, lay on his bed, and eagerly began to read Margaret's letter.

First about the International School: *I've received Desai's letter. I'm coming next year. Chander also plans to work in Bangalore …* Then about the weather: *It's been snowing without a break for the past three days. I feel like sitting near the fireplace all the time. I've put on weight; been drinking a lot of beer.* And then it was about the change in her father: *Father's been livelier after his retirement. Mother's nagging doesn't bother him any more. He has opened a store where he sells Indian things like curry powder, mango pickles, and papadams. In a strange way, he's finding his identity now. He gets up early, lights scented sticks to the god of Tirupathi, and does puja. And in the evenings, he goes to the Theosophical Society and listens to lectures. He's trying to build an organization that can make arrangements to invite* Harikathadaasas *and artistes who can play the sitar and the sarod at public recitals.*

I can understand why you're rebelling against God but you should also understand why Daddy needs God. I talked this over with Chander. He calls you a romantic. He says you're a product of the Nehru era. Crazy fellow! I don't agree with everything he says but he does have insight.

As Jagannatha came to the last paragraph, his face blanched.

Darling Jagan, we've decided to be open with each other, haven't we? You shouldn't feel hurt about what I'm going to tell you. Since the time you left, Chander has been pestering me for my love. For me, his jealousy, his intensity is a new experience; something I've never known before. I don't know why, but I've lost my heart to him and have given myself to him. I know you'll grieve over this. But only you can understand my weakness and forgive me, Margaret.

Jagannatha's hands were damp. He read the last paragraph over and over again, trying to deaden the pain by allowing himself to be stabbed in the same spot repeatedly. He got up from bed and came downstairs. Neelakantaswami was overseeing a placard being tied to the car. It announced a few speeches for the next day; so and so and so and so will be speaking at such and such a time, at such and such a place. Ranga Rao had placed a battery-operated mike in the car and was testing it: 'Hello, Hello.' Ananthakrishna of the Sarvodaya Movement was discussing Lohia[81] and Gandhi with some of the socialists. Shanbogh Shastri peeped out of the office, came outside, and said, 'I'll be taking the afternoon bus to Kanara district to get a few farmhands.' And having made a show of loyalty, he retreated indoors again.

Neelakantaswami was excited. 'The people are beginning to gather,' he said. 'What an opportunity! They're coming from all over the state and even from north India. We'll have to publicize this meeting as much as possible.' Ananthakrishna was beaming; he was looking forward to making a speech.

'This mike is no good,' grumbled Ranga Rao.

'Prabhu got it during the last elections for Gurappa Gowda's campaign,' said Sripathi Rao.

Jagannatha wanted to get away from it all; he walked up the cashew hillock. Suddenly everything had become pointless. He said to himself, *barely four days more. Then the Holeyaru will step into the temple. And stepping in, they'll change the course of centuries of history. But when I'm all keyed up and waiting for the supreme moment, what a blow you've dealt me, Margaret!*

[81] Dr Ram Manohar Lohia (1910–1967), a freedom fighter and one of the founders of the socialist movement in India.

Until now, he had not realized how much he loved her. It was excruciating to take it in; a naked body that his body had known was at this very moment lying in the arms of another man. *She'll talk to him intimately, she'll open herself to him, she'll moan with pleasure. I've become a cast-off, from this sky, from this moment, like a thing tossed out.*

Now, I'll have to do only what has to be done. There's no other go; I'll do it. I'll walk with the Holeyaru while cruel eyes reject me. Whoever they are, whoever I am, whoever God may be; there are no certainties. Someone else is touching and caressing everything I had touched and caressed. In destroying me, he has found his joy.

Jagannatha stood on the crest of the hill and stared vacantly at the pinnacle of the temple. Neelakantaswami's rasping voice coming over the mike reached him from a distance, inviting everyone to the next day's meeting.

'Attention everyone! Attention! Here's an appeal to the honourable citizens of Bharathipura. One of the leaders of our country, Shri Jagannatharaya, has committed himself to serve the Harijans, sacrificing everything to the cause. To support his struggle socialist leader, Shri Neelakantaswami, joint secretary of the Mysore Socialist Party, Shri Ranga Rao, and Sarvodaya leader, Shri Ananthakrishna, a close disciple of Gandhiji, will be speaking tomorrow evening at five, in the courtyard of the temple.'

Jagannatha was disgusted with the grating noise that was desecrating the stillness of Bharathipura. *If I don't take myself in hand now, all that I've worked for all these days will come to nothing. What sort of a person am I? But my anguish is real too. The only way to forget it is through action. I have to become detached; I must give up my personal life.*

He was startled to hear footsteps. Subbaraya Adiga had come up from behind and now stood beside him.

'I saw your face. I felt you were in pain and so I came.'

Adiga did not say anything more. When they were coming down the hillock, he did not ask Jagannatha what was bothering him. He did not pester him with questions. Jagannatha was grateful for the man's sensitivity; he really knew when to speak and when to be silent.

Chikki had made jilebis because Adiga had stayed for lunch. She must have been happy that he had ritually cleansed the saligrama of

Narasimha, installed it in the prayer room, and performed the puja. Besides, Gopala had come from Mysore. The students in his college were on strike. There was a clash between two gangs—the Lingayats and the Vokkaligas. The principal had sided with the Vokkaligas and so the other students were demanding his resignation. 'Hopeless fellows!' said Gopala, condemning everyone. Listening to him, Neelakantaswami and Ranga Rao regretted they were not in Mysore. To give an impression that he was beyond caste prejudices, Neelakantaswami condemned a Lingayat connected with the skirmish and praised another. Ranga Rao followed suit; he criticized the Vokkaliga principal and commended the Vokkaliga registrar. Jagannatha could sense a cold war between the two.

Adiga sat inside and had his lunch. Ananthakrishna was in great spirits and said nice things about the food.

When Jagannatha said, 'This evening you must speak to the Holeya youth,' Ananthakrishna was quite happy to oblige. 'I've written to Vinobha about you,' he said, 'If we get his blessings, it'll be a big boost to our campaign.' Jagannatha was in no mood to talk. Soon after lunch, he went upstairs and lay down.

Neelakantaswami had taken the car and gone out again to canvass for the cause. Jagannatha felt sick listening to his proclamations praising Ananthakrishna and his own self.

Towards the evening, he set out to visit Puranik. He looked for deserted lanes and took them, like a thief. After hearing Neelakantaswami's acclamations he was embarrassed to show his face to the people. He walked briskly down bylanes and soon reached Puranik's house and rang the bell. As usual, a Gurkha opened the door, got him to write his name on a slip of paper, and took it upstairs. Puranik came down and shook hands with him. He was wearing a tie; the collar of his shirt was frayed. But his well-pressed suit sat neatly on him. Jagannatha was amazed at his trim figure; Puranik had no paunch.

'I was feeling terribly lonely. Thanks for coming. My friend Avadhani is terribly ill, you see,' he said, as he took him upstairs. Ignoring Jagannatha's protests, he poured whisky into two glasses and added soda.

'For the success of your intended revolution,' he said, and clinked his glass against Jagannatha's.

Jagannatha savoured the whisky and tried to forget everything. But he could not help but hear snatches of Neelakantaswami's announcements that floated in, even into Puranik's room upstairs. He did not refuse a refill. He stretched out his legs and closed his eyes, but could not calm himself. His mind was turning over the last paragraph of Margaret's letter relentlessly. Puranik turned on the radio and some piano music wafted in from somewhere. Jagannatha lit the cigar Puranik had offered him and Puranik started talking:

'I have kept ready for you the material I once gathered on Bhootharaya. There is a curious folk song in it with two or three different versions. You know, only those women who have passed their menopause can go up the hill of Bhootharaya? The belief is that if a girl menstruates on the hill, she can't come down; she becomes the possession of Bhootharaya. This song describes the deluge and how it happens. A headstrong Brahmin girl goes up the hill and menstruates. Thus she becomes the possession of Bhootharaya. She isn't satisfied and sleeps with a Pariah. Bhootharaya is enraged. He comes down the hill and destroys the town in a furious dance. Not even his Lord, Manjunatha, is able to control him. Evil is let loose. In another version, which is more interesting, the Bhootharaya enjoys her in different forms; as a bull, as a horse, as a wild bear, and then as a Shudra, and finally as a Pariah. The girl refuses him in the form of a Pariah and so Bhootharaya is enraged and destroys the town. A very curious story. You must read it.'

Jagannatha took the bundle of papers from Puranik and left. When he reached home, Neelakantaswami, Ranga Rao, and their henchmen were chatting in the yard. Beyond the yard was blasting Ananthakrishna's speech to the Holeya youth. As soon as he saw Neelakantaswami, Jagannatha saw red. 'Hey, Mr Neelakantaswami, I didn't like the way you praised me just to give your party a boost in my town. It was a very vulgar thing to do. Don't bring your politics here, please.'

After he had said that, Jagannatha felt he had been needlessly harsh. But his face was red and his body was trembling with fury. Neelakantaswami replied shamelessly, 'Politics is new to you, Saar. That's why you're talking this way. You can't wear gloves when you start a revolution. You shouldn't feel squeamish about soiling your hands.'

'I'm sorry. Please don't exploit this situation for your politics,' Jagannatha said firmly.

It did not look as if his outburst had upset Neelakantaswami. Anyway, Jagannatha felt good about losing his temper. Deciding he would not be a puppet in the hands of these cunning politicians, he went straight up to his room. But, is Neelakantaswami the only reason for my anger? Jagannatha felt feverish. He lay down and closed his eyes.

TWENTY TWO

Jagannatha Visits the Holeyaru

Thrayodashi, the thirteenth day of the lunar cycle. Jagannatha woke up early, washed his face, put on his sweater, and stepped outside. He remembered that the sweater was Margaret's gift and all the anguish of the previous day engulfed him again. It was cold. He walked up the hill briskly. In the valley where Bharathipura lay, the morning mist was like fluffy balls of silk cotton as the sunbeams warmed it away bit by bit. For a while, the heavy mist had seemed to press down on the sunlight. But soon the rays had broken through and were glistening in the mist. The present scene evoked memories of a distant past. The same chill, the same mist, and the same sunlight, tender as a newborn baby, was here then, when I used to walk with my mother, holding her hand, even as it is now when I'm in agony. How warm the river would be when I'd go in for a bath! And little puffs of steam would come out of my mouth whenever I said ah-ah-ha. I've remembered all this many times over—the moss on the temple walls, the monkeys on those walls. When did I think of this plan of action? If it seems like evil, well, so be it. Pilla is the sharp blade of an axe and I'm the handle. He must gain and I must let go. And having gained, he must learn to let go. Then history will move forward.

They're singing the morning hymn to wake up God. I'm waiting for the town to stir and stretch its limbs. Today I'll go to the huts of the Holeyaru. Whatever happens … let it happen.

Jagannatha returned home and had his breakfast with the others—some uppittu and coffee. The ambience in the dining room was festive; Neelakantaswami, Ranga Rao, and their friends set out again to canvass for the evening's programme. He had not seen Chikki since the morning. He went to the kitchen to see what she was doing. Bhagyamma was chopping vegetables. Chikki was engrossed in moulding a three-in-one fireplace. It was well known in the neighbourhood that fire burnt very well in her clay stoves. Neither Bhagyamma nor Chikki had noticed him. He was astonished at Chikki's absorption. She had suppressed her anxieties and busied herself in cooking and serving the guests. Jagannatha felt grateful to her. He walked away silently, went up to his room, and sat down to write to Margaret.

He began with *Dear Margaret* and wrote a restrained formal letter. It sounded false. Her photo on the table brought back the pang of losing her—her hair falling over her cheeks as she leant forward to say something mischievous, her eyes smiling, behind her the apple tree in the backyard of their apartment. He had taken the photo. Lying under this tree, she had rejected him once. Now she had rejected him again, in deed.

Margaret must have the freedom to be an individual. And having that liberty, she must be my possession, and even when she's mine, she must remain independent. This is what I want. If I can't possess her, our love won't be fruitful, and, yet, love won't last unless she is distinct from me. Ambivalent, but true. That's why being in love is such a torture.

He wrote another letter beginning it with *Darling.* It was magnanimous; forgiving, full of love. But it seemed manipulative by robbing her of her liberty and making her guilty. The problem was to be frank with her without revealing his heartache. He tore up that letter and started again: *Dearest Margaret, while my liberal views have lost, his jealousy, meanness, and intensity have won. In this way, you've tested my openness once again. I understand my defeat. Because your individuality is meaningful to me,*

I'll try to understand why you want to leave me for him. There's no need for pity. The moment may come when you may truly want me. I'll wait for it, firm and whole, Jagan.

He went over what he had written. Why haven't I mentioned Chandrashekar by name anywhere in the letter? It was too painful. But wouldn't it seem petty to consider the man that Margaret loves as nameless? So he rewrote the letter, correcting it here and there, using the very name Margaret had so fondly used, *Chander.* Even as he was writing it he agonized as if he had seen the two of them together in the nude. '*I've won!*' he thought as he read what he had written. But a deceptive expansiveness had sneaked in through the changes he had made, giving the impression that he was not jealous of Chandrashekar.

He felt he had no other way. At the end of the letter he added: 'Today I'm making an attempt to go into the homes of the Holeyaru.' And then he walked straight to the postbox and posted the letter.

He felt light-hearted.

In the afternoon, when everyone had gathered for lunch, Jagannatha announced, 'I won't be speaking today. You carry on with the programme.'

'Oh, you can't back out like that,' said Neelakantaswami, shocked.

'It's not that I'm backing out. I've something else to do. Anyway, I feel there's no point in making speeches.'

'We should make the people of the higher castes relate to the Holeyaru with love. That's Gandhiji's objective. The people may be willing if you speak to them.' Ananthakrishna added his bit.

'But that's not my intention,' explained Jagannatha, 'It's more important to make the Holeyaru rebel. The Holeyaru have to become persons. That's the reason I've decided there's no purpose in talking.'

Sripathi Rao did not join in the discussion. After lunch, Jagannatha persuaded Neelakantaswami to go without him. 'You carry on with your propaganda. Don't misunderstand me. I've some other plans for the evening. Far more important than making a speech.'

But Ranga Rao persisted, 'People will come if you'll be speaking.'

Presently, everyone left to canvass for the meeting.

Jagannatha went up to his room and wrote in his notebook: *I must become tough for decisive action and yet I must also remain sensitive to pain and joy. I must understand Nagamani's death.*

He felt expansive and generous. He wrote: *People like Chikki really know the Holeyaru. She knows who's a shirker at work; who's pregnant; who is whose mistress; how many children she has; how many have died ... But I'm trying to understand them even deeper in another kind of a relationship. And for that I'm destroying everything—Manjunatha; my memories; the temple bells that ring inside me; the people's respect for me. I'll be alienated from all these, and in losing them I'll regain everything. Even they will gain and in gaining will learn to let go. My freedom will grow only in as much as I emancipate the lowliest of the lowly. And with this new reality, I'll regain Margaret.*

Sripathi Rao came up to him in a hurry, Jagannatha looked at him quizzically.

'Do you know who got the farmhands to quit working for you?' he asked, and then sat down to chew betel leaves and nuts while recounting Prabhu's machinations. 'You'll face trouble from him,' he warned as he went out to chat with Ananthakrishna.

Jagannatha waited for the evening. He knew that no Holeya would attend the meeting to listen to the speeches. He washed his face, changed into clean clothes, combed his hair, and set out towards the huts of the Holeyaru with a light heart. He remembered what his mother used to say when he was a boy: 'If Brahmins enter the houses of the Holeyaru, they beat them up and drive them away, fearing they'll be ruined.'

Jagannatha was apprehensive.

He walked up the hillock staring at the thatched huts. He thought of the moment when the Holeyaru would see him in one of their houses and broke out in sweat. He felt there was no other way but to face up to anything that might happen. He walked right to the shacks. He could see no one except a Holathi in her backyard, placing a huge stoneware pot on three stones that served as a fireplace and lighting a fire. Perhaps, she was heating water to bathe at night. A few children were playing around with runny noses and with no clothes to protect them from the evening chill.

'Pilla!' called Jagannatha, standing in front of a hut. Wonder whose hut this is? We use the same word 'gudi' for temple and for the dwelling of the Holeya. How strange!

'Pilla!' he called out again and turned back.

The Holeyaru appeared from wherever and stood about. With dishevelled hair and naked except for the loincloth, they stood petrified, like statues carved in black stone.

'Is Pilla here?' Jagannatha tried to smile.

There was no answer.

Fear touched him.

'I've some work with him. So I came to see him.'

They might have been even more stupefied by his gentle tone. No one moved. Only the children continued to play. The whole situation with the setting sun and the silence seemed surreal. The way the Holeyaru were staring at him, standing one here, one there, became unbearable to Jagannatha, so he asked authoritatively, 'Why are all of you staring at me like this? Where's Pilla? Tell me.'

Pilla must have arrived just then. He came towards him in a hurry, dressed in white and limping slightly.

He too looked terrified.

'Come, Odeya. Please sit down,' said Pilla as he headed towards his hovel. Elated with victory, Jagannatha walked with him. Opening a door of woven palm fronds, Pilla invited him in, 'Come in, Odeya.' Jagannatha walked in amazed that the situation had changed beyond his expectations.

Except for a few baskets hanging from the loft and a few pots, there was nothing else in Pilla's house. But the mud floor, gleaming as if it had been polished, was clean. Pilla felt awkward that he had nothing to offer his master to sit on, but Jagannatha said, 'I don't need anything,' and sat on the floor.

The Holeyaru who had been standing at a distance until now surrounded Pilla's hut. One of them, an elder, came in and said, 'It isn't proper for Odeya to come into our huts this way.' His voice was trembling with fear.

Looking at Pilla, Jagannatha said, '*You* explain it all to them.' Pilla tried, 'Odeya says he can also touch us.' No one seemed to understand him.

'Where are the other young men?' asked Jagannatha.

'They'll be coming now, Odeyare.' Jagannatha was happy to see Pilla at ease while talking to him.

'None of you should be afraid, Pilla. All of you should walk with me. You should be furious enough to fight, to be able to say you're not swine but men. Understand?' Jagannatha wanted to say much more but stopped himself. He stood up and in front of everyone he put his arm on Pilla's shoulder.

'Where's your father?'

Pilla pointed to his father standing at a distance.

'We'll get your son married next month.' Jagannatha was smiling now. It looked as if the Holeyaru were in a daze. *This is just the beginning; everything will be sorted out later,* he said to himself, and to Pilla, 'Tell the other men I'd been here,' he said before leaving. Pilla too went along limping to see him to his house.

Jagannatha was cheerful when he reached home. Change will naturally bring fear, to the Holeyaru and to me. It's only when we hold it by the horn and look it in the face that it'll begin to loosen its grip on us.

Neelakantaswami, Ananthakrishna, and Ranga Rao had returned in high spirits after making their speeches. They were discussing what each had said at the meeting.

'You spoke very well,' said Sripathi Rao to Ananthakrishna.

'But I don't agree with the Sarvodaya principle of politics by persuasion,' countered Neelakantaswami and argued his point well with valid reasons. Jagannatha also joined in the discussion. The question of caste came up, and Jagannatha said, 'One can say the Lingayats have about fifty per cent claim to contend for caste-based politics because there are still some who are backward among them. Perhaps we can say the Vokkaligas have some seventy per cent right. As for the Brahmins, they have no authority at all. The only people who are justified a hundred per cent are the Holeyaru. But the tragedy is that they're not aware of their predicament. And, so, the Holeyaru, Lingayats, and Gowdas fight for caste-based politics in their tussle to get jobs. That's all.'

Neelakantaswami supported Jagannatha's argument.

'Class awareness is better than caste consciousness,' contended Ranga Rao.

'Nothing works without love,' added Ananthakrishna.

Adiga, who had been engrossed in listening to the discussion, raised his bum and farted. 'Damn the gas!' he muttered to himself, 'But this body craves for gassy foods.'

The socialists looked down with embarrassment.

After dinner everyone went to bed. Jagannatha walked about on the front porch. In the sky were the two stars: Vashishta Maharshi and the Holathi, Arundhati. Jagannatha chuckled. On the chilly eve of the new moon day, the stars were sharp and bright like needle points. Jagannatha's heart bloomed with joy. He went in and opened the door of Chikki's room. Chikki was sleeping with just a sari covering her; she had not put off the lamp. 'Put on a blanket, Chikki. Aren't you feeling cold?' he asked, taking out a coverlet from a bench nearby and going to cover her.

Jagannatha laughed when she replied peevishly, 'Ayyo, why do I need it?' and insisted on covering her with a blanket. He lowered the wick of the lamp. Chikki was happy.

Perhaps I wouldn't have been able to rebel like this if Amma were alive or if I had had a younger sister to be married. And what if I had belonged to the middle class?

He came to his room, turned down the lantern, and lay on his bed. His body was warm; he did not feel like having a blanket over the shawl. That was the woolen shawl his mother had brought him many years ago. It was soft and brown, the colour of snuff. He had been wrapping himself with it for some twenty years now. It was worn smooth with use. He himself had darned some of the frayed patches. Margaret had also patched it up in two places though she had teased him about it. After father had died, mother had gone on a ten-month-long pilgrimage. She had bought the shawl in Kashi and brought it for him. Even now Jagannatha covered himself with it, lying on his side, crooking his legs, and tucking his hands between his thighs, just as he used to sleep as a boy. He had to sleep in this, his favourite position, to sleep well. Margaret had teased him saying he was a baby in the womb. She would press down his crooked knees with her legs; she would complain there was not enough space for the two of them on the bed if he slept that way; she would pull out his hands and straighten him, laughing. Jagannatha remembered, 'Even when she locked her toes in mine and pulled my legs down, I had to draw them up as I fell asleep.

"Please," I'd say, caressing her, petting her, as I drew up my legs and dozed off.'

He suddenly felt a twinge of pain as he tried to sleep but he was drowsy again. He was in deep sleep when he heard people screaming. He got up and rushed down. The others had already gathered in the yard before him.

TWENTY THREE

The Burning

Fire was raging on the hilltop. And beyond the yard stood the wailing Holeyaru. The farmhands had lit all the lamps available and brought them out—gaslights, lanterns, and the bed lamp. Jagannatha was bewildered. 'Where am I? Am I sleeping? Is this a dream?'

'All this is because they touched the saligrama,' he heard Chikki telling Adiga. Neelakantaswami and Ranga Rao were running around briskly, trying to get the situation under control. Ranga Rao brought a pot of honey from inside and smeared it on the burns. Some elderly Holeyaru were weeping. Neelakantaswami walked about scolding the Holeyaru, advising them, boosting their courage. Ananthakrishna accompanied one of the socialist youths to fetch the doctor. Jagannatha found Pilla and asked him, 'What happened?'

While everyone was sleeping, the huts had caught fire. Pilla had run out shouting. He had awakened everyone and brought them out. While they were coming away from the fire, some of them had suffered burns.

Jagannatha did not know what to say to the Holeyaru who were looking at him, distraught. He took Neelakantaswami aside and whispered, 'No one has died, I hope?'

'I think … one boy … But don't say anything until the doctor arrives.'

Neelakantaswami lit a cigarette. 'I expected such violence,' he said as he went out to console the Holeyaru. Jagannatha also went with him and helped smear honey on the burns. One of the socialists was describing an incident in Mandya where a Holeya's fingers had been chopped off. A Holathi was lamenting, 'Where shall we sleep? Where can we live? Whom do we turn to now?' Jagannatha tried to reassure her but failing, he scolded her.

What should I do right now? Daybreak is a long way off. The Holeyaru need a roof. They can't possibly sleep under the night sky; it's too chilly. And the other Holeyaru won't let them go anywhere near them.

'Neelakantaswami, take them to the long shed beside the house, the one in which areca nuts are skinned,' he said.

But the Holeyaru hesitated to enter it. Neelakantaswami's persuasion did not work; Jagannatha had to shout at them and send them in. Chikki felt she was making it difficult for them by standing there and went indoors.

The parents of the dead boy, however, sat outside with the body in front of them. They would not move even when Jagannatha asked them to get inside. They would not listen even when Neelakantaswami said, 'The doctor will come and treat him. You go in.' The child's body was full of blisters; his face was disfigured by burns. And yet they were under the illusion that he was alive. The father told Jagannatha how the boy had got burnt so badly:

'He was in the loft when our hut caught fire. On the loft was a bunch of bananas. This boy's crazy about bananas; he's used to stealing them and eating them. He'd never listen to me however much I'd tell him not to. Wretched fellow! When the thatch caught fire, the flames caught him right in the face. It's only when he fell down with a thud that we realized our house was burning.'

Jagannatha wondered how to tell the parents that their boy was dead. He tried, 'Look here, your boy …' He could not understand why the mother had stood up in fear even before he could finish. Crying loudly, she said, 'That bunch of bananas wasn't stolen from your farm, Odeyare. I'd gone to my mother's house last week. She gave it to me for us to eat. I'd kept it in a pot in the loft to ripen. If you want me to, I'm willing to swear on Bhootharaya. These bananas weren't stolen from your farm.'

It sickened Jagannatha to see her humbling herself. He was irritated that she thought he was talking about the bunch of bananas.

'Your son is dead.'

As soon as he told them in a hoarse voice, the parents broke down screaming and crying. And all the Holeyaru who were in the shed came running out as soon as they heard the heart-rending cries. Perhaps they were finding it as difficult to be in his house as it must have been inside their burning huts. 'Go in! Go in!' he said roughly but no one heard him. All of them surrounded the dead boy and wailed. 'Let them cry if they want to,' he said to himself and went off to stand in a corner of the yard. The doctor had brought some balm for the burns and was now sitting on the porch with Ananthakrishna, talking to him. Neelakantaswami and Ranga Rao, together with the socialists, were among the Holeyaru, looking for those who were seriously hurt and bringing them to the doctor. Seeing Jagannatha standing alone, Pilla came up to him. So did Adiga. Both of them stood quietly. The silence was intolerable.

'You believe all this happened because they touched the saligrama, don't you?' Jagannatha asked Adiga cruelly and looked at Pilla who stood at a distance in the darkness.

Adiga did not reply.

'Tell me. Why are you silent?'

'This isn't the time for anger, Jaganna.'

Jagannatha was disgusted with Adiga's phony gentleness. 'Give me an answer, Adigâre. I'm astounded at the way the minds of people like you work.'

'It's true that touching the saligrama is indirectly responsible for the death of the boy. If you hadn't put your hand to turn this wheel, everything would've been as it was, wouldn't it?'

On hearing Subbaraya Adiga talking so calmly, Jagannatha burnt with fury.

'Aren't you ashamed to spout Advaita here?'

'You should be sad because a boy died while eating a banana, not angry.'

'What if a Brahmin boy had died?'

'There's no need for discussion, Jaganna. Think of your responsibility in all this.'

'Your mysticism, your Shankaracharya—everything is an excuse to uphold this system. That's all.'

'Because of your anger, you're becoming a sham. That's all.'

The hiss of the gaslights burning in the dark, mingling with the wail of the Holeyaru, made the house on the hilltop like a burning ghat.

'You're unable to see what you have to see with your eyes wide open, Jaganna; your mind is agitated.'

Jagannatha did not reply. He looked at Pilla's face and tried to make out what he could be thinking at the moment. Adiga continued calmly, 'A sadhu in Dakshineshwar used to say, "Tell me what'll happen if you try to pounce on someone who's leaping on you? You'll hurt yourself. Instead, move in the same direction that he's jumping and step aside, don't try to push him from the front. Then, he'll fall flat on his face and you'll be saved." This is the secret of movement. The Holeyaru have been keeping pretty much to themselves. With their drink and their dance, they were happy. They had adjusted to their situation. "If you say you won't touch me, I won't touch you either," they said. In this way, they had learnt to tolerate their condition. Of course, it's greater to get involved than to adjust. When you see it from that angle everything seems frivolous, like a wanton sport—the fire, the suffering, you with your hand on the wheel to turn it—everything.'

Wonder how many centuries of intrigue are behind Adiga's pattern of thinking! 'Don't you ever get angry, Adigare?' Jagannatha asked with intense disgust. 'Don't you feel the man who's behind the arson when the Holeyaru were sleeping is a low-born worm? Prabhu might've done this work or perhaps Shetty, whoever. Anyway, why don't you get furious, tell me? Why don't you feel this caste system is stunting your very humanity, tell me? Only when the Holeyaru are like animals, willing to be kicked when they're kicked, do they merit your love, don't they? Why don't you think this is despicable, tell me? Your

Shankaracharya, Madhavacharya, your Paramahamsa, your Ramana Maharshi[82]—all of them are like you, arrogant.'

'Who am I, anyway?' replied Adiga without losing his temper, 'I've put on this costume to feed my stomach, that's all. I've no right to speak; I bash up my wife when I'm angry. But I have doubts about your rage. Is it burning steadily like the flame of burning camphor or is it smouldering like fire on damp faggots?'

Jagannatha was stumped for a moment. 'This sort of a discussion will make me look inward and become incapable of any action, he thought' as he walked away to talk to Pilla.

Subbaraya Adiga went towards where Ananthakrishna was seated.

Jagannatha was dispirited to see the way the Holeyaru were sitting in the yard and bewailing their loss. As much as there was genuine grief, there was so much cunning too in their attempt to exploit his sympathy. I really can't love these people sincerely, he felt.

Neelakantaswami called Jagannatha for some confidential discussion. He seemed to be in a flurry. Jagannatha was disconcerted at the way he was whispering secretively. Perhaps even as he bent close to his ear and muttered, Neelakantaswami's fingers were separating his hair, strand by strand, and tugging at it, as they did whenever he was agitated. Neelakantaswami said in the dark, 'Saar, we must make an issue of this. I'll go straight to Shimoga and send a press-telegram to Bangalore. It'll make front-page news. I'll take photos with my camera. I heard the boy's name is Chouda. We must make Chouda the hero of our campaign.'

Jagannatha felt it was immoral to have such dealings with a man like Neelakantaswami who was quite happy to capitalize on the situation without any scruples. It seemed as if all of them were together perpetrating some injustice; as if only he was doing something else, ignoring the truth he had to confront in this situation. But it was impossible for Jagannatha to think clearly with Neelakantaswami whispering persistently in his ear, 'Our enemies don't have your sensitivity, Saar. They'll set fire. Kill. Threaten. We can't afford to sit back. We have to disturb the conscience of the people. And, for that, we'll have to use the newspaper, the radio, everything.'

[82] A saint who stressed that truth cannot be taught, it has to be experienced.

'I know,' thought Jagannatha, 'but what about the boy, disfigured and dead? What about the responsibility I must bear? What about these naive innocent people?' He needed silence to internalize all this and to dwell on it so that some chaste action could emerge from it. He needed solitude. 'But, henceforth, I'll never have solitude. I've been cast out from the intimacy of curling up in the softness of the shawl Amma gave me and revolving round my own self. Now, should I say, "Yes"; should I say, "No"? Should I say, "No", and meditate with Adiga on the veranda?'

The wail of the bereaved mother was unbearable. 'Yes,' he said.

Neelakantaswami ran upstairs and brought his camera. Ranga Rao brought all the gaslights and placed them strategically around the Holeyaru. In the darkness of the night a corner of the yard was blooming in the artificial light. And in the light stood the naked Holeyaru, clothed only in their loincloths. Their hair stood out like black bushes. Neelakantaswami ran about taking pictures of the disfigurement and the agony from various strategic angles in the flare of the flashbulbs. He cajoled them into sitting in different poses, waited for their keening, and clicked the camera at the right moments. He called Jagannatha and said, 'Look at Chouda and tell me where he has wounds from the burns, Saar. I'll need to wire the details.' As Jagannatha examined Chouda's body, Neelakantaswami waited for the moment when his face expressed his anguish and clicked. Jagannatha felt dirty as the flash went off. Seeing Jagannatha straightening up enraged, Neelakantaswami said amiably, 'We need even that, Saar.'

Neelakantaswami and Ranga Rao drove off in the car to Shimoga. Ananthakrishna was all praises for the two of them, 'Neelakantaswami will surely win the next elections. Nanjanagudu, his constituency, has a sizeable number of Schedule Caste voters.'

As soon as he arrived, Sripathi Rao made arrangements for the disposal of Chouda's body. He calculated the materials needed to build new huts the very next day. There was an ample stock of bamboo and wooden poles in Jagannatha's house. 'It would be dangerous to thatch the huts again. We'll have to buy zinc sheets from that scoundrel, Prabhu. See how he's benefited from the arson he's planned. Even if we think of getting them from Shimoga, we'll have to use Prabhu's lorry.

In any case, whether he was behind the fire or Janardhana Shetty, it's irrelevant. The dead boy is dead,' said Sripathi Rao.

Jagannatha sat on the veranda, listening to him. Adiga, who was sitting with Ananthakrishna said gently, 'Jaganna, these politicians are a weird bunch, aren't they? Look at your Neelakantaswami, for instance ...'

Jagannatha was hurt.

'Adigare,' he said, 'Behind your spirituality is the temple, the money, the blind faith, and people who set fire to children and kill them in the dead of night. In the same way, behind me there are people who play dirty politics. But shall I tell you how I feel about the two? The work that Neelakantaswami's doing with his camera is more meaningful than your unworldly grief.'

Even if Jagannatha had any doubts about what he had said, he was able to overcome it at least for the moment. Adiga did not reply. Ananthakrishna spoke about Gandhi's philosophy concerning means and ends. Adiga noticed that it was nearly daybreak. He picked up his jug and got up to go to the river for his morning ablutions on new moon day. But before he left, he told them a story:

'I'll tell you a story to show you that our society has come to this state only because Brahmins have lost their respect for rituals. A mendicant in Gujarat told me this story. Once upon a time there was an agrahaara where a community of orthodox Brahmins lived. In each Brahmin's house there was the fire-pit for religious ceremonies. And each family ate only after the ritual sacrifices to the gods. And then what happened one day? A Brahmin, an elder, got his son married and brought the bride home. The daughter-in-law was a young girl. That was her first day in her husband's house. She woke up that night wanting to go to the toilet urgently. The house was new to her; the place was strange; she was scared to go outside. And, so, she pissed in the smouldering fire-pit and went in to sleep without telling anyone what she had done. The elder Brahmin woke up the next morning and saw a nugget of gold in the fire-pit. He got worried. How can there be gold in the holy fireplace? He was very upset that the place had somehow been polluted. At that moment his daughter-in-law came up to him looking very scared. She prostrated in front of him and told him she had peed in the holy place. The father-in-law was a good man. "Don't worry," he said to her and looked in the Dharmashastra. He found the way to propitiate the gods for the sin his daughter-in-law had committed. After he purified the fire-pit according to the stipulations and got back to performing the daily rituals, he had an idea. After all, there was a way to sanctify the fire-pit whenever it was desecrated. And so he asked his daughter-in-law to piss in the fire-pit again the next day. And she did. The Brahmin next door got to know of this. He said to his daughter-in-law, "Anyway, there's an approved way of ritually cleansing the fire-pit. So you piss in it too." In this way, the news went round and all the Brahmins in the agrahaara started this practice. But one poor Brahmin did not agree to this. Even when his wife pestered him, he did not comply; he moved out of the settlement. When his house fell vacant, his neighbour thought, "If I can get a nugget of gold from my fire-pit, why shouldn't I acquire his fire-pit too and get two nuggets and become wealthier than the others?" Then each Brahmin wanted to acquire all the fire-pits; it was the beginning of their greed. Eventually, the whole agrahaara was destroyed by fire.'

After his narration, Adiga might have wondered how the story was relevant to the situation. Suddenly, he walked away, saying, 'I'll be back after my bath.'

TWENTY FOUR

New Moon Day

Chikki brought four huge pots of gruel, a roll of banana leaves for plates, and some mango pickle on another leaf for the Holeyaru who carried their meal to a corner of the hill. They would not—could not—eat in her presence. Jagannatha called Pilla and his friends and told them, 'Look, we'll be going into the temple tomorrow. You shouldn't be nervous because of all that's happened. Right now I'm making arrangements to put up huts with zinc-sheet roofing for all of you.'

He wanted to ask Pilla what he was thinking about but, perhaps, the very word *think* would be new to him. Apart from Pilla, none of the other men were real to him as yet. Kariya? Mada? Basya? The only other person who had become real to him was Chouda, the dead boy.

Jagannatha had his breakfast and set out. The morning was chilly with a tender sunlight but his body warmed up with the walk. There were people all along the way. Among those returning from the river after their bath, there were some familiar faces and so many more unfamiliar ones. Sripathi Rao had taken the responsibility of getting the huts built and so Jagannatha could afford to relax a bit. He could stroll about watching pilgrims who had come from different corners of the country to fulfil their vows. No one seemed to be bothered about his plan of action. For centuries now, people have bathed in this way on this very day. They have told the same old story. They've told it to their children just as Amma used to tell me: 'Jamadagni, a sage, was a very short-tempered man. Sensing an unchaste thought in his wife, he asked his children to chop off her head; none of them came forward. None except Parashurama. He raised the axe and cut off his mother's head; he was bound by the principle that one should never disobey his father's orders. But she was his mother, wasn't she? And doesn't love transcend such rules? Pleased with his son's implicit obedience, Jamdagni told Parashurama to ask for a boon. He asked him to bring his mother back to life. And so his mother lived. But the bloodstain on the axe remained no matter in which river he washed it ... At last he dipped the axe in the Tunga that flows by Bharathipura. And the bloodstain vanished. Kodali Rama installed Manjunatha here in memory of his sin being washed away. In the swirling pool in the river where he had washed the axe, thousands of people immerse themselves on the morning of the new moon day. And then they walk about with a light heart, believing their sins have been washed away. This place as the destroyer of sin, this eddy; the belief and the love that rises beyond it ... Trying to regain the clear, pure conviction he had deep within himself when he had first taken his decision, Jagannatha stood on the bank of the river. How many thousands of people! The aged, the children, the women—pale, turmeric-smeared faces of women, tired out with countless birthings, hair dripping with water ... I used to run behind Amma's thick, black hair dripping with water, to keep pace with her.

Doubt should bloom in the minds of these people; they should also become aware. They should be able to kick God and stand tall. The power of Bhootharaya should surge in the Holeyaru. They should take responsibility for their lives. If only they could take that one step into the temple, these who have always been outcasts! Pilla's first step must agitate this ancient place of pilgrimage that has been hibernating. Whatever it is that has become accustomed to the daily ritual of ringing big bells and small bells will have to shudder and rise. Chouda's corpse, Pilla's blood, the burnt down huts—all these must carve out a new reality.

Jagannatha was happy no one had recognized him. He turned back. The chariot was decorated for the next day's festival. There were the same damp ropes to pull it. Under the same tree there was another man with a performing monkey. There was also a gymnast. And the shops down the street were opening their doors. What a gathering! If only there could be a slight crack in it to let a single doubt creep in; that should do. It could create a great rift.

Catching sight of him as he opened his sweetmeat stall, Vasu greeted him, 'Hey, how're you?'

TWENTY FIVE

Interview

'Mr Jagannath, may I ask you another question? Are you an existentialist? I'm asking you because your ideas are similar to what Sartre has preached on commitment,' asked PRT, a newspaper reporter who had come from Bangalore. Neelakantaswami's trunk-call to the press had worked. With him was a short, sprightly man with a loud guffaw, who looked much like Puck. He was darting about taking photographs of Jagannatha from different angles. PRT was taking down Jagannatha's replies to his questions seated in front of him, notebook in hand. Neelakantaswami was listening eagerly to whatever Jagannatha had to say while discreetly pushing his chair closer to Jagannatha's so that he could also be in the pictures.

'I don't like to explain my action in terms of the expressions you're using,' Jagannatha said, without any enthusiasm.

'So shall we say you're a Marxist?' PRT was well-known for getting ministers to talk.

'Our communists haven't ever been rooted in our own environment in their way of thinking; they been looking either towards Russia or towards China.'

'Then, are you a socialist of the Lohia School?'

'I feel Jagannatha Rao's way of thinking is very close to Lohia's.' Neelakantaswami had broken away from the Socialist Party in Lohia's name. So it served his purpose to make such a statement.

'It's true I like Lohia's ideas. But, as I'm not so interested in parliamentary politics, I haven't joined Neelakantaswami's party. I need the help of whoever believes in this campaign.'

PRT did not let it go at that. As he drank the coffee Chikki sent them, he got an export-quality Charminar cigarette from Puck, the photographer, and lit it. He offered one to Jagannatha.

'I don't smoke much, but all right,' Jagannatha too lit one.

'You're planning the entry of the Harijans into the temple right before the Chariot Festival tomorrow. Are you aware that there'll be a mighty revolution because of this?'

'Well, that's what I thought … but not any more. Before any revolution, I intend to rend the faith of this town. If that's fruitful, it would be the first step. Perhaps the Holeyaru may not step into the temple out of fear. Isn't that possible? My aim is to get them to revolt only because *they* wish to. Whether we win or lose tomorrow, I know the struggle has already begun.'

'That is correct.' Neelakantaswami praised him to show his approval.

'Another question. The crown that we see on Manjunatha in every picture is said to be a donation for saving your life. Any comments?'

'No,' said Jagannatha.

'Now, the reason for the burning of the huts: Some say it happened because the Holeyaru had touched the saligrama and some others say it's because one of your followers tried to rape a girl of the Bunt community. Any comments?'

'It's for the police to track down the guilty.'

'There's a rumour that a merchant from this town had a hand in it,' said Ranga Rao pointedly, trying to draw PRT's attention to it. PRT crushed the cigarette underfoot and asked, 'While some people say you're an idealist, a few others are of the opinion that in the next election you plan to stand from this constituency. All this is in preparation for that, they feel.'

Jagannatha laughed as he shook his head.

'I'll just carry on with this work of uniting them, that's all. First the Holeyaru, then the farmers ...'

'What's your opinion of the present council of ministers? Do you think we can bring in the socialistic pattern of society?'

'No, the President of our country washed the feet of Brahmins at Kashi and drank the water believing it to be sacred. He fell at the feet of the Sringeri Swami, who, I heard, doesn't give holy water to widows with unshaven heads. He's also a great devotee of this god, Manjunatha. It's my opinion that in this country we have to first free the people from the clutches of God.'

'Thank you.'

PRT stood up to go about the city with the photographer. Noticing the packets of Manjunatha's prasada in their pockets, Jagannatha asked them, 'Did you visit the temple before coming here?'

'Yes. A beautiful place. What a tremendous bell there is at the place! I heard your family gifted it,' said PRT. The photographer brought his palms together and bowed to wish goodbye and then laughed familiarly, shook hands, and bounded away behind PRT.

PRT returned to Bangalore with a story together with pictures: The crown that had saved Jagannatha's life featured prominently in the story. There were also bits about Jagannatha's study abroad; his acquaintance with E. M. Forster; his interaction with the New Leftists; his long hair, simple clothes, aquiline nose, and elegant bearing; and then about the saligrama incident; the attempt at molestation; the existential theory about taking the first step towards changing a centuries-old reality; the boycott of the farmhands; merchant Prabhu's anxieties about a breakdown of economic stability in Bharathipura; and about the power of Manjunatha's henchman, Bhootharaya—his power over every strife, every illness, his power to give the grace of motherhood to barren women. And then a poser: *Will Jagannatha contest the next election?* There were rumours and speculations and a pointer at the present MLA Gurappa Gowda's non-committal silence. He had also covered the fire in the huts, Chouda as victim of the arson, Pilla as Jagannatha's henchman, and Chikki's hospitality to the guests despite her disapproval of Jagannatha's stand.

He had added towards the end: *Bharathipura is an attractive little town nestling among hills. It has been sleepy and insular for thousands of years. It would be wrong to presume that now this ancient township is particularly alarmed; it conceals within itself the essence of Indian culture. As you walk these streets you see thousands of foreheads, all smeared with the kumkuma, Manjunatha's prasada. On the day of the Chariot Festival, ask any of them if the Holeyaru can cross the threshold of the temple. They will shake their heads without a trace of anxiety; they firmly believe that Bhootharaya will drag the Holeyaru out by their feet and that they will die, spitting blood. One of the men belonging to the Brahmin Youth Association said, 'If Jagannatha Rao was a true revolutionary, he should have boycotted the temple. There is no meaning in an atheist saying that the Holeyaru too need the temple.' Whatever that may be, it would not be wrong to say that this temple, which has received the President of the country as a devotee, has grown and now rests on the faith of the common people. The only ones who cut across class differences in India are gods and god-men. It is not Mr Jagannatha Rao's intention to make this god attainable to the Harijans too, but there are many instances in the country to show that this could also happen, overshooting his purpose. The district commissioner at Shimoga is himself a Harijan. He said to me, 'Our society has to be transformed through the non-violence Gandhiji believed in. Under the leadership of the President, the country is already treading the road to social progress peacefully. I believe the doors of the Manjunatha temple will be opened to the Harijans one day or the other. Has not Vedanta preached* panditthaaha samadharshinaha[83]*? It would be a failing on my part if I did not gratefully remember here that the temple committee had sent me the prasada when I took over as the district commissioner. Hostility is wrong. Communities should live together in harmony. The Harijans should become educated, put aside their differences, and create a prosperous society under the leadership of our President.*

In conclusion, PRT had said: *When I met Mr Satyaprakash in his house, it was early in the morning. On his forehead was the kumkuma. Wondering if it was Manjunatha's prasada, I mulled over my experiences at Bharathipura.*

[83] 'To the learned view, everything is equally valuable.' (Bhagavad Gita, chapter V: verse 18)

TWENTY SIX

The Letter

The three-piece clay oven had to be dry. Chikki had smeared it with a coat of diluted cow-dung mixed with black charcoal powder and was drawing small, delicate rangoli designs on it with white chalk powder.

In a corner of the yard, Neelakantaswami was busy with his friends readying the placards:

Banish Untouchability right now!
Victory to the Mysore Socialist Party,
Inquilab Zindabad!
Exploiter of Farmers, Bhootharaya!
Exploiter of Bhootharaya, Manjunatha . . . !

Ranga Rao was arranging the red-lettered placards in a line to dry. Sripathi Rao was busy getting new huts built for the Holeyaru.

A Holeya stood at a distance and called out respectfully, 'Odeyare.' He was not one of Jagannatha's men. Bringing his palms together, he begged, 'Because *your* Holeyaru are entering the temple our Odeya is angry; he says he'll throw us out. Odeyaru should protect us.' Even as Jagannatha was wondering what to say, Sripathi Rao tied the edge of his dhothi round his waist and said, 'Hey, Kogga, get away! If your master drives you out, who'll carry the baskets of shit on their heads to clean out his toilets, tell me? And that too now, during the festival! He may set your huts on fire at the most, that's all. Take turns to keep watch.'

Jagannatha was pleased with the way Rao had spoken. He wanted to tell the Holeyaru: 'Your lowliness is your strength. In your lowliness you're indispensable to this society. Say you won't sweep out the shit. Then you have the power to create a stench that can pervade every corner of the town and destroy the fragrance of joss sticks and frankincense that surrounds Manjunatha every day.' Jagannatha trembled. He looked out of the window at the mango tree, laden with flowers. 'Margaret, the frothy beer on the table, the pastime of heady confident talk about being able to make every human possibility bloom—henceforth, no more of all these. I'll have to use this cruelty, this dream, this penance that's withering me to locate the key points of Bharathipura's stability and crush them. If the awareness is born that even a mystic's shit would stink if there was no Holeya, then Time would move on. And, with the change, the production of iron will increase. And, with the increase, steel pipes will come into use. And, with that, there will be flush-toilets all over the country. The need for baskets of shit to be carried on heads will disappear. Gandhiji's and Basavanna's dream will blossom. Instead of human waste, these dark Holathiyaru will wear white jasmine flowers in their hair and, besmeared with sandalwood paste, they'll be attractive to Brahmin men. And Brahmin girls will fall for dark, broad-shouldered men like Pilla.'

Jagannatha was revelling in his illusions and felt ashamed he could derive so much pleasure from fantasizing. 'It's vital that I realize my own need to let go of my Self. Or else I can't become real; I won't be able to act resolutely. I'll become gooey. It's because I'm still an introspective demon that I'm disturbed by these scenes of cruelty. Once I'm totally engrossed in the act, I'll become a surgeon's keen-edged scalpel, without love, without hate, merely an instrument capable of cutting along the lines of purpose.

'So, if I have to renounce myself, how much of me should I let go?' Jagannatha entered another train of thought. 'Kaapaalikas and

Shaakthas are supposed to mate with corpses to attain special powers. They're believed to exhume the dead and eat them to become ascetics. Ascetics are perfect revolutionaries. Do I also have to take their path of renunciation? As Adiga says, is it really impossible to belong to society and be a revolutionary? The irony is that we have to enter the temple to destroy God's glory.'

Ranganna brought him the mail.

Jagannatha opened a long envelope, a local delivery. In it was a letter written in running hand on both sides of a foolscap sheet. In the top left hand corner was the conventional *kshema*, 'safe', and in the top centre, 'Shri Manjunatha *Prasanna*'. He turned it over wondering who it could be from. There was no signature. He began to read the letter with curiosity. He was used to reading clerk Krishnaiah's cursive writing and so it was not a strain to read this:

To Shri Jagannatha Rao, an eminent landlord of the town, the erstwhile trustee of the Shri Manjunatha Temple, the one responsible for the golden crown on Manjunathaswami's head in gratitude for saving his life, the one carrying the burden of protecting the citizens of Bharathipura like a father, to you comes this humble appeal from a poor man who has been a well-wisher of your family from your father's time ...

Jagannatha folded the letter, feeling bored. He was about to tear it up but was attracted to the charm of its old-world style and so continued to read it:

Jagannatharayare, it grieves this poor man greatly to write that you may not be your father's son. Your father was a devotee of God. The lady who married him, your mother, had no relationship with him at all. We do not know how your father endured this. Whatever that may be, in case you were truly your father's son, it is certain you would not have come forward to do such a heinous act, belonging as you would be to a high-class Brahmin family. Then do you ask whose son you are? You are the son of Krishnaiah who worked as a clerk in your house. It is not surprising that he was everything to your mother even though he was a Brahmin of the lowest class. But that is irrelevant to us as it concerns an over-sexed woman. It is said that the sin of the sinner is in the mouth of the one who speaks about it. But I have to talk about it; I have no choice. I am an eyewitness to the fact that Gopala, who lives in your house, is also your mother's son. You may be aware that when you were young, your mother left the town on the pretext of going on a pilgrimage with Krishnaiah and his wife. At that time, when I had gone to Madras on some work, I saw your mother pregnant. She delivered the baby there, named him Gopala, and they returned with the story that the baby was born to Krishnaiah's ailing wife during the pilgrimage. As she was childless, Krishnaiah's wife brought up Gopala as her own son without complaining. And especially after she died one or two years later, your mother carried on her sinful relationship with Krishnaiah unhindered.

The reason I'm bringing up all this is only to ask you to straighten out the mess in your house before you try to reform the town and not to sully your late father's revered memory. The shastras ask us to sacrifice a person to save a town. And so we have courage to believe that Shri Manjunathaswami will forgive us if we have to reveal the facts to curb your influence completely in this town. Reiterating that, had you been born as the son of a high-class Brahmin, you would not have come forward in this way to destroy the town, I end this letter with great sadness,

Always your well-wisher,

A resident of Bharathipura

Jagannatha went down the steps to the yard; he did not know why he was going that way. Neelakantaswami was sitting there, getting the posters made. Sripathi Rao was overseeing the supply of bamboo, wooden poles, and rope. Jagannatha stood quietly among them. Seeing him standing there, Ranga Rao came up to him. 'Why ... Saar? Aren't you well?' he asked, looking at Jagannatha's face anxiously. Even Sripathi Rao was worried. 'Go in and lie down,' he said. 'I'm okay,' said Jagannatha, trying to look at him calmly. And then he went up, lay on his bed, and closed his eyes. The letter was on the table. He tore it up and tossed it into the waste-paper basket lest anyone else should read it.

'Where's Pilla? What should I tell him about tomorrow? Their clothes are all burnt. I must get them new sets. Oh, I forgot to see to that. He came down again and told Rao they had to buy some clothes for the Holeyaru. 'White shirts and white dhothis,' he stressed.

'You don't look well. You lost sleep all of last night. Go and lie down,' said Rao.

Jagannatha sat on the porch. His legs felt weak. Seeing him sitting there, Neelakantaswami also came and sat beside him and said, 'Ranga Rao had been to the market. And, do you know, Mr Jagannath? No one there believes that the Holeyaru will be entering the temple tomorrow. They say Bhootharaya will appear and pull them out by their legs.' Neelakantaswami laughed as he lit a cigarette. Jagannatha took a cigarette from him, lit it, and sat with his eyes closed. He tried to smile at what Neelakantaswami had said and got up saying, 'I've got to see to something.'

'You don't look well. You've lost sleep. Go and get some rest,' said Neelakantaswami as he went back to getting the posters ready. As he was walking away, he said, 'I'm getting a big poster done that says *Change is the dharma of life*.'

Jagannatha scolded himself for his stupidity: Look at the way I'm fretting over a letter from some poisonous worm! *Thuth*! Gopala was in front of the mirror in the hall, combing his hair. He turned and smiled warmly and, seeing Jagannatha staring at him, said, 'Did you want something, Anna?' Jagannatha started. 'What if it is true? Or is it a lie? Truth or falsehood, there's no one to tell me. Probably Rayaru will say it's a lie; even Chikki may tell me it's untrue. But how can I believe them? And yet, how can I trust this venomous creature's letter? So is it true or false? There's no place or time that can free me from this speculation.'

Jagannatha went up the stairs without saying anything to Gopala. 'I must talk to Pilla about tomorrow. Tell him about what? Everything seems pointless. It's true I'm in agony. I have to stare this turmoil in the face, there's no other way; that's also true. And it's also true that I'll be turning this question over and over again inside me with no respite; going around it over and over again. And I'll live looking at me going around it over and over again until I die.

'If there was no room for doubt, would I have possibly dwelt on it this way? I always slept by Amma's side. I was in middle school at that time. I couldn't sleep. Amma sat up and was munching betel leaves and nuts. She wasn't supposed to chew betel leaves after Appa died and yet she used to. She put the betel leaf in her mouth and went out. I was still awake. Did I wonder why Amma had put the betel leaf in her mouth and gone out? I don't remember. But, then, why do I remember even now that I was awake that night? She returned after a long time and slept beside me. Where had she gone? To Krishnaiah's room beside the office or to the toilet? Krishnaiah's wife, Sakamma, used to sleep in the room next to the kitchen. She used to see to things like milk and ghee. She was Krishnaiah's elder sister's daughter—with very small eyes and a crooked face. Did Chikki live with us then? Yes, she did. Upstairs, in another room—in the same room as she sleeps even now. If Chikki didn't suspect anything at all, then whatever's said in the letter isn't true. If she did she wouldn't have respected Amma so highly. And even Rayaru, what great regard he had for Amma! So she must've gone only to the toilet and returned. But I know for sure that she never would chew betel leaves before going to the toilet. When Amma came back and slept again beside me, was she perspiring? Was her hair all tousled?'

Trying to stop his mind from agonizing over the muddle, Jagannatha looked out of the window. Rayaru, Neelakantaswami, and Ranga Rao were engrossed in whatever they were doing. The volunteers were laughing as they went about their work. Pilla was limping towards Rayaru. 'No, this is like spiralling down an endless tunnel perpetually. This is true agony as there's no respite from it.

'Amma used to play dice with Krishnaiah. And Chikki too would join them. And Sakamma too. Appa died when I was in primary school. Appa too used to be with them when they played dice, but I don't remember him playing or singing. Krishnaiah used to read Kumaravyasa's[84] *Bharatha* beautifully and explain it. Chikki says Appa trusted Krishnaiah very much. When I was in the middle school, Krishnaiah, Sakamma, and Amma had gone on a tour of India for about eight or ten months. Chikki was with me then. When they returned, Gopala was a tiny baby. Sakamma used to pet him. Amma too. That's why everything is surely a lie. Amma knew Hindi. She brought me a shawl from Kashi. It's a blatant lie that she was in Madras. The one who's written to me that he saw Amma pregnant there is a despicable worm.'

Jagannatha sighed deeply and stretched his legs in bed. He wanted to toss about; he was so happy. 'Amma was wealthier than Appa. Three-fourths of the property we have now is hers. Appa was a good agriculturist. I've heard Rayaru say he used to wonder who the real landlord was: Appa who worked with the farmers with his dhothi tied high at knee-length, or Krishnaiah who went about to the court and the offices in his silk jubba and fine Finlay dhothi.

[84] Naranappa of Gadag, an epic poet of the fifteenth century, who wrote ten cantos of the Mahabharata in six-line stanzas. His *Bharatha* is known for its narrative and poetic power.

'I'm surprised I'm suspicious like this; I've seen different possibilities in man-woman relationships in England. Perhaps people were jealous of Krishnaiah. How normal! But it could also be equally natural to be suspicious.'

Jagannatha got up feeling light-hearted and came down again. He took another cigarette from Neelakantaswami and lit it. 'You've given a new dimension to the movement. I am very grateful to you,' he said. He was happy to see Neelakantaswami looking gratified. He gave Ranga Rao some money to buy clothes for the Holeyaru. 'Come back soon,' he said as he smoked, walking about in the yard looking at the posters.

Suddenly, the anguish struck again. He was irritated with the way Neelakantaswami was tugging at his hair. 'That day Amma didn't go to the toilet with the betel leaves and nut in her mouth. She's certainly not the kind who'd go there with anything in her mouth. Did this happen before she went on the pilgrimage? Or was it after? What was the colour of the sari she was wearing that night? Trying to remember every detail of that incident, Jagannatha walked up to a jackfruit tree and stood under it.

'Amma sat up. She touched me. Why did she? Did she touch me to make sure I was asleep? And then she sat chewing the betel leaves. She took the leaves from the plate that was by her pillow. It's the same plate that is used even now. No, she chewed the leaves after she returned and before she went to sleep. I loved the smell as she crushed the stuff in her mouth; the aroma of the juices of cardamom, clove, sunna, tender betel leaves, and areca nuts blending. No, she munched on the leaves after she returned from the toilet—not before. But Amma wasn't the type who'd chew anything in bed. She wouldn't let me lie down and eat. I used to love to stuff the pocket of my shorts with kodubales and eat them in bed, crunching them one by one. But Amma would scold me. She used to go to Krishnaiah's bedroom every day. Every day she'd go without Chikki knowing about it.'

Adiga returned from the river after his bath. 'There seems to be a lot of excitement,' he said to Jagannatha but, looking at his face, he went straight in. *Now he'll worship the saligrama. And all my efforts will be fruitless like offering a homa of water instead of fire.*

He felt as if green snakes were crawling all over him. 'I'll ask Rayaru about it. That may ease my heartache. He'll laugh it off as an outright lie. Then I'll be so happy; my burden will drop from my mind with a thud.'

He tried to take a few steps towards Rayaru. 'But then I'll be sowing seeds of suspicion in his mind. Of course, he'll tell me it's a lie. But even he may start wondering like me if it could be true. Then I'd be doing Amma a great injustice.'

He stood staring vacantly at the jackfruit tree. Some labourer had slashed a branch with a knife; sap had oozed from the gash, it was sticky. 'Though the tree's old, it still yields fruit. Red segments of fruit, sweet as honey. Appa loved farming. When Sri Krishnaraja Wodeyar[85] had come to pay his homage to Manjunatha, he's supposed to have eaten the fruit of this tree and been so pleased with it that he had given Appa a medal. I can't remember how Appa looked.

'I think of Appa. But who's my father? When Appa died Amma wept, Krishnaiah wept. Why did they cry? No, I'll never be able to resolve this question: is it true or false? Amma had got a gold chain made for Sakamma. She would wait for Krishnaiah to return from Shimoga by the last bus; Sakamma too would stand waiting for him.'

Suddenly, out of the torment in his mind, a clear insight burst open like a pearl. Jagannatha went straight up to his room and sat writing it down in his notebook:

'Just look at this! A person like me who wants to expose these people to great distress by desecrating the glory of Manjunatha just so that they may take responsibility for their lives, even I am agonizing over the suspicion that my mother could've committed adultery. The crucial question is: why am I so upset? Though I'm fully aware I have no way of resolving this uncertainty either within myself or outside of me, why am I in turmoil wondering if it is true or false? When Pilla reached out his hand to Kaveri, I said it was right. I offered the saligrama to the Holeyaru. I gathered courage to alienate my family from the whole of this community. Despite all this, my anguish shows that sentiments like class, caste, family still matter to me. Or else, I wouldn't have been troubled that I'm not a legitimate son—that I could be a bastard.

'When I want the Holeyaru to penetrate the womb of God just to deal a blow to the people, why do I want only the one who took my

[85] The erstwhile king of Mysore.

mother's hand in marriage with Agni as witness to enter her vagina? Do I have the right to desecrate the dark recesses of the temple when I'm agonizing so much over the possibility of a stranger entering my mother's? I'm trying to find out whether this is true or false as if my spirit were all afire; will I anticipate a revolt with the same intensity? When I feel fire coursing through my veins at the very thought of someone else caressing the mole on Margaret's bottom, do I have the right to expose the fondly held beliefs of the people to disarray?

'But it's true that even when I'm thinking this through clearly, I'm grieving. My mind says my feelings are unjustified, but my feelings stand tall trampling my thoughts; I'm caught on the horns of a dilemma.'

Jagannatha stood up, having written so much. Now that his mind was lighter, he continued thinking: 'I can't love the Holathi who pleaded that the banana her son, Chouda, was eating on the sly wasn't from my farm. Some day all these Holeyaru will be educated; some of them will become like Satyaprakash; the young men will wear tight-fitting trousers; the need to carry shit on their heads will disappear; instead of Manjunatha, they'll get high on LSD ... When I think of it this way, any change seems meaningless. The soothing darkness of Manjunatha's compassion must have given Amma some comfort. Perhaps every melodious quiver in her songs was filled with all the pain in her life. Since I'm caught up in the struggle to fulfil my life through changing the times, the pain and pleasure of daily life seem inconsequential. Like the one who received holy ash[86] even when he fingered a vagina, I may eventually have to become a demon obsessed with a single purpose.'

Jagannatha was beset by the same trend of thought even while he sat for lunch with the others. 'Until now the wealth and eminence of my family had been my protection. Now that I've stretched out my hand to destroy these, my ears should be prepared to hear anything. While I nestle in the shawl Amma gave me, I should be ready to get up on hearing someone wailing. I suppose in the final analysis what Adiga said is true; it may not be possible to be a revolutionary without being an ascetic.'

[86] Reference to an episode in which Kinnara Bommiah tests Akka Mahadevi by making such amorous advances towards her.

During the meal Ranga Rao said, 'Do you know, my mother gets angry with me when I invite Brahmins to eat at our place. "Why should they eat with us and lose their caste," she feels.'

Adiga, who was eating in the kitchen, said, 'I'm sitting here only in deference to my priestly profession. While on my way to Rishikesh, I've eaten in all sorts of places. You know as the saying goes, be a Roman while you are in Rome.'

Everyone was in a jovial mood during the meal. Jagannatha washed his hands and walked about in the backyard, trying to clarify his thoughts further. 'There's no point in wondering if I fully believe in what I've undertaken to do because this kind of faith should deepen only as I go along. I have to endure these hindrances to create a humane community where my parentage becomes insignificant. As long as concepts like my mother, my son, my wife remain in their present connotation, so long will notions of caste and wealth remain, or as long as the idea of caste and status exists, so long will the present attitude to relationships also stay. Trying to alter even the very nature of these concepts is revolution. Henceforth, I stand committed to a conscious struggle—ready to see everything, prepared to go through anything.

'I shall await the new man from within me—seeing with one eye the present reality with compassion and, with the other, cruelly lancing it in a bid to transform it, loving it passionately and yet being detached from it; understanding why there's a caste system even within me, but trying to overcome it through action, I shall await the man who walks tall with his head held high. Letting go and at the same time embracing; gradually getting into shape; walking in the wake of cruelty, abuse, greed; dissipating Manjunatha, I shall see that the baskets of shit come down from the heads of the Holeyaru. Let a Brahmin boy desire a dark-skinned Holathi with flowers in her hair. Let a Brahmin girl long to be embraced by a coarse-haired, dark-skinned Holeya. Until now an Indian has had no real dignity. Over the bhootha of the Holeyaru stands the bhootha of the Shudras and over him is Manjunatha and on Manjunatha's head is my crown. In Adiga's eyes is His radiance, in His worship was Amma's wet hair, and in His providence, adultery, birth, death, mating, children, baskets of shit on the head—I must redeem everything He has taken. I must reclaim Him as harvest, as metal, as milk-filled breasts, as the heat of loins. I must make Him shine as electricity in light bulbs. In this way I'll overcome the anguish of who might have fathered me through Amma's vagina. Tomorrow, with the help of the Holeyaru, I shall sow this new truth, as yet unformed, between the thighs of Time and wait.'

Sripathi Rao was standing in the veranda, smearing sunna on tobacco. Seeing Jagannatha on his way to meet Pilla, he said, 'Today I'll meet the young Holeyaru and talk to them. You go up and lie down. You don't look well.'

'Rayare,' said Jagannatha, fumbling for words as he had been caught up in his thoughts, 'All that I'm expecting from the entry into the temple tomorrow may not really happen. But I feel the struggle has begun. Time has started moving. I must tell you what I've decided to do. Eventually I'll be handing over the affairs of the property to Gopala. It's a burden. Even today, the Holeyaru call me, Odeyare, Master. I want to create a union; I must unify the farmers. I must make them refuse to give whatever tenancy payment the landlords demand from them, fearing the wrath of Bhootharaya. But no change can come about dramatically; I must learn to wait.'

Rao put the tobacco into his mouth and smiled saying, 'I wanted to tell you something. Nothing may happen whatever you may do—that's the nature of this soil. And, yet, I've decided to walk with the Holeyaru in their procession to the temple.'

Seeing tears of gratitude in Jagannatha's eyes, he teased, 'Maharaya, this doesn't mean I agree with everything you say. It's just that I may have to live in shame until I die if I back out in fear when you've girded yourself for the fight. This is just my way of saving my face, that's all.'

Jagannatha felt exhausted. He went to bed and fell asleep.

TWENTY SEVEN

Ganesha Bhatta's Protest

The chief priest of Shri Manjunatha temple, Seetharamaiah, was mumbling some mantra as he walked quickly towards his house in a lane behind the temple. His cousin Nagaraja Jois had become arrogant these days, saying he would not hesitate to go to court to contest his right to be the priest of the temple. When Prabhu's nephew, Venkata Rao Kamath, had stopped him to whisper the news in his ear as he was returning home after finishing the puja, Seetharamaiah was apprehensive. 'Tell me why no one has gone to the court for anything until now, Seetharamaiahnavare. Isn't it because they were terrified of Bhootharaya? Yes or no? When Jagannatharaya destroyed that dread, how can the fear of sin possibly remain in the people, tell me. Don't you know Jois's nature? Isn't his son a lawyer after all?

Let the Harijans enter the temple tomorrow, I'll see what sanctity remains in Seetharamaiah's puja? I'll surely sue him, Jois said when he had come to the store. I told my uncle what Jagannatha's doing is like helping a monkey in the garden with a ladder.'

Seetharamaiah had not let Kamath see that he was scared. 'Well, there was a suicide in his family .... God will see to everything,' he had said and gone home.

Seetharamaiah was an impressive man with diamond studs in his ears, a thick tuft of long grey hair down his back, rudrakshi beads set in gold round his neck, and Manjunatha's special prasada—kumkuma mixed with musk—adorning his brow.

Usually, as soon as he heard his father's footsteps, Ganesha would hide *Devadasa*, the novel he was reading by the corner window in the inner room, and pretend to be absorbed in cutting the plantain leaves to size or in making leaf-cups. But that day he was so engrossed in the story, he did not notice his father entering, nor see or sense his father close by, staring down at him. His father slapped him, pounded him on his head, tossed aside the book, and hauled him upright. Ganesha stood up hissing. He was furious enough to want to knock his father dead but he could not express his anger because of his stammer. All he could do was to stare at Seetharamaiah with repressed rage. His eyes filled with tears of frustration: 'This monster has gobbled up the tender sentiments the novel had aroused in me; he has dragged me from my world of make-believe where I mingled with the characters with dignity and self-esteem; this demon has tossed me back into this vile reality.'

His father's usual litany of curses began with, '*Mundedhe*, wasting your time reading novels. Aren't you ashamed of yourself? Don't you have any self-respect? Is it enough to eat and grow fat? Why don't you have some sense even after getting married?' As the curses landed, so did the slaps on his cheeks, like the bilva leaves a devotee casts on a linga during worship, one by one. Ganesha's wrath was also rising. He was thinking of the propitious moment when the whacks would have to end; of the instant when his hand would rise and take a swing at his father's protruding teeth to knock them out as they moved up and down with the berating lips; when there would be peace. He was vaguely aware of the barrage of complaints and expected to get into an uncontrollable temper when he saw his wife peeping at the door, indifferently taking in his condition, and disappearing. That was when Subbaraya Adiga walked in and said, 'What is this! Seetharamaiahnavaru has taken on the Rudra avataara!' As soon as he heard Adiga, Seetharamaiah's fury swung to the other extreme; he began to shed crocodile tears. 'Look at this, Adigare! How long will I have to slog like this? This scoundrel sits with some filthy book all the time. If he doesn't have a sense of responsibility even after marriage, what can I do, tell me?'

Ganesha knew his father's sob story would continue relentlessly: 'But even that'll have to end; soon it'll be time for lunch and he'll be hungry. And then it will be time for my afternoon bath before puja. In the mornings, I have a cold bath in the river, but in the afternoons I can have a hot bath at home. If Appa wasn't at home, I could've shut the bathroom door and bathed naked without even the loincloth; *I could pour plenty of hot water over my naked body.*' Ganesha sat making the leaf-cups from banana leaves desiccated over embers.

Subbaraya Adiga spoke softly, 'I too have a grown-up son. He too is disobedient. But there's no point in beating them. If you keep beating him, Ganesha may have a nervous breakdown again, Seetharamaiah.'

'After I die, he'll have to take over as Manjunatha's chief priest. If he behaves like this, what else can I do, tell me? I'm not saying this for effect, Adigare, but I've been feeling out-of-sorts lately. And yet I've been officiating at weddings, thread ceremonies, at every ritual. As for this fellow, he has no sense of ritual purity, ritual pollution ...'

Ganesha tried to forget his humiliation as he folded each leaf-cup at the corners, secured them by pinning bits of broom sticks into the folds, and stacked the cups into neat piles, setting them one into the other. 'Every time Appa talks, he has to refer to the chief priesthood. After Amma died, he got married again only because we needed a woman in the house to look after me who would be Manjunatha's priest some day! Is it my fault that my stepmother, who's just a few years older than me, has no sons? That both her children are daughters? Not just that, even my wife is my stepmother's elder brother's daughter. And why? Because it was always, "After Appa dies and you become the chief priest, do you want a girl from a good family who will help you out with your daily priestly duties in ritual cleanliness, or would you rather have someone like those Konkan girls who part their hair on the side and go to movies?"

'There's not a single place in Bharathipura where I can smoke a beedi in secret. Once a farmhand who'd seen me had told someone else in secret and the news spread throughout the town, reaching Appa's ears; he whipped me until I had welts on my back.

'It's always, "For a man who's going to worship Manjunatha as chief priest, where's the need to know English? To read novels? To see movies? To have a wife who loves him? To wear a shirt with collar? To wear slippers? ..." My wife, Yamuna, sleeps with my stepmother; she's allowed to sleep with me only on certain propitious days of the month. But, when I'm always aware that I'm beaten in her presence and that Appa's sleeping nearby and might shout at me any moment, what would I want to do to a wife who curls up beside me? All the descriptions in the novel *Natasaarvabhouma*[87] can only feed my fantasy while masturbating; that's about all.'

Yamuna brought him another pile of dried banana leaves and left. 'The smell of desiccated leaves is forever in my nose. But, thank God, Appa's not ranting at me any more; he's venting his anger at Jagannatha Rao, who's like the heroes of some of the best novels I've read.'

'Will any son born to his father take on such a heinous act, tell me, Adigare? Anti-Brahminism is rampant everywhere. The amaldhar hates Brahmins, the district commissioner hates Brahmins, and the whole cabinet of ministers is anti-Brahmin. And, now, if even he who used to be the trustee of the temple goes against Brahmins ...'

As Ganesha expected, Seetharamaiah took off on Brahminism, 'What does Vedanta say?

One is born a Shudra
One's karma makes him a Dwija
One's reading of the Vedas makes him a Vipra. That's all.
One's knowledge of Brahma makes him a Brahmana.

'I always tell Ganesha, "Look at the filthy books you read? What can these writers write about all this in Kannada? Have you seen anything that matches even a sloka in Sanskrit from *Lalitha Sahasranaama*?"[88] What descriptions of the female body, Adigare! The thing is, we're in Kaliyuga[89] now. If not, how can the son of a high-class Brahmin family forget that this god's crown saved his life and want to bring beef-eating Holeyaru into the temple? It's shocking! Do I have to tell you all this when you know the rituals of the first installation of God's

[87] Novel by Kannada writer A.N. Krishna Rao.
[88] The thousand names of the Divine Mother.
[89] The fourth age of the world according to Hindu cosmology.

idol in the temple? Jagannatha can turn cartwheels if he wishes, but it's just not possible to allow the chandalas to enter the temple. How many lakhs of years has this temple existed! They say, apart from Kashi, there's no other place as sacred as this. You know how they say, "for a hundred years, for a thousand years, for a hundred thousand years, for eternity" when they consecrate an idol? Parashurama installed Manjunatha for ever and ever after all the ceremonious immersions in grain, curd, milk, and water. He is not born yet who can destroy such a Manjunatha ... nor will he ever be.'

Ganesha watched the way his father's buck-teeth moved up and down pressed against his lips. Adiga stood up and said, 'I've got to be going.' Suddenly Ganesha was in a panic again. 'What if Appa starts raving again because some leaf-cup is crooked or that I haven't ground enough sandalwood paste? What if he says, "Which whore's son gave you that book?"'

With a towel round his waist and another on his shoulder, Ganesha got up quickly and went into the bathroom. His father's words, 'He is not born yet who can destroy such a Manjunatha ... nor will he ever be,' were stuck in his mind. Gathering courage to bolt the bathroom door, he took off his clothes and stood naked in front of the fire. His father would scold him even if he slept without his loincloth at night. Now, he smeared some coconut oil between his thighs and delighted in massaging the oil all over his body in the warmth of the fire. His stepmother might have complained; he could hear his father screaming at him, 'What're you doing behind the locked door, you demon? Are you bathing without a loincloth like a Muslim?'

Ganesha could remove his loincloth only twice during the day, when he went to the toilet and when he bathed. *Even during such intimate moments Appa yells.* Ganesha stepped into the bathing area and poured hot water slowly on himself. He felt a great pleasure as it trickled down, looking for the oily parts of his body. He had heard that the pleasure-loving Ravana[90] had asked for a boon that his body be covered with an itch whenever he had a bath. As he cleansed his body of oil with soap-nut powder, Ganesha cleaned his gold girdle, the gold for which had been stolen from a donation to the temple for Manjunatha's crown.

[90] The king of Lanka who abducts Rama's wife Sita in the epic, Ramayana.

'Not just this, even stepmother's studs, her chain, the earrings of her two girls, and the gold in which Appa's rudrakshi beads were set—all these were made from the crown given for saving Jagannatharaya's life.'

Ganesha laughed to himself as he noisily filled the mug with hot water and poured it on himself. 'They say the town will be burnt to ashes if Manjunatha is desecrated. Nonsense! Am I not the only one in the inner chamber whenever Appa goes out to officiate at weddings or some such ceremonies? I can get up early and go in there any morning, shut the door if I like under the pretext of getting things ready for worship, and sit there alone, can't I? The only other place I can be alone is when I go to the hillock to relieve myself.'

Ganesha had experimented with many different ways of desecrating Manjunatha; that was his way of venting his anger against his father. His hair stood on end as he remembered one of those sacrileges. It had to do with when Ganesha had seen the mute linga in the semi-darkness of the inner sanctum lit by the ever-glowing wick-lamp. 'Bastard!' he said, giggling at the memory as he quickly poured water on himself and stood in front of the fire, towelling his body. He enjoyed the beauty of the different shades of fire as it burnt the dry coconut shells.

'Haven't you finished yet?' his father was calling again. He could hear his stepmother scraping coconut and Yamuna coughing while seasoning the dish. Ganesha took his own time drying himself and leisurely stepped out of the bathroom.

His stepmother might have stopped scraping the coconut to talk to his father about him bathing in the nude; his father started his harangue again. And then the inquisition, 'How did you get this novel, *Devadasa*, with Jagannatha's name on it?' Ganesha did not reply. His father raised his hand to slap him for being silent, but remembered that his son was in ritual purity after his bath. He went to the bathroom to have his own.

That night Ganesha lay in bed thinking: 'Wherever I may go, Manjunatha won't let go of me. I'm sunk in His prasada. This womb of God stinks with stale oil, camphor, joss sticks, kumkuma. The house smells just as bad with the kumkuma set aside for worship, the chickpeas to be offered to Manjunatha soaking and bloating in water. It's all I eat when I'm hungry. That and fresh coconut—mounds and mounds of pieces, every day. And there's nothing cooked in the house without a reckless use of the free coconut we get in plenty from the pujas; it's in the curry, in the vegetable, in the chutney, in the cucumber salad.' In his entire life, Ganesha had not known the joys of eating spicy potato-onion curry, deep-fried potato bonda, or oily masala dosé. He could only imagine such pleasures while reading the novels of A. N. Krishna Rao.

'What if Jagannatharaya loses? What if the Holeyaru refuse to enter the temple? Then Appa will win. After he dies, Manjunatha will crush me as if He were an oil-press. That will be my state until I die. And stepmother will keep griping that Yamuna didn't have a son. The same chickpeas, the same vegetables, the same kumkuma, the same worship.' Ganesha felt sick; he drew up his legs under the blanket and shivered as if he would puke.

He held his breath and slyly removed his loincloth. 'Appa's in that corner. Perhaps he's guessed what I'm at. In the dining room, stepmother, her daughters, and Yamuna are sleeping. Tomorrow the ranting will begin again, the walloping will start again. Yamuna will be involved in her duties even as she looks on. She'll check the almanac for the propitious days and come to sleep beside me. But Appa will be snoring in the same corner. And I'll be holding back my craving to read the rest of *Devadasa* until I can get away from Appa's prying eyes for some time.

'No, I will NOT allow it,' said Ganesha to himself and sat up. 'Bastard! Bastard!' he chanted. He tied his knee-length dhothi and wrapped himself in the blanket and stood up. It was chilly outside. 'The key to the inner room of the temple should be somewhere near Appa's head. Is it under the pillow? Or beside it? If he catches me and kills me, let him.' Softly, he groped for it. 'God's mercy!' The key was near his head, not under the pillow. He felt his way to the kitchen. If the insomniac demon of a stepmother asked him what he was doing, he decided he would say he wanted water. He drank some too, to avoid suspicion. Without making a sound, he picked up the crowbar lying beside the grinding stone. He opened the backdoor. 'Damned door!' It creaked. Ganesha heard his father cursing in his sleep. '*Daridra Shani*!' he must have said. Ganesha pretended to go to the toilet; he dipped the mug noisily into the boiler for water. He poured it into the bucket and lifted it with a clatter to make sure it registered in his father's mind that he had gone to the toilet. Then he bolted the backdoor and walked towards the temple, crowbar in hand.

The beggars in the temple yard were still awake. Ganesha saw the pilgrims arriving in the dead of night to attend the Chariot Festival the next day and thought, '*What fools!*' He feared he would arouse suspicion if he went into the temple wrapped in a blanket and so he tossed it to a beggar under a tree and walked on. No one would suspect the son of Manjunatha's pujari; they would assume he was there on temple business. If anyone were to ask him why he carried the crowbar, he would say he needed it to dig holes for posts that would hold the oil-lamps.

Ganesha opened the big door of the temple, went in, and shut it. No one was there. It was dark. Silent. He unlocked the door to the innermost chamber and entered. He closed the door and bolted it. The two ever-glowing lamps were burning. There was a huge mask over the small linga, a genial smiling mask. A gold crown on its head. Since his thread ceremony, Ganesha had spent most of his time here. It all seemed so easy!

It's eternal, they say, lasting as long as the moon and the sun last; eighteen feet below it are the power circles of Shri Sakthi, they say, with a pit filled with the nine gems and gold coins. It's secured by the mantra that binds the spirit in all the eight directions, they say.

'All Appa's fables; they must be ravaged. Right from the roots. Or else I'll be destroyed. There's no other way. When Jagannatharaya brings the Holeyaru in, I'll shout, "Everything's demolished! Now we're all free!"'

Ganesha dug around the linga with a crowbar. He was sweating. He turned up the lamp-wick, for better light. *There's a slight crack at the base; only Appa and I know about it. Nagaraja Jois had also got to know about it somehow, but Appa had insisted there wasn't any.*

The sound of the crowbar seemed as if it were pounding him. *If Appa comes and sees this, I'll die right here or I'll kill him.* The blows damaged the linga. *What could be worse? Now, it doesn't matter who comes or who sees,* he thought as he continued digging around it.

A mouse scurried across his feet, scaring him. He looked for it to kill it but it disappeared down the drain meant for the holy water. 'Let it die! Let it die!' chanted Ganesha as he dug like a man possessed.

The linga came off the pedestal. He wrapped it up in a length of cloth ritually cleansed and spread out by his father to dry, and lifted it up. It was not all that heavy; he was able to carry it together with the crowbar. He came out, shut the door of the inner chamber, and walked straight to the river. There were people even on the river bank but no one recognized him. He tossed the linga into the eddy that had the power to cleanse all sins and came back.

He was perspiring. Until he entered his house through the backyard, he was not aware of what he was doing. It was only after he had pushed open the back door and was just about to step inside that he felt there was someone standing there in the dark; his heart sank.

'Where were you all this while, you wretched plague,' said his father. Ganesha felt a resounding slap on his burning cheek and reeled. His father must have got up to go to the toilet and might have known for a long time that he was not home. Ganesha did not realize what he was doing; he raised the crowbar and threw it. He did not know where it had struck his father. He just heard him scream, 'Ayyo!' and ran. Not quite knowing where he was going, feeling it was too far to Jagannatharaya's house, he ran back to the temple, entered the inner sanctuary, bolted the door, and sank to the floor. The silence was so profound he could hear his heart thumping. His father had not come after him; perhaps he was dead. 'Amma!' he sighed deeply, closed his eyes, and stretched out his legs. 'I'll hide here until Jagannatharaya comes with the Holeyaru tomorrow,' he decided and slept on the stone floor, breathing through his mouth.

TWENTY EIGHT

The Revolution

It was the day after the Chariot Festival. Jagannatha sat scanning the special issue of the newspaper, *Jagruthi*.

Fruitless Revolution
And, yet, the strength of Jagannatha Rao's resolution remains steadfast

He was not interested in the details. The people who had besieged his house continued to shout. The police would be exhausted blowing the whistle and trying to control the mob.

What absurd slogans!

Victory to Ganesha Bhatta!
Boycott the atheist!

And there were bhajans too:

Jaya Manjunatha! Jaya Bhootharaya!
Jaya Ganesha Bhatta! Jaya Deva Deva!

Jagannatha looked out of the window. New faces, mostly. It was funny to see the same banners his men had used the previous day being held up now by some other men, but with different slogans: *Release Ganesha Bhatta, the saviour of God's sanctity!*

Jagannatha laughed. Poor Ananthakrishna, his voice was hoarse with all the talking. Now, only Sripathi Rao was out there straining to calm the crowd. Even as Jagannatha was about to go down to help out, Neelakantaswami came up in a hurry saying, 'I feel it's proper to send Ganesha home.'

Neelakantaswami was tugging at his hair; he got on Jagannatha's nerves. 'Please sit down,' he insisted. And after he sat down, Jagannatha continued calmly, 'That's impossible.'

'Prabhu's plotting something, do you know? For now the people may be under the impression that Ganesha is the incarnation of Bhootharaya, but what if his mind clears and he explains his intentions? Prabhu's worried about it. Naturally. And so he's planning to lodge a complaint that we had abetted Ganesha's vandalism and that he has stolen gold from the temple.'

Ranga Rao and Ananthakrishna also came up. Tugging at his khadi shoulder wrap, Ananthakrishna suggested, 'Why don't you issue a statement? It's better that yours comes before Prabhu's. State that there's no connection between the hatred with which the priest's son has uprooted the linga and thrown it away, and our peaceful protest. Later, perhaps ...'

'No, I'm indirectly responsible for what Ganesha's done,' explained Jagannatha, looking through the window at the crowd that believed Ganesha was the incarnation of Bhootharaya. Who's responsible for this new frenzy?

Ranga Rao stood closer to Jagannatha to curry favour and said, 'It's not that, Saar. It's not the right tactics to antagonize all the Hindus. Just give a statement that Ganesha Bhatta might have had a nervous breakdown and done this. That way, we won't be saying he's wrong in what he did, nor will we be taking on people of all castes by saying he's right.'

Ananthakrishna agreed, 'Not just that. You will also be addressing these people with blind faith who believe Ganesha is the incarnation of Bhootharaya; it's just that he's had a breakdown.'

Neelakantaswami refined the argument further, 'Ganesha had a personal grudge against God. His is not an ideological rebellion like ours. So it's not wrong for us to say we don't want to identify ourselves with his neurotic action.'

Ananthakrishna accepted this argument and added his bit, 'That's the way it also happened, didn't it? Ganesha opened the door only after *you* asked him to. Whatever he may have told you, whatever the pilgrims might've heard, the story that ultimately spread was that Bhootharaya had entered Ganesha and made him do this. Because the deity wasn't in the inner sanctuary when the Harijans entered it, these crazy people danced for joy because it hadn't been desecrated at all. Everything went haywire. What can we do? That's the nature of this soil.'

In his anguish, Jagannatha imagined the future: 'Ganesha in a daze, sitting on the temple platform with a mound of kumkuma in front of him; his eyes are blinking but he doesn't raise his hand even to shoo away the flies crawling on his lips. After worshipping Manjunatha, the pilgrims bring their palms together before him in obeisance and take a pinch of the kumkuma ... In course of time, Pilla or his son will become a minister. He'll unveil my portrait in Bharathipura. I'll be somewhere writing about revolution. Perhaps in Delhi; perhaps with Margaret ... Ganesha, now an old man, will still be sitting on the platform. Or, if he dies, the wooden board on which he sat will be worshipped as a relic. They'll build a girls' school in my name. With progress, electric bulbs will glow in the inner sanctum of the temple. Prabhu will make speeches praising me. Then, the same people who are booing me now will clap their hands.'

He stood up; he was worried that Sripathi Rao had been at the task of controlling the restive crowd for too long.

'Don't go. Seeing you the people may get enraged,' Neelakantaswami cautioned him.

'These people are not even capable of violent rage,' said Jagannatha and as he came down the stairs, a police inspector came up to him. He held a warrant to arrest Ganesha. Prabhu had lodged a complaint that Ganesha had vandalized the temple and stolen gold that belonged to God. 'Really, what a crafty person he must be! The point is, he feels it's dangerous for him that the priest's son is with me.' The inspector politely requested Jagannatha to hand over Ganesha. Asking him to sit down, Jagannatha explained, 'Ganesha has had a nervous breakdown.'

'We know that, Sir. But we haven't been able to control the crowd. They won't budge from your house. Later you can bail him out. You can take him to hospital. The district commissioner has personally asked me to tell you this.'

Jagannatha was silent. Two policemen walked out with Ganesha who was in a daze and did not seem to be aware of anything around him. He just stared vacantly as he walked. The moment the pilgrims saw Ganesha being led out, they chanted his praise and surrounded the police van. The police had to push them aside and make way for the van to move out. As it sped away, they surged after it.

Jagannatha sighed as he came into the house. Sripathi Rao, Neelakantaswami, and Ananthakrishna went upstairs with him. With the help of the socialist volunteers, Ranga Rao went about chasing away the few demonstrators that were standing about under the trees. It was more difficult to control the outsiders who had come for the festival. Ranga Rao asked the police to continue to keep watch and went upstairs.

Jagannatha checked with Gopala when he had to go back to Mysore and walked about in the hall trying to remember and understand every detail of what had happened the previous day when he had gone to the temple with the Holeyaru: 'Early in the morning, some ten of the young men had assembled in the yard with Pilla as their leader—all of them dressed in white. Even as I drew closer to talk to them, I could smell liquor. They had been drinking, to brave the ordeal. When I said, 'You shouldn't be afraid,' Pilla had said, 'Oh, no!' with an unusual swagger. Though I was sure their entry into the temple wouldn't be a conscious, voluntary act, I also knew there was no turning back. I stood helpless. Was I scared then? Did I accept that it was impossible to keep a community act pure?' Feeling it was pointless even to speculate this way, he went upstairs.

Sripathi Rao, Neelakantaswami, Ananthakrishna, and Ranga Rao were seated on a mat, engaged in deep discussion. Chikki brought them some coffee and kodubales on a tray and left. The men had been discussing the events of the previous day in great detail, but, on seeing the newspaper from Bangalore that had arrived on the mail bus, they became quiet; their attention was diverted. Neelakantaswami was happy they had made front-page news. After eagerly scanning the headlines, he said, 'This PRT is a rascal, a reactionary. He twists the news. *Jagruthi*'s reporting is so much better.' And he began to read aloud:

Fruitless revolution in Bharathipura

Harijan entry into Godless temple

'We won't step back from the struggle,' says Jagannatha.

'Anyway, Bhootharaya saved God from defilement,' say a group of devotees.

Ananthakrishna craned his neck to look at the paper and said, 'Read on.' Sripathi Rao listened as he opened his bag of betel leaves and nuts, and prepared the mixture for munching. Jagannatha suddenly remembered something. 'The police are guarding the Holeyaru, aren't they?'

'Some ten or twelve policemen are there with them. I met Pilla. Asked him to come to the meeting this evening,' replied Ranga Rao enthusiastically.

'No one here can understand my anguish. They don't even have to. It's easier for them to be caught up in action. How intently they're listening to Neelakantaswami reading the news! Perhaps they're under the illusion that whatever they did is real only because it's been reported in the papers.'

Neelakantaswami read with great excitement:

Bharathipura is beautiful as sunlight like a broom sweeps away the morning mist. This play begins as pilgrims from many regions wait in the chill for the Chariot Festival. Bhootharaya is the henchman of Manjunatha who has even the President of the country as His devotee. Can the Holeyaru cross the Lakshman rekhe *drawn by Bhootharaya's authority? The eyes of the pilgrims watch keenly—with curiosity more than eagerness.*

Jagannatha was irritated. Ranga Rao was appreciative. 'Fine writing!' he said.

'It's immoral to write like that,' commented Jagannatha, as he lit a cigarette and sat listening:

It was seven when a procession of young Holeyaru, clad in white, and their leader, Jagannatha Rao, reached the Chariot Street to destroy the glory of Manjunatha. Following them was a car with a mike blaring slogans of victory:

Inquilab Zindabad!

Victory to Jagannatha Rao!

Down with Bhootharaya's exploitation of farmers!

Victory to the Mysore Socialist Party!

These were the chants of revolution in Bharathipura where Vedic chants have been reverberating for centuries.

As he was reading, Neelakantaswami's face fell and his voice dropped. Jagannatha had been so disgusted when he had heard a slogan on the mike with his name that he had left his place at the head of the march and had got into the car and taken Neelakantaswami to task. He had given strict instructions that it was to be a silent procession. He noticed now that Neelakantaswami was still smarting under the previous day's insult. Pretending to have forgotten the incident, Jagannatha sat looking down. Neelakantaswami faltered for a moment and then carried on reading:

Police on either side, with Jagannatha Rao leading the march, tall and impressive, London-returned, belonging to the family of temple trustees. Behind him, ten Holeya youth, and following them, the veteran Congress leader, Sripathi Rao. After him the Sarvodaya leader, Ananthakrishna; Mysore Socialist Party leader, Neelakantaswami, and his following.

Except for Ranga Rao, all the others were smiling. 'This kind of verbless prose is so irritating,' he said to Jagannatha. Ananthakrishna added his comment, 'Everyone's abusing Siddanavalli's prose[91] these days.'

The devotees make way for the protestors, taking care not to touch the Holeyaru lest they be prevented from pulling the chariot. The procession winds past the decorated chariot and up the steps of the temple. Whispering everywhere, commotion of police trying to control the crowd. A village woman screams in frenzy, 'There's no way the Holeyaru can get in. Bhootharaya will drag them by their legs. He'll make them spit blood.'

'At last some verbs,' sighed Jagannatha, stood up, and walked into his room. Neelakantaswami continued to read aloud. Jagannatha looked out of the window. The blossoming mango tree. A few curious stragglers coming up the hill hoping to get a view of the atheist. He had never anticipated this moment. Even when he had thought it could get out of hand, he had not thought it would happen this way: 'Pilla

[91] Siddanavalli Krishna Sharma was a journalist who wrote short, terse sentences, some of them verbless. His style became popular in the journalism of his time.

was at the threshold of the temple. I waited for the step that would change the course of centuries, the one step that would let the outcaste become an insider. I was aware that thousands of eyes were drawing Pilla back. I looked at him as if to deride their cruelty, their stupidity. I stared at him as if to tell him only he could take that step. The strange thing about that moment was that I was as curious as I was anxious—curious to know if Pilla was prepared. Perhaps the bravado of booze had evaporated. I stood staring at him with yearning; if only Pilla will take just one step now with all these eyes as witnesses, Bharathipura would roll into a new reality. I tried to tell him, "If you don't become firm, I can't." As a witness, as a partner, as an agent, I stood searching his eyes. But Pilla turned away and looked at his companions; he looked at the thousands of people watching him. He said to the one behind him, "You go in first." That fellow said the same thing to the one behind him. And so it went on until they who had stood in single file gathered as a group. They tried to wheedle one another; then they started fighting.

'What did I want to do then? Why did I stand there dumbstruck?'

Neelakantaswami criticized PRT's report severely, 'See how subtly this reactionary has exaggerated things.'

He read on: 'With the speed of lighting a mighty change in the crowd. Some shouted, "*Jai Manjunatha! Govindhaanu Govinda! Govinda*!" And someone else, "Push forward! Pull him down!" Perceiving the distress of the Holeyaru, some danced for joy; some wept. Some others shuddered as if Bhootharaya had possessed them. A rumour spread everywhere that Bhootharaya had dragged the Holeyaru by their legs. In their ecstasy the people got out of hand; they broke the police barricade and rushed forward.'

Jagannatha stood listening to the report. 'Yes, that's true. I stood there, arms folded. What I couldn't do, Neelakantaswami did. Panting, he went towards Pilla, grabbed him by the hand, and dragged him into the temple. The others followed. The ritual of entry was accomplished.'

Neelakantaswami was reading angrily:

When this reporter asked, 'Do you approve of this forced entry?' Sarvodaya leader Ananthakrishna replied, 'Was it possible to compel them in the end? That's a matter of opinion.' GOOD. But from Jagannatha Rao, who was a passive spectator, the only response to my question was a sorrowful silence. 'NO,

Mr Jagannath, you will have to issue a statement denying this.' To which he said, 'My question now is, is it important to know how I really feel, or is it more important to somehow fulfil the purpose I believe in? Until this confusion is cleared, I can't say anything. But the only thing I know is that even this problem can be sorted out only through action and not through speculation.'

Jagannatha went into his room and stood at the window once again. He could see Subbaraya Adiga approaching in the distance. He went downstairs, fearing the police might keep him from coming into the house, looking at the way he was dressed.

'No, I don't think I would've done what Neelakantaswami did. But then, what else have I been doing from the beginning? I never imagined the outcome of my action would be so outlandish; that's the vital flaw in the way I had thought this through.

'When I went in with the Holeyaru, the scene was bizarre. Prabhu and Seetharamaiah were right in front of the inner sanctum, the womb of God. Seetharamaiah's head was bandaged. Now as I recall the anxiety on their faces, it occurs to me that they must have been exhausted begging Ganesha to open the door. Ganesha may have been in no state to say anything clearly. It was only when Seetharamaiah screamed and raged, "The Holeyaru have come in, don't open the door," that I realized something had happened. "What can we do? Through God's persuasion his son has bolted himself in. He's not opening the door even when we call him," Prabhu had explained, theatrically.

'I went straight to the door, knocked on it, and said, "Ganesha, it's me, Jagannatha. I'm here. Open the door. Don't be frightened." The door opened. Ganesha walked out unsteadily and collapsed at my feet.'

His face expressionless, Subbaraya Adiga said, 'I've come to see Chikki.'

'She's inside.' Jagannatha sent him in and went back upstairs. The discussion had become quite fierce. Neelakantaswami was talking loudly, 'Just look at this! Look at the way he's reported this: *"Manjunatha disappeared, knowing the Holeyaru would be coming in," this is the rumour that spread among the people. Shri Neelakantaswami announced over the mike that the one who had uprooted and thrown away the linga was the purohit's son, Ganesha Bhatta. But the people danced in exultation, believing that Bhootharaya had entered Ganesha Bhatta and through him had transported Manjunatha to the river the previous day so that He may not be desecrated through the entry of the Holeyaru into the temple. The faith of the Indian is so deep that* ... He talks only about devotion to God, that rascal. Has he reported all that *I* had said at that point? I had said, "Don't be victims of the dead Puranas. Jagannatha Rao and Ganesha Bhatta, both are revolutionaries. The deceit of the priests and the traders who are turning this revolution into a myth will not work. Bhootharaya's exploitation of farmers will have to stop. This is only the beginning of the revolution. That's all." Has he reported a bit of what *I* said? Some of the people in the crowd accepted what I said; Ranga Rao is witness to that.'

Jagannatha came downstairs and walked about in the yard. It was almost time for the meeting. Pilla and his friends, and perhaps, the other Holeyaru may come. Ranga Rao had announced in the papers that there would be meeting of all the oppressed classes. But Jagannatha would have to strive much more before the farmers would be willing to attend a meeting with the Holeyaru.

Upstairs, the friends continued their discussions with great gusto.

Thinking of the decisions that had to be taken about the union at the meeting, Jagannatha went towards the bathroom to have a wash.

Adiga was explaining to Chikki the arrangements being made to re-install Manjunatha.

In Conversation

U.R. Ananthamurthy and N. Manu Chakravarthy

N. Manu Chakravarthy (NMC): Let us go back nearly a decade before *Bharathipura* (1973) to *Samskara* (1965). Now, four decades later, when you reflect on your creative process and your understanding of India as a culture and a society, what was the crisis you were trying to confront at that time? You wrote *Samskara* in England when you were preoccupied with a different intellectual scheme, working on the relationship between politics and fiction as reflected in the works of a few British writers of the 1930s.

U.R. Ananthamurthy (URA): I shall try to recount what was happening to me then. My constant companion, Kailasapathi, a Marxist and a communist, was of the view that individuals do not matter in history and that only certain economic and political forces do. I argued that if individuals did not resist or fight for change, the shape of things would have been different. But by saying individuals do not matter, you are making history an automatic kind of process and, if that is the case, it is very convenient for an intellectual brought up on science and modern analytical tools to say that what happens next is predetermined. I would say to him that I couldn't be a writer if I didn't accept the role of the individual in history. I was also very moved by George Thompson, a sage-like person who cycled to the university and had even organized the Indian workers. He was a professor of Greek and I was particularly fond of him because he had fought for the Gallic language in Ireland. I realized that there were many ways of relating to the world in which we lived. I knew that mine was very different. India was very different. So it was a challenge for me to relate to India. My mind was working like that. But the reason for writing *Samskara* was very accidental. I used to go to the London Museum Library and read all the newspapers of the nineteenth century. Things began to intermingle; the bits came from everywhere, like weaving. I do not weave at the structural level alone. I want to weave at the textual level.

NMC: While writing *Samskara*, you have referred to many unexpected magical moments in the creative process. The novel is located in the Brahminical area, the agrahaara, and its protagonist Praneshacharya is a strong and pure representative of the orthodox Brahminical order. In fact, in writing all these, there is no irony in the text nor any kind of scepticism because he represents its true values. But the text also has a different world. It is this world that makes the text very symbolic, allegorical, which is what you referred to. This happens when you weave into the novel many disparate elements of decadence, confusion, disorder. And this is what the closed Brahminical society experiences. In other words, the novel constantly juxtaposes notions of purity and pollution, order and chaos, of a community marking the transition in a changing social order. This also represents the existential turmoil of an individual and I think when you turn to *Bharathipura*, it furthers all these in a more drastically altered environment. But the two novels portray the altering destinies of individuals and communities, and both are foregrounded simultaneously and there is no privileging of either of them. Now, much as you talk of your creative processes at a very conscious level, how were you able to achieve this integration so successfully in the two novels?

URA: It is a bit difficult to answer this question because, whenever I try to write, I abandon a strictly conscious self because I have not been able to do precisely what you said I have—solely through my conscious self. Then ... my nature is kind of *chanchala*, a wandering unstable self, totally identifying myself sometimes with one way of thinking and then on to another way of thinking. You know that constantly happens within me when I write. I have abandoned many versions of several texts, but with *Samskara* there is only one version. I had no problem. There were many emotional reasons for it. Perhaps I was weary of having to speak English all the time and, then, when I sat down and wanted to write in Kannada, all my Kannada past came back to me. It was just the sheer delight, that element of joy in writing. With *Bharathipura* I think the writing was a little more deliberate than *Samskara*. That again is because of my lifelong preoccupation with Gandhi—even during those days in England when Marx and dialectics were attractive. And then Sartre became more attractive to me. I read a lot of Sartre those days because of his own problems with the need for action and also the need for reflection, between which there is a strange connect. This I felt could be integrated in a story which I had heard in my school days.

The story was what the Brahmins used to tell me. There was an attempt to take the Dalits to Dharmasthala temple and that was resisted. In my village a man called Shyam Aithal had tried to lead Dalits into the temple. He had made that attempt. And in my own town, Thirthahalli—Gandhi had come there at the beginning of the twentieth century—there was a group of Brahmins from orthodox families who were all Gandhians. They must have also gone through a lot of conflict of this kind. But, again, among the Brahmins there were two sorts: one, the *loukika* Brahmins and, the other, the *paramarthika* Brahmins, the priestly Brahmins. The priestly Brahmins did not get into much trouble. But the loukika Brahmins, those of the world, acting in the world, joined the Congress and invited Gandhi. There is a pamphlet which is still with my friend. It is a remarkable document where the Brahmins of Thirthahalli tell Gandhi, 'We have been able to implement charaka; now we have khadi. But we have not been able to remove untouchability. We have not been able to take the untouchables into temples. You must pardon us.' This confession to Gandhi was printed. Around this time I used to hear stories that some Dalits were taken into a temple, that the Dalits went as far as the temple. Then they got scared and came back. They could not cross the threshold. Metaphorically, that became important for me. The day the Dalits crossed that threshold was for Gandhi the beginning of the liberation of Dalits. Even Ambedkar tried to do that. He managed to get people to share the same water. That was a long struggle, not just between Brahmins and Shudras but between the Hindu castes and the *Panchamas*. That became for me a point of contemplation. I tried to imagine a Dalit going as far as that and not going into the temple.

The pollution and purity thing has been a constant preoccupation of mine and it has gathered other meanings over time. This is something that my friend Prof. Martin Greene saw in my writing. He read some translations and made me conscious of it. He said, 'From the beginning you have had almost an obsession with the idea of touch,' and I said, 'Yes, that is true.' In *Samskara*, there is 'the touch'. Even before that, I had written 'Ghatashraddha' while I was in Mysore. There is an incident where this boy, Naani, is going into the forest in search of Yamunakka, a widow, because she has just disappeared, and he takes a Dalit who is holding the burning torch. Suddenly the boy thinks of him as a supernatural being. He wants to make sure for himself because he is afraid. He tries to touch the Dalit, but the Dalit says, 'You cannot touch me.' He leaves the place and runs away. The touch theme is there in one sense. And then Yamuna is touched by Naani. He clasps her belly which carries a child. The widowed woman becoming pregnant is negative and also positive. And the boy wanting to touch the Dalit is positive, but eventually it becomes negative. The theme of touch is related to the caste system. It is sociological among other things. So you find it all through my writings, mainly because of my own notion of pollution and purity that I shared in my house, and my grandfather who had his own very complex notion of it. I was so impressed when he told me a story. He used to carry me on his back when I was tired, when we went to the forest to gather firewood. One day he told me, 'We Brahmins had the *shapanugraha shakti*. We could give *shapa*. We could also give *anugraha*. We have lost both.'

I asked, 'Ajjayya, Why?'

He said, 'Because of my desire for coffee.'

He was very fond of coffee. So coffee was a polluter. For me a little thing like that triggered many ideas. So coffee in itself begins to have many ideas around it. Caste has many people living under such notions. I used to know people who sincerely lived like that. There is some strange metaphorical connection I have with that kind of a world. And, so, I could not become entirely anti-Brahminical as some people make of me. I became what they call a sceptic or a questioner or, to put it differently, living through it myself like a guinea pig. A writer is a guinea pig who experiments on himself.

All these things enter my consciousness. Coming back to *Bharathipura*—because I had come under the influence of Marxism, etc.—I thought temple entry should be a process of deconstruction. We must deconstruct the myth—demythify. That was also very fashionable. We must demythify the temple. The Brahmins believed the temple was so sacred that if one entered the temple in a state of pollution (s)he would vomit. My hero wants to prove that a Dalit could go there and nothing would happen; and all those beliefs about the power of this god is meaningless. But when I was writing that novel, many ideas came to me. And my hero Jagannatha begins this deconstruction by first giving away papers that had given his family a hold over all the tenants through *levadevi*. He tears them all up, one by one. So he wants to destroy. In that sense it is not a Gandhian novel. In a Gandhian novel the hero becomes a part of the community. In my case he wants to destroy God. Otherwise, the village will not begin to develop. So, in a sense, I was a modernizer, a Westernizer. The Navya movement was full of modernizers. I was also one of them. I am not a simple modernizer in that novel. The novel's thrust is in a different direction. I give full scope to my ideological position. But the novel questions it, reflects on it, interrogates it, and turns the other way. That should happen in the process of writing. And I magically get it sometimes. Even my story 'Suryana Kudure' (The Stallion of the Sun) was written like that. I was reading Marx, in whom I had come across the term 'village idiocy'. He wants conflict, he wants cities to grow so that human consciousness can develop. Otherwise, there is an Asiatic mode of production. History is not moving as fast as it should. I was worried about it, could not accept it, and had a constant dialogue with these things at a simple level. It is in a village that an insect like this is connected with the world of animals, the sun, and the earth. This kind of a connection of all of nature—interconnecting and creating a word suryana kudure—is a metaphor in itself. Marx does not know that villages create languages, villages create Homer. Great poetry comes from very ancient societies where the mode of production is not as evolved. So all those ideas become a story. There is always that kind of a process in what I write; the process is not always successful, but the ideas become important.

NMC: You were referring to the constant preoccupation with touch. This element of touch figures in many ways in your works. But it is not such a simple affair. For example, it figures in different contexts in different ways, going by each character. Praneshacharya is touched and that is a different kind of experience for him. When you come to *Bharathipura*, touch figures in a radically different way. Here the untouchables have to touch the saligrama, the sacred object, and emerge from their state of pollution. But it also means that if they touch the saligrama, they are polluting it. Jagannatha wants to use the saligrama as a symbol, a living image, of oppression, injustice, and inequality, and wants to pollute it. It is through pollution by the so-called polluted people that Jagannatha is trying to establish equality and justice. I want you to keep these things in mind and focus on *Bharathipura*, for it brings us face to face with a number of issues of the Nehruvian and post-Nehruvian era. Looking back on all these things three decades later, what were you trying to suggest in relation to all these very complex contradictions of the Indian society?

URA: I thought the sacred had to be destroyed. Again I go back to my childhood. Everything was sacred. We were told the stone under a tree was sacred. There were many things we could not touch. I thought all these had to be deconstructed and overcome. Many of us used to experiment going into the *smashana* in the night and come back and feel we had overcome the notion of the bhoothas and so on. Also, we used to urinate on the bhootha stones to prove to ourselves that they were not sacred. They were very existential symbols. I believe an author should be able to interpret his very symbolic actions in actual terms as well. So Jagannatha for me represents—what you said so well—all these. He does want God to be destroyed, that god which is the curse for the little temple town. There is a passage there where I say the whole town has been controlled by God and areca nut. They cannot grow anything but areca nut. They have not experimented with other forms of agricultural products because areca nut brings them money. The progress of history has been stalled. So I am still with the old Marx, that unless you move with the capitalist system into a kind of *nagareekarana*, we will not overcome feudalism. I used to meet a man called Ranganatha Rao who said, 'Nothing will happen unless we urbanize.' I used to meet communists who were very active in the Bhadravathi iron factory. I was under the influence of all kinds of people. So, somewhere in my mind, along with my Gandhian ideals, I was also getting urbanized: one way of going beyond caste and ...

NMC: ... the feudal order ...
URA: ... and local loyalties, local gods, and their power, and so on. So, in *Bharathipura*, a big kind of experiment is going on. Beginning with the Nehruvian age, the whole of Indian civilization was undergoing a certain change. I worked on it both unconsciously and consciously. I say consciously because in the work there are conscious ideas. People complained that the novel was burdened with ideas. I never thought it was burdened with ideas because ideas are also characters there. So you are right in your description of the work. The reason for it was my upbringing in Shimoga.

NMC: Were there other elements to enhance your creative impulses too?
URA: I also had very noble examples. One becomes a writer only if one sees both sides. So what is it that makes me so related to tradition, in a critical sort of way? It is language. When I read a Kumaravyasa, a Pampa, the *Vachanakaras*, or when I listen to Purandara Dasa or Kanaka Dasa, it moves me. Bhakti moves me. This is something strange. When we talk of tradition, we should know there is music, there is painting, there is temple architecture—something rich, which represents in a perennial sort of way something very valuable to which you can always be attached. I am sure you understand what I mean. All these happen because I write in Kannada. If I had begun to write in English, I could have taken the modernist thought with great glee. But because I write

in Kannada, it gives all my writing, all my thinking, a certain rootedness. I do not think these two novels would have come in any language other than an Indian language. It can come in English as an idea. But a work of art chooses its own medium and, I think, for an Indian, the Indian language is the medium. You see R.K. Narayan does not have these struggles at all. He is not unaware of these struggles. He is not a foreign writer. Raja Rao is not a foreign writer. They are all aware of these things. But the kind of stress to be put into certain things you will find only in Karanth, in Kuvempu, in writers like us all over India. So it is also my argument that we must keep these languages alive, for they keep quite a few centuries alive. There is a certain continuity. I certainly find that even when I see myself as an existentialist, I do not merely relate to Western existentialism. I relate to certain Upanishads, to *Vachanakaras*, to *Allama*, to several things within my own tradition. And hence there is a certain richness. If you take Kannada literature, every writer has had a fascination for other writers. Kuvempu had a fascination for Wordsworth, and every writer has been interested in Shakespeare. And each of us goes back to Veda Vyasa, the Mahabharatha, and the Ramayana. So that way we are a very stable civilization. That is the nature of the Indian languages. I must pay very great regard to it. It is not merely something happening between me and my actual experience, but me, my actual experience of life, plus my reading.

NMC: All that you have said so far applies largely to an ambivalence towards modernity which is also a critical sensibility through which you revisit the past. But something fascinating happens when we just extrapolate many more things out of this. Jagannatha in the modern world is breaking the past. But look at a tale like *Samskara*. With its relatively suspended time and space, a kind of a past, and Praneshacharya at the centre of it. In *Bharathipura* Jagannatha moves into the past from the present to break it. However, in *Samskara* new forces of history make their entry into this old world order. And, so, Praneshacharya has to make an onward journey—out of the agrahaara, out of his pure self—and enter the new world, which could be called profane, secular, and rational, much to his amazement, disbelief, and shock. This is very fascinating. There is a certain dynamism, a certain tension in *Samskara*. One could almost say it is Praneshacharya who moves to become Jagannatha and it is Durvasapura, Parijatapura that becomes *Bharathipura*. So what have you to say when I ask you to comment on how the past moves into the future, for all along you have talked of the need to revisit the past? What would you say of that sense of the past, the Indian past, traversing a very new, unknown territory and moving into the future, which is what *Samskara* is all about? There is something very remarkable in the two texts—that the present moves to review the past whereas the past has to move out of its own suspended area. This is an extraordinary kind of creative dialectics. Can you talk about this process?

URA: You amaze me by describing it like that because it makes a lot of meaning. I had not thought this out as clearly as you have. You have brought great clarity into all these in a certain way whereas I have worked without being fully conscious of it. But I tell you in *Samskara*—like in *Bharathipura*—structurally, somehow, I have worked with different layers of modernity entering into the novel before Praneshacharya goes in search of that. Naranappa, who has gone to the town, and his gang that is very fond of art, defy Praneshacharya. They also belong to the world which Praneshacharya later enters, but they are already there in the background. And there is one more person (Praneshacharya's boyhood friend who is in Kashi, called Mahabala) who just gives up the whole thing and goes and lives in a prostitute's house. Praneshacharya is always bothered by that reversal. In Naranappa also he sees the same challenge. The profane world may be as profoundly attractive as the sacred world. It has that kind of an attraction for the human soul. There was no question of good and bad and evil. He had seen it in Mahabala. And now he sees it in Naranappa. And too many things happen. Putta enters the novel. Once Erikson told me, 'Are you aware that Putta is a *tadbhava* of *putra*? Praneshacharya does not have a son. Here comes a son for him, a putra.' He was thinking in terms of the great film *Wild Strawberries* by Bergman. He thought that *Samskara* was more like *Wild Strawberries*. I had not seen *Wild Strawberries*. I tried to tell him Putta is not just putra. He is an in-between; he is a *Maalera*. Even in caste he is neither Brahmin nor the other. He is from an in-between caste. He is the opposite of both Naranappa and Praneshacharya. That was what I was conscious of—that I was creating a world in which there were complications even within the so-called traditional place. And, also, I was influenced by Hegelian dialectics because, I told you, in England I used to go to Prof. Thomson's classes and talk to Kailasapathi, the true teacher. In dialectics, sometimes one becomes the opposite of what one is. In a certain excess, what is a quantitative change becomes a qualitative change. This is a very hidden text for me. Now I can talk about it, about *shraaddha* itself. In our families, when you burn a body, you have to do all the other rituals, making the dead man a *pitru*. This is something most Brahmins who attacked me did not even know. So the Brahmins in the agrahaara, because they are deeply traditional, hesitate to do that because they have to not only burn the body but also do the other rituals. Actually it begins on the seventh day. First you bring back the thighs and then the navel, construct the whole body, and then the *preta* becomes a pitru. '*Gaccha gaccha* preta' which means you ask the preta to go away. So to make Naranappa, whom they hated, into a pitru was impossible. But Praneshacharya begins to do just that. Once he is exposed to the secular world, he repeats all the actions of Naranappa. So, in a way, a shraaddha is performed to Naranappa. He is including Naranappa within his own consciousness. It is a simpler kind of a tale than *Bharathipura* for me. I have never been able to write like that again. Somewhere things are allegorical, simpler, and there are hidden things. I was wondering if in the Vedic past there was a certain truth about us, which we have lost by making it into a tradition, etc. Was there something absolutely free from all this? These were the things which I was consciously working out aesthetically.

NMC: Let us examine the range of all these because you were talking of *Samskara* being a simple tale, and there being many allegorical elements in it. I would like you to respond to this observation for a particular reason. Beyond a certain point *Samskara* becomes increasingly symbolic and allegorical both in thematic and aesthetic terms, while *Bharathipura* almost entirely moves on the realistic plane from the beginning to the end. This perhaps explains—as you have already pointed out—why the dilemma of Praneshacharya becomes more and more internal and metaphysical, while Jagannatha's dilemma becomes increasingly political. Many people identify you with the Navya movement, but there is always this allegorical and lyrical quality in you that defies such reductionist descriptions.

URA: I will approach this question in my own way. When I wrote *Bharathipura*, I took the risk of writing on a very contemporary subject of Dalit emancipation. There were other views on Dalit emancipation than taking them into a temple. I knew that the novel would not be discussed as fiction but as a project. It was seen purely as a project that I was giving, that the Dalits should go into the temple rather than do anything else. Another friend of mine, who is a critic whom I like, G.H. Nayak, said something else when the novel appeared. He compared it with the excellent writing the Dalit writer Devanooru Mahadeva was doing then. He said that there is the quotidian reality in Mahadeva but no intellectual and philosophical dimension. He argued I had that dimension, but not the quotidian reality. He was wrong. I tried to argue with G. H. Nayak. My problem in the novel is Jagannatha does not know the Dalits at all. It is an attempt on the part of this highly modernized, Westernized landlord trying to come to terms with the reality of the Dalits. That is why he begins to teach them, give them clothes, make them touch the saligrama, go into their area, and become friendly. He does not even know their names. I told G.H. Nayak that I was aware of their reality, but there was something that I had to examine. I meant to put ideas into practice. For me it was very important. Only later did I begin to write urban-based stories. Then Mahadeva told me, 'Sir, you should write like *Bharathipura* and not move away from it. Get involved with that.' This delighted me because I could see that the Dalit movement itself wanted some philosophical dimension to it, and I remember giving Mahadeva a copy of Paramahamsa to read, because I did not think of Dalits as pure Dalits who needed to be fed and taken to the Parliament and had to be politicized. Truth is many-faceted. When I wrote *Bharathipura* there was Basavalingappa (a minister in the Karnataka government who was a Dalit) who had read the novel. He told me at a meeting in Thirthahalli that he read it and liked it. He said when he read it, he was not responding to its aesthetics, etc. 'I should at least stop Dalits carrying shit on their heads. I have decided I will stop it.' He said that in a lecture, and you know what—he did. That gave me greater joy than any criticism. That is the kind of person I was when I wrote it. I am perhaps less so now. When Basavalingappa stopped the practice, the question was: who will carry the shit? What will happen? He said, 'Let it grow behind your house. You live smelling it. It is not the business of my people to do it. You do it.' Oh, the anger! He incurred the wrath of everyone. Later he said something against Kannada and there was a big movement against him. I stood by him in my articles.

NMC: Our discussion of *Bharathipura* has taken us back to the 1970s. You have made a reference to what the critics thought of the novel, of how a very conscientious Dalit politician reacted to it, and of how your contemporary fellow writers responded to the work. We have done a contextualization of *Bharathipura*. But when we go into this new translation almost four decades later, how would you recontextualize the work? So many things have happened to the Dalit movement, which itself is at a crossroads. In Karnataka it is divided between the Left and the Right. *Bharathipura* is a place, but it is also Bharati, Bharata, India. There is something very symbolic about the title. But four decades later, several things have happened to your own creative processes, your own understanding of tradition, culture, and, in recent times, without being apologetic, you have daringly revised many things you said in the past. You are always interrogating yourself, much as people try to misrepresent you. It seems to me that your views on the caste system, on language, have not been understood at all. There are many fissures, contradictions within the Dalit movement, and writers like Siddalingaiah and Devanooru Mahadeva have moved towards Dalit folk tales and legends, and have been reconstructing Dalit mythology. Siddalingaiah has moved away from his position of rage and anger to metaphors, and Mahadeva, of course, with his *Kusumabaale*, has brought the metaphorical, the allegorical element into the Dalit imagination. As somebody very deeply involved with contemporary life, I want you to recontextualize *Bharathipura*.

URA: The realistic world which I bring in, with which I am so intensely, seriously engaged, tends to make *Bharathipura* look dated. But the other thing that you have been saying the work contains, may still make it relevant. I didn't plan intensely for it to be relevant in future also. It just happened and I have no regrets. But the work has lived because it has a symbolic frame. Long ago, when I was writing this, I used to have intense discussions with Dalits. Devanooru once told me,

'Sir, there is no difference between us, Vokkaligas, and Lingayats. We speak the same language, we look alike, we live the same life. If you are poor, you are the same as any other. I wonder about this all the time ...' As a part of the ruling class, they will be as good or as bad as any ruling class.

NMC: Such a character figures in *Bharathipura*—the IAS officer Satyaprakash.

URA: Yes. Not that I am not aware of it. Once I remember a communist asked Devanooru Mahadeva, 'When you Dalits become a little fortunate you forget your own people.' Mahadeva gave him a very simple answer, 'Why should we be special when it is so with everyone? We are also like the others. Do you make a conscious attempt to be very close to all the poor people in your caste? No. We, too, don't ...' I have been encountering this argument with that kind of a reality. I used to have some sympathy for those who argued that the caste system would vanish only through urbanization. I think we took a revolutionary step in India: the government of independent India promulgated universal adult franchise and declared that those who refuse temple entry can be punished. If a temple refuses entry to Dalits, it can be punished, at least in law. That law cannot be made now because somebody will go to the court and say it is a private affair like a private school, a private college, and we have the freedom to make our own rules. In the past, the Dalit cause was a national cause because of Gandhi and Ambedkar. Hence, the temple entry law was passed that cannot be passed now. When we talk of Dalits, we do so of only those fortunate ones who have entered the cities. There are others in very large numbers in villages. They still depend on land, agriculture, and they have all these problems in the villages. The media may not really give the importance that is due to it. But it is there. In the villages they are agricultural labourers. If you go to any village, the caste system is still prevalent. The Dalits come to pluck out the weeds. Somebody else comes to harvest the crops.

NMC: There is another reason why I ask you to recontextualize your work. In *Samskara* and *Bharathipura* you deal with actions, choices of Hindus, the upper-caste Hindus, especially the Brahmins. Let us try to recontextualize and resituate these elements of the text. It is possible for the two novels, through Praneshacharya, to describe the journey of a Brahmin with some kind of an authenticity. It is possible for Jagannatha too. Failure or success does not matter at all. It is inconsequential. They, at least, move towards a realm of action through a new kind of consciousness and certainly through conscience—the honesty of Praneshacharya, the integrity of Jagannatha. I personally feel the texts are about converting the ethics of knowledge into ethics of action. For Praneshacharya, the new knowledge, the new awareness, propels him towards an ethics of action. So too with Jagannatha. What would the ontological, existential position be, as regards moral choices, for an upper-caste Hindu today, especially for a Brahmin, for that matter, in sharp particularity? The two novels are very great paradigms about these struggles involving the ethics of action. Given the number of choices available for upper-caste Hindus, how would you recontextualize *Bharathipura* considering the principles of conscience or consciousness which I think is a major preoccupation for you as a writer?

URA: Once my very dear friend Subbanna tried to answer this—not this question, but this kind of an investigation about untouchability and so on. He said, 'I am a Brahmin. I am a landlord. I live in a village.' There are very few Brahmins who live in villages now. My Jagannatha could also have moved away. With the land settlement, etc., even the sociological world has changed. They are more urban. That has to be taken into account. My grandfather was a priest. Consequently I had to deal with non-Brahmins every day. There was a certain relationship with them, which, I thought, was vitiated by untouchability. I could deal with all that with a certain denseness. If I recontextualize my novels, the Dalits and the tribals who are losing their land because of development will certainly shape my thoughts. I would recontextualize my works by the experience of my living in a society where a certain degree of functional inequality exists. And, hence, my whole attention has shifted from the *Bharathipura* kind of world to the modern world where *development* has to be critiqued and not *tradition* with the same intensity. Perhaps, if I were in a village, I would have to critique tradition with some intensity. That is why when I read works in the Indian languages about people in the villages, they bring a different reality into my consciousness. Many of our young writers also happen to be Dalits. For them and for all of us, creativity hereafter will have to be rooted in the contradictory realities of our age, if it desires to be historically, ethically committed to what I call the *shashwatha*, the eternal. There was no time in India when the concern with the shashwatha did not exist. This has been a continuous concern and the Buddha himself had to deal with social questions even when he was preoccupied with eternal questions. There are some people who think that the Buddha was kinder to the Kshatriyas because he wanted some kind of stability in society and, hence, was not critical of them. But such people forget that he also saw the destruction of the tribal world. There is a story of Ajatashatru who wanted to raid a tribal kingdom. He comes to the Buddha, the great guru, for permission to do so. That would have meant the annihilation of an old world. It is a profound story. Buddha calls Ananda and asks him, 'When the members of this tribal group take a decision on anything, do they still have meetings?'; 'Do they discuss what is to be done openly?'; 'Do they come to a consensus and then do it?' Ananda replies that they have meetings and do arrive at a consensus before doing anything. The Buddha says, 'Then such a people cannot be destroyed.' The Buddha deals with spatio-temporal questions even during his monumental engagement with eternal questions. My works try to capture this confrontation of the individual with the temporal and the timeless.

NMC: Keeping the contexts of creative processes in mind, what would you say is the burden for writers of the 'post-colonial' world and what are the additional burdens for Indian writers writing in the Indian languages? You say that writing done in English is very different from writing done in the Indian languages, the bhashas. I am asking you to comment on the engagement of the creative writer, keeping in mind the changing scenario in the light of the choices made by the nation itself. This leads to another kind of recontextualization of your works.

URA: People say that Kannada writing has declined. But I don't feel so. Younger writers now are trying their hand at doing exactly what you said just now. There is an influence of Latin American writing. They do it in several ways. One, they write tales, not realistic stories, but a tale that is a mix of myth and imagination. And much of it comes from the rural world, although it is written by people who live in urban centres, but whose childhood was in the rural areas. But, again, this is threatened. I have said this several times. If you do not go to a government school, you will never get to know this kind of a thing and you will never write in your languages.

NMC: Let me help you extend this argument. Is it only that they do not have the poetic element in them, or is it that all these young writers who are doing the critiquing are just politically correct? They write about what is generally acceptable. You and others of your generation were controversial because you were all taking risks as creative writers. For instance, you created a very different kind of cultural polemics. Even your contemporaries did not understand you or they misrepresented you. The society at large did not understand you and you were regarded as anti-Brahmin by the Brahmins, and you were a reactionary for the so-called progressives. You took risks. That too I understand as a kind of inner poetry. Are you also trying to say that Indian writers, young writers in particular, while they lack the poetic element in a literal sense, are also playing safe, by not taking great risks and not accepting challenges that would create a new kind of cultural polemics?

URA: They are indeed playing it safe. I used to put it in a simple manner with my contemporaries. If you want to be nice when you write, you cannot write really well. Being nice, being pleasant, giving a certain satisfaction happens when you work with the reader without disturbing him. Many of these things that are good writings do not deeply disturb anyone.

NMC: Could you explain what precisely took you into the realm of political fiction in *Awasthe*?

URA: There is a continuation of Jagannatha's search into *Awasthe*. When I write, I also wish to introduce events whose significance I do not fully understand myself. I leave it at that. I mean you should not be a *sarvaantaryaami* writer. That is a very arrogant kind of position. For instance, there is an incident when my hero encounters a sadhu who lives in a cave.

NMC: Sarpasiddheshwarananda ...

URA: Yes. It is an incident where there is violence—the killing of a snake. I have not fully understood it. But my hero is searching for a way out of politics, and, at the same time, is undertaking a spiritual quest. My fiction was greatly shaped by an incident in Gopala Gowda's life. I think he gave up his studies when he was doing his Intermediate. Once he had very high fever. He was a poor student and had to go back to his village. He got down at a railway station after Sagar and stayed in a hotel—not a hotel but a roadside eatery. The owner of the eatery asked him to get out and not sleep there. Gopala Gowda refused to budge. The shop owner threw him out. Gopala Gowda cursed him. Fifteen days later he heard that the hotel was burnt. So he thought he had godly powers. He threw off his clothes, became naked, and began to worship Goddess Durga. I have seen this in my village. There is a tantric undercurrent in rural areas—wearing a yantra or worshipping a devi. I had seen it in my father himself. He would suddenly begin worshipping for two or three days, staying in some place, and performing elaborate rituals. Gopala went through all these and even used to write short stories on these. He was conscious enough. I had an intimate kind of relationship with such wonderful people. I have been very fortunate in that sense. All these go into the novel, fortunately not just as biographical details of a psychologically interesting character, but as someone who represents a deep search for a cleansing of life—outside and within. Such things are very important for me. The whole of *Awasthe* is built on the desire that there should be a strong socio-political movement. Many of my political ideas got clarified while writing the novel, which is not just a political novel, just as *Bharathipura* is not a novel only about Dalits. Even when I went to the West as a student I did not do so with a feeling that we were empty and had to find enlightenment there. Such confidence came from Prof. C. D. Narasimhaiah, our teacher. While at Maharaja's College we discussed Eliot, Hopkins, and others, and in the coffee house I used to meet Adiga. At times, Adiga seemed more important than Eliot. When I say influences, I want it to be understood that for me an unknown man in my village, who was a great celibate, figures in my world of ideas as importantly as anyone I have encountered elsewhere. This is where I think all Third World literatures—Latin American, African,

Indian (primarily in the Indian languages)—meet. I don't think any of these things meet in Europe. Only at a certain point of time did the Buddha or the Upanishads become very important for European writers like Yeats and Eliot. The Eastern antiquity had some meaning. But Europe can do without it now. It means Europe can do without the Third World. We are not like that. We need to critique Eastern antiquity and reject and accept some of it. At the same time we critique the West and reject and accept some of it. This was possible for me as I did not privilege one over the other. They happened simultaneously and one connected with the other.

I am a very chanchala (fickle-minded) kind of a person. I don't mind it when I am working on anything. I remain naive and allow things to dominate me and move me. It is like going through everything imaginatively, to feel as intensely as possible. You know you cannot do that, and you also know why you cannot do that. You know you are also a product of other kinds of consciousness. A capacity to do this was there in me intensely in my younger days. I would be very intense about something and turn against it in my writing, during the process of writing. Turn against it in order to enrich it. I think I do it even now. For me Adiga was a poet who meant a lot. Adiga was searching very intensely for metaphors, etc., in the ancient Vedic lore. Long ago, when I had just passed my honours, I had to write a foreword to his poetry and I am very proud to say that it still remains one of my best writings. I marvel that I wrote it. I had just come out of honours and then he sent me his poetry. I said that his way of thinking is *arshadrishti*. The Indian languages we use as writers have been preserved—I wrote this once—through illiteracy, preserved through backwardness. Once I went to a seminar in Germany and I said I am not afraid of you taking us over because there are enough illiterate people in India. We have enough backwardness. I almost saw it as a virtue. I have that kind of a political inner current in me, relating me to them, which has saved us from total colonization. So that leads to other kinds of politics. You fight for your language and see the importance of it. I cannot be anti-Sanskrit. But all those who are for Sanskrit, for Vedic knowledge, etc., I feel, are those who are highly Westernized. That used to be slightly my quarrel with Raja Rao and Prof. C.D. Narasimhaiah. For them it was Sanskrit and English.

So we live in several 'times'. A lot of writing comes from that kind of a world and also the urban world. Maybe the two meet in my later works. You have asked me this question. For me it was a journey from an intense agrahaara to a middle town. *Bharathipura* takes place in a small moffusil temple town. In *Awasthe*, I come to Bangalore. Then I go back to the West. In a way I have been increasing my estate. That makes it necessary for me to include certain ideas which have been there all along in me. Actually, in a novel, the detail, the character, the locale, the place where it is happening—they begin to determine what you can put into the work and what you cannot. The language also determines these things. You have to get that language and you have to make it possible for your language to include experiences of that kind. Kannada has grown because it can take a lot of Western experience. I don't think any European language is growing as Indian languages are, taking more and more territory into their threshold. So changing the language and making it pliable for that kind of a thing is essential. It happens constantly. I am reading Brecht. I am told, when Brecht began to write in the 1920s, he made it possible for the German language to say certain things it could not express before him. Eliot has the line, 'To cleanse the dialect of the tribe.' It has to be done constantly and I am always at it.

Glossary

agrahaara	Brahmin settlement in a town or village
Akshathadige	third day in a lunar fortnight; the day the demon Aksha was killed
alaapana	the first movement in Indian classical music; an initial elaboration of notes
Alwar	Tamil word meaning immersed in devotion to God. There are twelve such alwars or saints
amaldhar	revenue collector
Anna	elder brother
Athige, Athige	sister-in-law
Ayyavare	Master!
Badri	a pilgrimage centre in north India
Balipadya	annual festival celebrating Vishnu's victory over King Bali
Besh	an expression of approbation

bilva	a tree, the leaves of which are offered to Shiva in worship
Bombay Show	travelling show of dancers set up during fairs
bonda	snack; slices of vegetables, dipped in batter and deep fried
chakkuli	deep fried snack made from rice flour
chandalas	outcastes
Chariot Festival	a car festival; a procession of an idol mounted on a decorated chariot
chombu	a small round vessel used as a mug
choultry	free lodgings
daffedar	a police constable
Dakshineshwar	a pilgrimage centre in Bengal
Daridra Shani	demon of misfortune
DC	district commissioner
Deeva	toddy-tapping community
devadasi	a temple dancer
Dhanigale	Master!
Dharmashastra	code of law
DSP	deputy superintendent of police
Esur	a tiny place in Karnataka where a fierce struggle against the British was organized
Finlay	a textile company, reputed for its fine, white dhothis
Ganeshachowthi	fourth day in the lunar fortnight, celebrated as Ganesha's birthday, the god with an elephant's head
Gouri Puja	the worship of Gouri, another name for Parvathi, wife of Shiva
Govindhaanu Govinda	choral chant invoking God
Gowdas	the farming community
Gurkha	Nepalese soldiers; Gurkha ex-army men are frequently employed as guards
Harikathadaasa	performer who narrates legends with song and music
jai	victory, implying, Victory to India!

jilebi	a sweet, fried in ghee and dipped in sugar syrup
Justice Party	the first anti-Brahmin movement set up by a reformist group
Kaapaalika	mendicant belonging to a Shaivite sect
kachche panche	a formal way of wearing the dhothi, taking the edge between the legs and tucking it in at the back at the waist
kakay	a creeper that bears berries
Kali	a popular deity in Bengal. Kali is the name of Devi, Shiva's consort, who has two aspects, one fierce and the other, benign. Kali represents the fierce side
kedage	a variety of agave plant with scented leaves, used in worship and to adorn women's hair; snakes usually haunt a kedage grove
kheer	a creamy dessert
Konkan	a person from South Kanara, Karnataka
Krishnashtami	Shri Krishna's birthday
kshema	safe and sound
linga	the symbol of Shiva's creative energy, in the form of a phallus; it represents Shiva in temples dedicated to him and is worshipped by Shaivites
Madurai	a pilgrimage centre in Tamil Nadu
Mahalaya Amavasye	worship of the moon in the latter half of the month of Bhadra
Maharaya	a term of address
MLA	member of the legislative assembly
mundedhe	son of a widow!
Mysore Socialist Party	a faction of the Socialist Party that originated in Mysore
Narasimha	fourth incarnation of Vishnu; half-man, half-lion
New Moon	first day of the first quarter on which the moon is invisible

Odeya	master
panchagavya	five items from the cow (milk, curd, ghee, urine, and dung) sipped as a ritual of cleansing
parijatha	small white flowers with orange stalk, associated with Krishna
payasa	a sweet dish
pinda	a ball of rice offered to ancestors
Ramanavami	birthday celebrations of Rama
Rameshwara	a pilgrimage centre in Tamil Nadu
ravike	tight-fitting blouse worn with a sari
rayare, rayaru	rayare and rayaru are suffixes denoting respect. Rayare is a term of address and rayaru is a term of reference
Rishikesh	a pilgrimage centre in north India
Rudra avataara	Shiva in his destructive form
Saar	Indian version of Sir
Sahebru	boss
sampige	slim yellow-gold flowers with a heady scent, used to adorn the heads of gods and women
Sarvodaya movement	a movement aimed at promoting cultural harmony, leading to socio-economic revolution through non-violence
Shaaktha	worshipper of Durga or Kali
Shastrigale	a term of respect used to address a Brahmin priest
Swathi rainwater	rain that falls when the sun is in Swathi, an auspicious constellation
taluk	division of a district
teertha	water sanctified by washing the idol in it
thali	a symbol of marriage, a pendant in gold
Tirupathi	a pilgrimage centre in Andhra Pradesh
Twenty-eight	a card game
Udupi Krishna Almanac	a calendar comprising solar and lunar days, named after Shri Krishna of Udupi, Karnataka

ullai, pidhai	words in Tulu, a language spoken in South Kanara. They mean inside, outside
uppittu	a spicy breakfast snack
Urvashi	a dancer in the court of Indra
Utthaanadwadashi	an auspicious festival after Deepavali. It celebrates the union of Lord Krishna and Tulsi, the goddess associated with the herb of the same name
Vashishta	One of the celebrated Vedic sages, composer of several hymns of the Rig Veda; Rama's priest, in the Ramayana; he married Arundhati, a low-caste woman who became a symbol of chastity
Vidhana Soudha	the secretariat in Bangalore that houses the chief minister's office and the two houses of legislature
Vipra	a truly wise man who has understood the nature of the body, world, and mind
vishnukranthi	a tiny, bluish wild flower that grows wild with grass